93-94
96

# ASSESSMENT IN SPECIAL EDUCATION

**John T. Neisworth**
Pennsylvania State University
University Park, Pennsylvania
Editor

AN ASPEN PUBLICATION®
Aspen Systems Corporation
Rockville, Maryland
London
1982

Library of Congress Cataloging in Publication Data
Main entry under title:

Assessment in special education.

Includes bibliographical references and index.
1. Handicapped children—Education—Evaluation—
Addresses, essays, lectures.   I. Neisworth, John T.
LC4019.A74   1982   371.9   82-11455
ISBN: 0-89443-808-5

Copyright © 1982 Aspen Systems Corporation

Library of Congress Catalog Card Number: 82-11455
ISBN: 0-89443-808-5

*Printed in the United States of America*

1   2   3   4   5

# Contents

# Preface

Assessment, whether spontaneous or planned, intuitive or objective, goes on every day. Teachers and therapists "size up" their students or clients, do things to them (i.e., intervene), and then estimate the effects of the intervention. It may be acceptable for us to "size up" the weather before deciding what coat to wear or to "guestimate" how much food to prepare for company. But the assessment of intervention needs to be more precise, especially as intervention becomes more effective. The development of a science demands a rejection of intuition as a fundamental means for decision making. Rather, modern empiricism requires that intervention efforts be guided by objective, publicly verifiable, accurate, and reliable assessment. We would not expect a surgeon to casually size up a patient before cutting; surgeons are guided by dependable assessments that describe the illness and predict the success of intervention.

In teaching, the effects of cursory, subjective assessment are not as immediate or drastic as in the case of the breakneck surgeon. The effects of teaching or nonteaching are usually delayed, undetected, or dispersed. But as instructional objectives become more explicit and more important in development and as treatment becomes more effective, assessment assumes a more crucial role in directing and evaluating intervention. In fact, many professionals—especially those involved with directive instruction—argue that assessment should be an integral part of instruction.

All teachers, whether they favor traditional psychometrics or direct (i.e., behavioral) observation and recording, need to deal with the concerns of the development, selection, administration, and interpretation of assessment procedures and devices. The concerns multiply as assessment becomes more critical in the lives of children. Such concerns include: Should assessment be direct or indirect? Process or product? Quantitative or qualitative? Historical or contemporaneous? Formal or informal? Criterion or norm referenced? Personal or environmental? Trait based or situational? Genotypic or phenotypic? Standardized or adapted to a child's handicap?

The answers to these questions depend largely on the purpose of assessment. The characteristics and degree of precision of descriptive assessment are different than those of predictive assessment. Instructional planning and teaching require yet another kind of assessment. Assessment for instructional purposes can be viewed as the bottom line for assessment, at least within the schools and clinics. When the semantics and theoretical disputes are set aside, it becomes clear that the real purpose of assessment is to develop hypotheses about, give direction to, or make plans for individual and group programming. Unfortunately, assessment practices and devices are not as helpful in instruction and therapy as they could be. In fact, assessment in the schools is often irrelevant as far as the teacher is concerned.

There are three reasons assessment is often irrelevant in instruction. First, traditional assessment typically uses global, norm-referenced measures of general potential or capacity. Such an approach lacks the precision and curricular relevance necessary to guide instruction. Use of these traditional measures to help teachers learn is like trying to fly an airplane with gauges that register the general capacities and conditions of the plane rather than immediate and specific flight information.

Second, traditional assessment is usually used to measure assumed conditions or traits. It attempts to describe what the student *is* (e.g., retarded, disturbed, or learning disabled) rather than what the student *does* (e.g., skill in communication, interpersonal competence, work skills, and task persistence). Thus traditional assessment merely assigns a child to a clinical category. As is often stated in the contemporary literature, labeling a child does not help the teacher teach the child. Children within a category are not all at the same educational level, and furthermore, instructional methods and materials are not category specific. However, analyzing what a child can or cannot do helps the teacher develop specific curricular objectives and select appropriate teaching methods and materials.

Third, traditional assessment results are usually reported in ways that confuse the teacher. Often, such reports are test centered, vague, and loaded with psychological and psychometric jargon.

The articles in this volume will not solve all the problems or answer all the questions concerning assessment in special education. But they will identify and highlight trends and problems, present alternative models and approaches to assessment, and suggest some ways to assess specific groups of individuals.

Assessment within special education forces a kind of distillation of the general problems of assessment; it focuses attention on the issue of instructional and therapeutic relevance and alerts us to the need for assessment procedures that are in keeping with the philosophy, methods, and goals of science.

*John T. Neisworth*
*Editor*
*August 1982*

# PART I:
# PROFESSIONAL TRENDS AND ISSUES

# Legal Issues in Assessment for Special Education

*Reed Martin, Esq.*
*Attorney*
*Houston, Texas*

FEDERAL LEGISLATION and judicial decisions have changed the roles of special education evaluators. The traditional diagnostic role has been broadened. Professionals may find themselves in a new role as "independent evaluators." Prescription decision making is shared among many in the new forum called the individualized education program (IEP) planning meeting. In addition, evaluators will likely be required to participate in emergency disciplinary proceedings and called to testify in the administrative trials known as impartial hearings.

## THE GOOD OLD DAYS

Not many years ago schools asked evaluators to perform in an individual effort. An evaluator using a single criterion often made judgments that brought about dramatic changes in children's lives. Testing instruments were often normed on

4

children so unlike the subjects being assessed that serious cultural and racial bias issues were raised. The administrators of tests received virtually no instruction in accommodating the needs of the handicapped; and, as a consequence, it was not unusual to find bright learning disabled or physically impaired children who were erroneously thought to have intelligence in the retarded range.

The diagnostic label hung on a child dictated the placement in which services were offered and thus carried the potential to be a self-fulfilling prophecy. Reevaluation typically occurred on a triannual cycle, so mistakes could be felt for a long time. Such mistakes were shielded from the check and balance of nonprofessional scrutiny because schools jealously guarded their files, stamping them "for professional use only." They routinely turned down parents' requests to find out what was being written about their child.

Communication with parents was typically minimal. For example, the author met a woman who had been told simply that her son was in an EMR program. She deduced that EMR stood for English, math, and reading—which were indeed the three areas in which her child was weakest! Professionals often laugh appreciatively at that true story, thinking it says something about the intelligence of the parent. Rather, it says something about the school.

## COURT CASES AND LEGISLATION

A dramatic change in the not-so-good old days began in California in the early 1970s. Revelations that large numbers of black children were being swept into classes for the retarded on the basis of a single administration of an intelligence test led to the filing of a law suit, *Larry P. v. Riles* (343 F. Supp. 1306 [N.D. Cal. 1972] aff'd 502 F.2d 963 [9th Cir. 1974]). The preliminary relief granted in *Larry P.* banned placements on the basis of a single criterion. Although the case did not reach a final decision for another 7 years (3 EHLR 551:295, N.D. Cal. 1979), it had alerted the country and Congress to a serious problem.

Revelations about parents' being denied permission to see their children's records also came to the attention of Congress. The resulting Buckley Amendment became the Family Education Rights and Privacy Act (PL 93-380, codified at 20 U.S.C. 1232g, with implementing regulations at 45 C.F.R. 99). The resulting right of access gave parents an opportunity to see all information that affects evaluation, placement, or programming of their children. The right extends to all personally identifiable educational records collected, maintained, and used by the school, without regard to who within the school system has possession of the file. Further, parents can demand a change in any record they find inaccurate, misleading, or violating their privacy.

During the first half of the 1970s Congress passed two other significant pieces of legislation influencing evaluation: the Education for All Handicapped Children Act of 1975 (PL 94-142) and Section 504 of the Rehabilitation Act of 1973. Legislative history makes clear the congressional concern over nonbiased diagnoses and effective prescriptions.

## THE EVALUATION PROCESS

All schools have standard referral processes that are used when a teacher's observation or other screening technique identifies a child as in need of evaluation. But PL 94-142 adds two other situations: (a) when a parent requests evaluation, and (b) when environmental or social conditions warrant evaluation.

### What Conditions?

In two recent cases, *P-1 v. Shedd* (3 EHLR 551:164 [D. Conn. 1979]) and *Mattie T. v. Holladay* (3 EHLR 551:109 [D. Miss. 1979]), the condition warranting more evaluation was student misbehavior serious enough to call for expulsion. In two other recent cases, *Howard S. v. Friendswood* (454 F. Supp. 634 [S.D. Tex. 1978]) and *Stuart v. Nappi* (443 F. Supp. 1235 [D. Conn. 1978]), the federal courts suggested that persistent truancy from a supposedly appropriate special education program warranted a closer look at the child. Deciding what conditions warrant evaluation and reevaluation in a school district should be a priority for assessment personnel.

### What Is Evaluated?

Every area of suspected disability must be examined, but evaluation is justified only if there is reason to suspect a problem. Federal law recognizes that the act of testing can itself be stigmatizing. Furthermore, the concept of using the least drastic means of evaluation (familiar to school personnel in choosing place-

ment options as the least restrictive alternative) requires that only as much testing be used as is needed. The diagnostic inquiry clearly must not be limited by the evaluator's prejudgment of what is available prescriptively. For example, a hearing impaired child should be assessed for aural and oral ability even when the school currently offers only manual instruction through sign language and finger spelling. The diagnostic process must not change to accommodate programs the school chooses to make available; rather, the programs must accommodate the needs of the child as shown in an honest, comprehensive assessment.

### Who Conducts the Evaluation?

The effort must be a multidisciplinary one, with an evaluator who is knowledgeable about each suspected area of disability. The multidisciplinary nature of the process is reaffirmed in the placement decision making, which must be based on information from a variety of sources and made by a group of people.

### What Is Used for Evaluation?

*Larry P.* clarifies that a variety of information, ranging from formal tests to teacher observation, must be used. Regulations under both Section 504 and PL 94-142 specify the concern of Congress that whatever evaluation materials are used should not discriminate on the basis of irrelevant criteria (e.g., race or sex). *Larry P.* concerned racial and cultural bias, but the real challenge today is bias on the basis of handicap. Test manufac-

5

6

turers do not currently seem to be helping evaluators meet this challenge. For the next few years evaluators will have to approach their education agency to determine how to deal with tests that do not reasonably accommodate the needs of the handicapped.

## What Is Produced by Evaluation?

Courts are beginning to recognize that a full evaluation produces not only diagnostic data but also information useful for the development of a prescription. Some schools disagree, viewing the prescription process as the province of the IEP meeting. Other districts forbid evaluators to write prescriptions, fearing the district would be bound to recommendations as stated in prescriptions. The district is only bound by the shared decisions in IEP meetings. The decision is a group-determined program based on individual evaluation data available to the team. In one recent case, *Winfield v. Fairfax County Board* (3 EHLR 551:269 [Cir. Ct. Fairfax Co., Va., 1979]), the court ordered an evaluator to write a prescription. The court held that a diagnosis alone did not meet the requirement for evaluation under PL 94-142.

One regulation overlooked by many districts involves a special written report as a product of any inquiry into a sus-

---

*Courts are beginning to recognize that a full evaluation produces not only diagnostic data but also information useful for the development of a prescription.*

---

pected learning disability. When the bulk of the regulations under PL 94-142 were promulgated, the formula for determining a learning disability was still being debated. The final decision was published in a separate set of regulations unknown to many districts. These regulations require written reports when children are assessed for learning disabilities. Team members must sign and indicate their agreement with the group conclusion. If members dissent, they must state their dissension in writing.

## What Is the Parents' Role?

Parents, being the child's primary caretakers, have information useful to the evaluation process. A complete evaluation must document contact with parents and information received from them. The proposed program for the child must be communicated to the parents in a written statement. The notice must include a description of each evaluation procedure, test, record, or report the agency uses as a basis for the proposal, and it must be written in language understandable to the general public. Thus parents will be a source of information and will participate in programming decisions based on the evaluation data.

## INDEPENDENT EVALUATIONS

Schools no longer "own" the evaluation process. An outside source, known as an independent evaluator, may be brought into the process. Congress, recognizing that schools often make mistakes, established as a check and balance the right of parents to have an independent evaluation. Although that right was established in PL 93-380, it was not clarified until regulations were promulgated under PL 94-142.

The sole definition of "independent evaluator" is that the person not be employed by the agency responsible for the education of the child in question. The parent then has the right to have the results of the evaluation considered with respect to decisions regarding a free, appropriate public education. The challenge for evaluators is not only that they might face an independent evaluator at an IEP meeting or impartial hearing but also that they themselves might be an independent evaluator in another district.

*Parents' Rights*

When parents procure the independent evaluation, they have a right to study the data and decide whether to share them with the school. The procedure is often misunderstood by school personnel, who must always share evaluation information without regard to whether the data affirm the school's position. One problem with parent-procured evaluations is that the independent evaluator may use tests or gather data in a manner unlike that required by the state. The statute and regulations make clear that even in such a case the school must consider the data in any decision made with respect to the provision of a free appropriate public education.

Parents also have the right to obtain the independent evaluation at public expense. If done at public expense, two

conditions apply: (1) the independent evaluator must be a "qualified examiner" meeting the same qualifications as those imposed on the agency for a similar evaluation and (2) both the location of the testing and the criteria for testing must meet agency standards. An independent evaluation at public expense can be obtained in three ways. First, parents can ask the agency to procure one. Second, an impartial hearing officer might, of his or her own volition or at the parents' request, order an independent evaluation at public expense. Third, parents can obtain one on their own.

When a parent asks, the school must provide information about where the parent can acquire an independent educational evaluation. If parents believe the school's initial evaluation was inappropriate, they may send the bill for the independent evaluation to the school (which must pay the bill or initiate a due-process hearing and show that the school's evaluation was appropriate). Even if the school proves that its evaluation is appropriate (and the parents pay the bill), the independent evaluation must still be considered in the school's decision making.

*When Evaluations Clash*

Thus an evaluator might find himself or herself in an impartial hearing defending the appropriateness of his or her effort. The test of the evaluator will include, at a minimum, his or her compliance with all state and federal guidelines; and it might extend, at a maximum, to the quality of the diagnosis and prescription in comparison with that of the independent evalua-

8

tion. If there is a discrepancy between the type of disability identified by the school and that identified by the independent evaluator, the appropriateness of the school's evaluation would be in question. Another problem may occur if the school's and independent evaluator's evaluations disagree, however slightly, about the degree of disability and, subsequently, the type of service delivery that is most appropriate. In that case the decision as to the "appropriate" evaluation would be the decision of the hearing officer.

### Emergency Discipline Judgments

A new role awaits evaluators in cases where "discipline" of the handicapped student is judged necessary. In *Stuart v. Nappi* and *S-1 v. Turlington* (3 EHLR 551:221 [S.D. Fla. 1979]) the courts considered the expulsion of handicapped students. In *Stuart* the Connecticut court held that expulsion would be a change in placement. In *S-1* the Florida court held that prior to expulsion a determination must be made whether the offending behavior was related to the handicapping condition. In either case, the court required the reconvening of the evaluation personnel to determine whether the misbehavior warranted further evaluation or if it indicated that services should be carried out in a different placement. Both cases make it clear that PL 94-142 supersedes local board policies on discipline. Thus the evaluators will be deciding the student's placement when previously the school board would have met to contend with the child.

It is a role many school board members will dislike. Many evaluators also will not welcome the added responsibility. If the misbehavior were so outrageous that there was pressure to work with the child immediately, then time for the evaluation would be very limited.

One case mentioned earlier, *P-1 v. Shedd*, creates a role for special education evaluators to assess a student, not identified as handicapped, who commits an act that warrants a recommendation for expulsion or suspension totaling more than 15 days in any school year. In such a case the child would be referred to an identification team to determine if the child is indeed handicapped. The special education process (IEP and placement) takes place in lieu of the established discipline process.

### TESTIMONY AT TRIAL

One final role awaits evaluators. The new federal laws create a forum, the impartial due-process hearing, which is conducted in many states like a minitrial. These laws authorize parents to go to court to redress grievances. Evaluation personnel should become aware of the possibility of their being called to testify. Most evaluators with whom the author has discussed this prospect say they are ready and will simply tell their story. But the trial forum does not work that easily. If the questions directed toward the witness are poor, so is the witness.

Would it not be tragic to play the other roles of the evaluator properly but fail in this last role, resulting in an unjust placement for a child? The final role for evaluators is to work with school district personnel or school district legal counsel or enable them to understand how to use evaluators effectively as witnesses.

## CONCLUSION

Evaluators have a variety of roles. Their diagnostic efforts must be comprehensive, open to parents, and merged into a multidisciplinary process. They must be prepared to respond to the challenge of an independent evaluation conducted by someone else or even to be an independent evaluator themselves. They must share the prescription process with parents and other education personnel in the IEP meeting. Finally, they must be ready to express their opinions in an emergency disciplinary session or in the artificial forum of a trial. Handicapped children will need their best efforts.

# General Assessment Competencies for Special Education Teachers

*Gaye McNutt, Ph.D.*
*University of Oklahoma*
*Norman, Oklahoma*

*Linda Higbee Mandelbaum, M.Ed.*
*Bowling Green State University*
*Bowling Green, Ohio*

REGARDLESS OF AGE, grade level, or educational placement of students, or of the subject matter being taught, educators who work with handicapped students periodically engage in assessment activities. The purposes of the assessment, the particular techniques used, and the amount of time expended may vary; but the success of any assessment effort depends on the competence of those individuals involved.

Competency statements for particular groups have been delineated by both individual authors and committees of professional organizations. Several lists of competencies have been published within the last few years. For example, the Division for Children with Learning Disabilities (1978) developed an extensive list of competencies for teachers of the learning disabled and is now collecting data related to them. Cegelka (1978) focused on competencies for persons responsible for the mentally retarded, and

11

12 the International Reading Association (1978) proposed a list of guidelines for reading teachers. Many universities and colleges also have developed assessment competencies keyed to their specific training programs. In some cases, these competency lists have been designed for only one type of teacher (e.g., teachers of the learning disabled) and usually for teachers who work at one particular age level.

The purpose of this article is to suggest areas of competence that would be useful for teachers of any type of handicapped students and for teachers of any age level of students. More specifically our purposes are (a) to briefly review four major knowledge areas that are prerequisite to the assessment competencies, (b) to propose a set of general assessment competencies that all special educators should acquire, regardless of educational philosophy, and (c) to outline implications and future directions that may result from these prerequisites and competencies. A definition of assessment is needed to clarify the purposes and our discussion related to them.

While there are many definitions of *assessment*, we have chosen to focus only on assessment activities that are used by teachers to acquire information concerning students' instructional needs. This definition is, admittedly, narrow in scope, because other types of assessment (e.g., assessment to identify students according to handicapping labels or assessment to evaluate the effectiveness of a program) are not included. However, assessing students to determine their instructional needs is a task *all* teachers normally

undertake, while other types of assessment are not used by all teachers. Additionally, many of the competencies that are related to assessing for instructional purposes are useful when assessment is used for other purposes.

## PREREQUISITES

Before assessing students, educators should have a well-formed understanding of (a) educational philosophy, (b) educational goals, (c) child and adolescent development, (d) subject matter content, and (e) terminology. At least a minimal level of proficiency in these is essential before educators can consider the assessment competencies.

### Educational Philosophy

An educational philosophy is a theoretical approach to education that an individual gradually develops. This philosophy includes beliefs related to how students learn and how they should be taught. Once a basic educational philosophy is developed, the specifics (e.g., choosing various methods or materials) become easier primarily because each is first judged in terms of whether it adheres to one's philosophy. The educational phi-

---

*Before assessing students, educators should have a well-formed understanding of (a) educational philosophy, (b) educational goals, (c) child and adolescent development, (d) subject matter content, and (e) terminology.*

losophy held by an individual helps ensure that all educationally related decisions are theoretically consistent with one another.

While many philosophies exist today, they are constantly changing. Some are gaining adherents and becoming stronger; others, ebbing. The philosophies prevalent among special educators today can be grouped into three broad categories: (a) ability training, (b) atomistic education, and (c) holistic education. Following is a brief discussion of each, based on an unpublished paper (Hammill, Brown, Brown, Gray, Hresko, Larsen, McNutt, Poplin, Reid, & Wiederholt, 1979) and a recent speech (Hammill, 1979).

### ABILITY TRAINING

Essentially ability training assumes that certain presumed mental functions or psychological processes within the brain must be intact before individuals can efficiently learn specific educational content (e.g., reading or writing). If these abilities are not intact, the assumption is made that the weaknesses or problem areas can first be identified and then remediated or circumvented. Therefore application of this philosophy generally focuses on assessing and training basic mental processes or abilities such as attention, auditory or visual discrimination, memory, closure, sequencing, and ocular pursuit.

The various theories related to this basic philosophy are many and can be traced to ancient times. However, the educational application of this philosophy did not become dominant in special education until the 1960s. Tests and materials by individuals such as Frostig, Getman, Kephart, and Kirk are examples of its application in special education. Research has generally failed to substantiate the usefulness of the tests and materials resulting from this orientation (Arter & Jenkins, 1979; Hammill & Larsen, 1974; Larsen & Hammill, 1975).

### ATOMISTIC EDUCATION

Atomistic education basically assumes that (a) whatever is to be learned can be broken into discrete and independent segments or components, (b) the segments can be put into an orderly sequence, (c) these individual segments and rules can be taught, and (d) the learner will generalize these into a usable whole (i.e., the whole equals the sum of the parts). The various theories within this philosophy can be identified in the works of Pavlov, Thorndike, and others; but their application in special education was not strongly evident until the late 1960s and the 1970s. Application of this philosophy results in completing task analyses, creating scope and sequence charts, using behavioral objectives, and so on.

### HOLISTIC EDUCATION

The holistic philosophy is based on three general assumptions. First is that the whole is different from the sum of its parts, and therefore teaching discrete segments (e.g., particular phonic skills in reading) will not necessarily result in learning being successful at the more general task (e.g., comprehending what is

14

read). Second, learners can construct and verify their own rules (e.g., the rules young children possess but cannot state when learning to speak). Third, when teaching any task, that task must maintain the characteristics of the general content to which it belongs (e.g., reading tasks should require comprehension in meaningful context). Individuals such as Vygotsky, Piaget, Bruner, and Chomsky have presented theories related to this philosophy, but it is only beginning to influence special education in terms of practical application.

## Educational Goals

Long-term educational goals should focus on the possibilities that exist for students after they complete the traditional 12 years of schooling, and enter the working world, sheltered employment, and so on. The important point related to this prerequisite is that teachers must consider what they are teaching and assessing in terms of its relationship to and effect upon the long-term goals. Tasks having little relationship to or effect on these goals should be seriously questioned in terms of their validity for being included in the curriculum.

Educators should develop a general perspective concerning (a) possible long-term educational goals and learning requirements related to obtaining each goal, (b) curricula that would result from attempting to reach the various goals, and (c) which goals are most important for the majority of the involved students. Maintaining flexibility in applying these goals to individual students is also important.

## Child and Adolescent Development

Educators need a general knowledge of child and adolescent development to determine expectations for students and to decide when to assess these expectations. For example, a general knowledge of child and adolescent development enables teachers to set and assess reasonable expectations related to the attention span of the students, their ability to interact with one another, and other social and emotional variables.

## Subject Matter Content

Whether the area to be assessed is academic (e.g., math, reading) or nonacademic (e.g., independent living skills), a thorough knowledge of that area is needed. For example, if mathematics will be assessed, the educator needs a basic understanding of number theory, computational processes, measurement, problem solving, and so on. Naturally, individuals' educational philosophies as well as their knowledge of child and adolescent development will influence the knowledge they gain in the content area.

## Terminology

When professionals discuss the problems a student is having, difficulties often arise when different terms are used to describe the same problem or when the same term is used to describe different problems. For example, one teacher may define *dyslexia* as a problem of reversing letters in words; another may think of it as a difficulty in comprehending what is read; and yet another may define it as existing when words or entire lines are skipped during oral reading.

How individuals define various terms obviously affects their communication with one another and the assessment procedures that will be undertaken. Because the trends in special education appear to be toward mainstreaming, increasing interdisciplinary work, and using teams of professionals with each student, the ability to precisely define terminology and to recognize that a variety of definitions may exist for a single term is necessary if assessment and subsequent remediation procedures are to be effective.

Each of these prerequisites influences what will be assessed, how the assessment will proceed, and how the information will be used. These prerequisites also influence the actual instructional process.

## GENERAL ASSESSMENT COMPETENCIES

The assessment competencies are presented as global statements so that they may be adapted by teachers of various age levels or types of handicapped students. Additionally, we present global statements because highly structured competencies represent only a particular philosophy and are difficult to incorporate into other philosophies. (See Blackhurst, 1977, for a model of how more specific competencies lead to behavioral objectives and curriculum development.)

The competencies are grouped into three categories: (a) techniques, (b) application, and (c) synthesis. The first category is factual information that all teachers should possess regardless of their philosophy, educational goals for students, or other prerequisites. As a rule, attaining skill in these techniques is not greatly influenced by the opinions and positions that result from the prerequisites. However, the latter two categories (i.e., application of the techniques and synthesis of the resulting information) are influenced by the opinions and positions that result from the prerequisites.

### Techniques

All assessment data can be organized and obtained through one of three basic techniques: (a) analysis of a product, (b) interviewing, or (c) observation. Although each technique may be applied in many ways and contributes particular types of assessment information, there is some overlap in terms of the various procedures within each of the three categories.

#### ANALYSIS OF A PRODUCT

Analysis of a product is examining work completed by an individual. For example, when teachers score and interpret tests, grade essays, or check homework assignments, they are analyzing products.

Educators need to understand the differences among three types of tests and should be skilled in four knowledge areas related to each. The types of tests are norm-referenced, criterion-referenced,

---

*All assessment data can be organized and obtained through one of three basic techniques: (a) analysis of a product, (b) interviewing, or (c) observation.*

16

and informal; the knowledge areas are test selection, construction, administration, and interpretation.

According to Gronlund (1976), norm-referenced tests allow a student's results to be compared with some known group's performance (the norming sample). Because norm-referenced tests have a highly quantitative nature, they are not particularly useful in assessing for instructional planning. Criterion-referenced testing is more qualitative. It compares the individual's performance with a specified content domain (Anastasi, 1976). Informal tests are usually teacher-made and may be in the form of short-answer objective tests or more subjective written tests (Wallace & Larsen, 1978). Educators should possess skills in each of the following knowledge areas as they apply to the three kinds of tests:

1. Test selection focuses on determining which type of test is more appropriate and choosing particular tests within one of the categories. Skill in making judgments about reliability, validity, norming samples, what test results to expect, and so on are necessary for proficient test selection. Mastery of the other knowledge areas related to tests is also necessary.

2. Test construction is most useful in creating criterion-referenced and informal instruments. Although most teachers are not involved in constructing norm-referenced tests, knowledge related to their construction is helpful when selecting such tests. Some of the basic information about construction of tests includes how to create a pool of items and eliminate inadequate ones, determining and improving reliability and validity when pos-

sible, and delineating administration and scoring procedures.

3. Competency in test administration includes not only how to appropriately administer various tests but also how to judge if a test was properly administered when given by another individual. Naturally, the results from improperly administered tests must be viewed as possibly inaccurate or misleading.

4. Proficiency in interpreting test results should be obtained only after other knowledge areas related to tests have been mastered. The interpretation and subsequent application of the results affect the instructional planning for individual students, which is a major reason for undertaking assessment procedures.

Tests are only one of the products that can be analyzed. Analyzing classwork or homework for patterns or types of errors (e.g., failure to use semicolons appropriately) is included in this area, as is analyzing work for particular strengths. Other products to analyze may be creative acts or their results (e.g., art work or music). Educators may also analyze past records of the student. In general, competency in analysis of products other than tests is closely related to mastery of informal testing and proficiency in the prerequisites of content knowledge as well as child and adolescent development.

INTERVIEWING

While interviewing is one way to gather assessment information, skillful use of its techniques enhances the cooperation of all those concerned with a student. Closely related to these skills is the general ability to get along well with people.

Following are examples of interviewing competencies:

- Asking specific questions that are easy to understand and that will provide the needed information.
- Questioning in an informal manner so that the interviewee does not become defensive.
- Listening and responding appropriately to the answers and questions of others.
- Making note of or remembering pertinent information.

## OBSERVATION

Observing provides educators with information not obtainable in other ways. For example, interaction between the regular classroom teacher and the student can be determined through observation, because either the student or the teacher, or both, may view the situation differently. The following are some of the competencies needed for effective observation:

- Being inconspicuous or unobtrusive when observing. Generally, an outsider must visit a classroom several times before students become accustomed to his or her presence. This is particularly important because the behavior of students is often different when an outsider is present.
- Selecting the appropriate behavior(s) to be observed and identifying other relevant behaviors that may affect the one selected.
- Using appropriate recording or measuring devices for the observation of behavior. These may be highly

structured or, at the other extreme, they may rely only on clinical judgment or insight.
- Being objective.

In attaining these general competencies, individuals with an atomistic philosophy might use Hall's (1974) or others' techniques for applied behavior analysis. Individuals adhering to a holistic philosophy might rely on the section entitled "Analysis of the Learner in the Classroom" that appears in *The Resource Teacher* (Wiederholt, Hammill, & Brown, 1978).

### Application

Before determining which of the basic techniques to use and actually gathering the information, special education teachers must be able to make decisions related to the following questions.

- What area is going to be assessed (e.g., reading, social interactions, math)? Aspects of the area to be assessed should be as specific as possible and will likely be influenced by the individual's educational philosophy, knowledge of the content, and knowledge of child and adolescent development. For example, individuals with an atomistic educational philosophy might consider assessing phonics skills, sound blending, or structural analysis within reading. In contrast, individuals with a holistic educational philosophy might focus on comprehension abilities when different types of reading materials (e.g., newspapers, recipes, history tests) are used.

18

• What types of information are needed? Student performance on actual tasks is usually gathered. Other types of information might focus on attitudes and expectations held by the student or his or her parents.

• Which individuals should be included in the assessment? The assessment process usually focuses on the student. However, assessment information can also be gathered from teachers and other professionals, the student's peers, and the parents.

By making these decisions and applying them to the techniques of assessment, special educators should be ready to actually gather the assessment data. In some instances, other individuals may also assist in gathering the data (e.g., when information is gathered to write an individualized education program).

### Synthesis

Synthesis is probably the most crucial of the three assessment categories and is highly dependent on the previous two. Despite its importance, it is seldom mentioned in competency statements or textbooks for special education teachers.

Proficiency in this category means the ability to take all of the previously gathered assessment information and combine the separate data and ideas to form a cohesive whole. This then becomes the basis for instructional programming. Following are some of the skills that may be required to accomplish this:

• Separating information that appears to be accurate from that which may need verifying.

• Determining if conflicting assessment information is present; if so, deciding which information should be considered more accurate and finding why the discrepancy exists.

• Eliminating information that is redundant or not useful for instructional planning.

• Comparing the information to draw up an order of importance for remedial action.

## IMPLICATIONS AND FUTURE DIRECTIONS

This article is an initial attempt to consolidate and add to currently available competency statements so that they can have broader applications. We have attempted to state a general order (i.e., prerequisites followed by assessment competencies), broaden the competencies to include any type of special education teacher, and to avoid highly structured statements that lock individuals into a particular educational philosophy. On the basis of these initial competencies, there are three major implications to consider.

First, the competencies presented here focus only on assessment for instructional purposes. We hope that a comprehensive set of competencies will be developed in the future and that relevant data will be gathered. If all special education programs related their specific competencies to a general set, contrasting particular programs would be easier. This would also enable individuals to choose the program that seemed best suited to their own needs and beliefs.

Second, individuals may wish to take these initial competencies and judge their own abilities relative to them. If they detect weaknesses, they may wish to pursue further study. Such study might take the form of attending university classes, reading independently, or attending relevant conferences.

Finally, a variety of special education organizations and other professional organizations have alluded to national credentialing of special educators in the future. However, each organization may have different beliefs related to competencies required for credentialing teachers. Therefore developing a set of general competencies may serve as a framework for initial communication.

## REFERENCES

Anastasi, A. *Psychological testing* (4th ed.). New York: Macmillan, 1976.

Arter, J. A., & Jenkins, J. R. Differential diagnosis-prescriptive teaching: A critical appraisal. *Review of Educational Research*, 1979, *49*, 517-555.

Blackhurst, A. E. Competency-based special education personnel preparation. In R. D. Kneedler & S. G. Tarver (Eds.), *Changing perspectives in special education*. Columbus, Ohio: Charles E. Merrill, 1977.

Cegelka, W. J. Competencies of persons responsible for the classification of mentally retarded individuals. *Exceptional Children*, 1978, *45*, 26-31.

Division for Children with Learning Disabilities. *Competencies for teachers of learning disabled children and youth*. Reston, Va.: DCLD, 1978.

Gronlund, N. E. *Measurement and evaluation in teaching* (3rd ed.). New York: Macmillan, 1976.

Hall, R. V. *Behavior modification: The measurement of behavior* (rev. ed.). Lawrence, Kan.: H & H Enterprises, 1974.

Hammill, D. *The field of learning disabilities: A futuristic perspective*. Speech given at the National Conference on Learning Disabilities, Louisville, Ky., October, 1979.

Hammill, D. D., Brown, L., Brown, V., Gray, R., Hresko, W., Larsen, S.C., McNutt, G., Poplin, M.S., Reid, D. K., & Wiederholt, J. L. *A model for classifying instructional strategies*. Unpublished manuscript, 1979. (7701 Cameron Road; Austin, Tex. 78752.)

Hammill, D., & Larsen, S. C. The relationship of selected auditory perceptual skills to reading ability. *Journal of Learning Disabilities*, 1974, *1*, 429-436.

International Reading Association. *Guidelines for the professional preparation of reading teachers*. Newark, Del.: author, 1978.

Larsen, S. C., & Hammill, D. D. Relationship of selected visual perceptual abilities to school learning. *Journal of Special Education*, 1975, *9*, 281-291.

Wallace, G., & Larsen, S. C. *Educational assessment of learning problems: Testing for teaching*. Boston: Allyn & Bacon, 1978.

Wiederholt, J. L., Hammill, D. D., & Brown, V. *The resource teacher: A guide to effective practices*. Boston: Allyn & Bacon, 1978.

# Multidisciplinary Team Approaches in the Assessment of Handicapped Preschool Children

*Charles Orlando, Ph.D.*
*Board of Cooperative Educational Services*
*Allegany County*
*Belmont, New York*

THE REGULATIONS implementing Public Law 94-142 (Federal Register, August 23, 1977, Part II) require that whenever a handicapped child is evaluated for the first time (Section 121a 344) the process involves school officials, the child's teacher, a person knowledgeable of the evaluative measures to be used and other personnel at the discretion of the parents or the school. It is reasonable to believe that those most knowledgeable about the evaluation are the professionals who administered the evaluative tests and measures to the child. These individuals are commonly involved in multidisciplinary approaches to the identification of handicapped children (Maitland, Nadeau, & Nadeau, 1974). Multidisciplinary evaluation teams, however, have had many functional problems related to their goals, organization, roles of the team members, and the development of program plans (Fenton, Yoshida, Maxwell, & Kauffman, 1979).

## OBJECTIVES OF
## MULTIDISCIPLINARY TEAMS

Multidisciplinary teams have been used in assessing young handicapped children for the following purposes:

- screening to predict failure (Keogh, 1973);
- screening to determine eligibility for specific programs (Fenton et al., 1979);
- screening and assessment to determine individualized special educational program needs (Daggett, 1979; Hayden & Gotts, 1977; Maher, 1979; Maitland et al., 1974).

### Prediction of failure

The prediction of failure is a nonproductive goal for multidisciplinary teams. It is both useless and potentially harmful to identify children as probable failures. Such labeling can result in self-fulfilling prophecy (Keogh, 1973), or worse, the exclusion of children with special needs from school (Kephart, 1974) solely because the school is not ready to program for them. Teams oriented to failure prediction seldom obtain information for programming efforts, and fail to assess situational variables that impinge upon the child in a task-oriented educational program (Keogh, 1973).

### Determination of eligibility

To determine a child's eligibility for handicapped programs is only a first step. Unless the assessment is extended to use accumulated information to design an appropriate individual education plan (IEP), the child will not be helped to function better in the learning environment. Haring and Ridgway (1967) found that a multidisciplinary team approach using a battery of standardized tests did not distinguish children with special education needs from children who needed no special help.

They concluded that behavioral analysis might be more effective in identifying program needs.

### Program determination

Much of the available information on multidisciplinary teams relates to team functioning and information gathering in programs for school-aged children. How this information is translated into program goals, however, has not been much studied—despite the fact that Maitland et al. (1974) found that 44% of 581 school districts they surveyed said they used the information gathered by multidisciplinary assessment teams to develop indi-

---

*Much of the available information on multidisciplinary teams relates to team functioning and information gathering.... How this information is translated into program goals has not been much studied.*

---

vidualized programs. Multidisciplinary team assessments for preschool programs have not found their way into the research literature, perhaps because of the relative newness of public school programs for handicapped preschoolers.

## PROBLEMS IN TEAM FUNCTIONING

The literature on team functioning (Brassell & Dunst, 1978; Sahin, 1978; Conner, Williamson, & Sieppe, 1978; Fenton et al., 1979; Maher, 1979) reveals a number of problems. These appear to be related to procedures for establishing goals, interpersonal relationships, and role perceptions.

Yoshida, Fenton, Maxwell, and Kauffman (1978a,b) analyzed a number of multidisciplinary teams in terms of their make-up and how they translated the information they gathered into special education programs. The teams usually consisted of school psychologists, social workers, speech and hearing personnel, principals, counselors, medical personnel, and special education teachers. All the assessment information was transmitted and received orally. Any program plans were usually communicated orally to the teacher, who often was not present at the team meeting.

In reviewing multidisciplinary teams, Fitzsimmons (1977) found major problems in the interpersonal relationships among team members. These included inability of certain team members to accept and explore comments about a child from other team members with different professional backgrounds, difficulties arising from differential status of team members, and team disagreement about the amount of time to be committed to developing goals.

Fitzsimmons (1977) also identified role encroachment as a problem in team functioning. Conner et al. (1978), on the other hand, advocate a multidisciplinary assessment model which requires that all participating professionals release their roles to others who appear to be in a better position to work with the child or the parents, and are thus better able to integrate the various aspects of the assessment information within a special education program. However, they state that specialists should not relinquish accountability in their fields. These two points appear to be contradictory. It is apparent that team members do not perceive their individual and team responsibilities in the same way.

Fenton (1979) recommended that each team have a written statement of goals, and a periodic review of each member's perception of his or her role in relation to other team members and to the stated goals. The literature would seem to suggest that for a team to function properly and determine team goals

and procedures, a capable and efficient team leader is mandatory.

## IMPROVING PRESCHOOL TEAM ASSESSMENTS

A number of authors have recommended ways to make preschool team assessments more effective (Keogh, 1973; Dickenson, 1978; Bagnato, Neisworth, & Eaves, 1978; Karnes & Lee, 1978; Orlando & Grund, 1974. One suggestion is that assessments be broadened to include factors external to the child, such as the teacher, the school climate, and the child's previous experience.

### Importance of classroom teacher

Bagnato, Neisworth, and Eaves (1978) make the point that while the various professionals on a team should assess a child's abilities in their respective areas of expertise, a classroom teacher is probably in the best position to gather information about a child's daily interactions. This is especially true in relation to the tasks that a child needs to be able to do to learn appropriate behaviors and cognitive skills in the classroom.

### From assessment to program

Screening by multidisciplinary teams, if it is to be used at all, should select children for more intensive multidisciplinary assessments that will identify handicapping conditions, determine program goals, and monitor intervention programs. However, such screening can also be used to develop individualized programs for all children screened, rather than the relatively few children with special needs (Orlando & Grund, 1974).

How should the bridge from assessment to program be made? Bagnato and Neisworth (1979) describe the need for "forging links" between developmental-diagnostic information gathered via multidisciplinary team

24 assessment and individualized programs for preschool handicapped children.

Bagnato, Neisworth, and Eaves (1978) designed a Perception of Developmental Skills Program (PODS). They outline a 7-point rating system for assessing communication, self-care, motor, and problem-solving behavior. The subjective impressions of all professionals involved in screening are included in these ratings. Bagnato et al. (1978) suggest that team members can develop an understanding of each professional approach to evaluation and of its strengths and weaknesses; over time, they will evolve basic guidelines for team functioning. Such an approach requires team members to work together over a period of time, share the goals and objectives of the team, and function as a *team* rather than a group of individuals.

The preceding information and ideas yield the following conclusions:

1. The major goal of a multidisciplinary team is to translate assessment information into an IEP.
2. A strong team leader is needed to maintain the focus of the team.
3. Professionals on the team should—within their area of expertise—assess both the child *and* the child's relation to the learning environment.
4. For the team approach to be effective, much more time must be allotted to team meetings and evaluation procedures.

### Translating assessment information into an IEP

Individual program guidelines for teachers can be provided by using the PODS system described above, or by other screening and assessment activities—such as Portage, Behavior Characteristics Progression (BCP), and Pines Bridge—which describe developmental skills in a hierarchial sequential order. They should also provide a framework to writing specific objectives for IEPs. The programs derived from these sequential development descriptions emphasize a child's skills and interaction with the learning environment. They provide an important first step in educational interventions. However, any statement of specific program objectives is only the first step in the process. Once the child begins to learn and function in the environment, the objectives shift and change, requiring constant monitoring of progress.

It is difficult to assess a child's ability to perform within a learning environment, but it can be done by using the team organization described by Orlando and Grund (1974). Their assessment program brings a group of children into the classroom for two half-day sessions. Team members assess the children individually and observe them in the learning environment in which they will need to function when they enter school. This model can be used in nursery schools, kindergartens, and programs for preschool handicapped children. The method of assessing developmental skills can be selected from the systems discussed already or from the multitude on the market, but the system is not as important as how the teacher and the team select and utilize priority objectives for designing programs. The priority objectives selected by the team from the developmental information gathered on each child (usually those skills the child may be able to perform but not on an automatic level) are then written in IEP form for discussion with parents. Once a child masters the objectives, the next one in the sequence is used, while earlier objectives are reviewed and integrated.

A difficulty with sequential developmental objectives programs is that they tend to teach skills in an isolated, limited way. Karnes and Lee (1978) suggest providing the child with a variety of learning experiences related to the desired skill. Otherwise, the child may learn a repertoire of isolated skills which cannot be transferred to novel situations.

### Strong team leaders

Either the classroom teacher or, as a second choice, the program coordinator, should serve as team leader because the assessment information must be translated into a feasible written IEP. This may cause some problems because the teacher often has lower professional status than other team members. Proper inservice training can overcome this. The classroom teacher is primarily responsible for monitoring a program's effectiveness and should call the team together when problems arise.

### Assessing the child and the learning environment

Team members should observe the child and assess the child's performance within the learning environment. If a child cannot be seen during the initial evaluation, then the team members should wait until the child can

Goals:  1. Identify handicapped children
2. Develop IEP
3. Monitor and evaluate IEPs

| Team member | Responsibility | | |
|---|---|---|---|
| | Assessment | Program | Evaluation |
| Teacher-team leader | Developmental objectives | Help select priority objectives<br>Provide experiences related to objectives | Evaluate learning in relation to objectives, on an ongoing basis |
| School psychologist | Intellectual ability, socialization objectives | Help select priority objectives<br>Assist with development of behavior management objectives | Observe child's progress and learning situation in relation to objectives |
| Speech-language therapist | Language and speech assessment, audiological assessment | Provide language experiences, resources for teacher and parent re: objectives | Monitor progress by sampling language behavior periodically |
| Health professional | Heart, lungs, vision assessments, immunization time test | Help select priorities<br>Assess physical progress<br>Refer to appropriate specialist<br>Provide needed modifications | Monitor progress<br>Follow-up on referrals to health specialists |
| Parent | Developmental history | Help select priority objective, home activities to develop identified skills | Relate perception of progress to team |
| Other professionals | As determined by team referral; reason for referral qualified | Help select priority objectives<br>React to recommendation of team | Review programs and recommend program modification |

Figure 1. A proposed model for multidisciplinary team organization.

26

be evaluated in the learning situation before developing the IEP.

For these procedures to be effective, all team members need to respect one another as professionals and as equals, and work together to make the team as efficient as possible.

**Time constraints**

Currently most teams put little time into assessing children and formulating educational programs. The successful multidisciplinary team approach demands a substantial commitment of time, during which members

---

Date of Plan _____          School _____

Child's name _____          Handicapping condition _____

Date of birth _____          Parent's name _____

Home address _____          Phone number _____

| Service | Program | Teacher | Location | Beg. date | Program review date |
|---|---|---|---|---|---|
| Special class related services | Preschool | | | | |
| _____ | | | | | |
| _____ | | | | | |
| _____ | | | | | |

Long-term educational goals:

Extent to which child can participate in regular education programs:

| Area | | Hours per week | Location |
|---|---|---|---|
| Transportation | _____ | | |
| Cafeteria | _____ | | |
| Physical education | _____ | | |
| Other | _____ | | |

Suggested parent role:                          _____ Individuals attending conference

Signed: _____

_____

_____

_____

Figure 2. IEP, Preschool Program for Exceptional Children (page 1).

can work together and discuss all aspects of each child's program. This requires more personnel than are presently used. It also means changes in scheduling to allow for open-ended discussions on problems and procedures. Many school officials will say that they cannot afford to extend schedules because of already overburdened budgets. In order for IEPs to be effective, however, the schools cannot afford *not* to see that teams have sufficient working time. Time spent in initial program planning is usually saved later by the use of appropriate goals and the decrease in trial-and-error programs.

## A PROPOSED MODEL FOR MULTIDISCIPLINARY TEAM ORGANIZATION

A proposed model for effective multidisciplinary team functioning is found in Figure 1. Although it was designed for prekindergarten assessment, it can and should be extended to preschool and school-age handicapped children as well.

The stated goals must be accepted by all team members to ensure some degree of success in developing a functional multidisciplinary team within this model. Assessment, program, and evaluation responsibilities are defined for each team member. While an individual variation may of course occur within the model, the basic outline is useful because it provides the necessary focus and structure for optimum team functioning.

After the assessment procedures have been accomplished, team discussion should yield a determination of whether the child has a handicapping condition or not. If a child is identified as handicapped, the proper placement and priority goals must be recommended. A concise two-page form is illustrated in Figures 2 and 3. This form contains all the information required by law as well as a statement of the learning objectives selected for initial programming. More than one copy

Date _____

Child _____   DOB _____   School _____   Teacher _____

Long-term goals

Instructional objectives          Current functioning          Methods of assessment          Methods/materials

**Figure 3.** IEP, Preschool Program for Exceptional Children (page 2).

28

*Models for effective multidisciplinary team functioning can crucially influence the outcome of multidisciplinary assessment teams.*

of Figure 3 can be used when many priority objectives have been selected, either because the child is more severely handicapped or requires services (e.g., speech therapy, occupational therapy, counseling) from more than two professionals.

With experience, the team will learn to choose an increasing number of appropriate priorities for a child, based upon the type of handicap and behavioral manifestations. Team members will also learn to become more efficient in the selection of assessment instruments useful with handicapped children of preschool age, and to match these instruments with the varieties of educational programs provided.

Models for effective multidisciplinary team functioning, such as the one presented here, can crucially influence the outcome of multidisciplinary assessment teams—teams that are likely to be increasingly important as more effort is directed toward special education and its downward extension to preschool-age children.

## REFERENCES

Bagnato, S.J., & Neisworth, J.T. Between assessment and intervention: Forging an assessment/curriculum linkage for the handicapped preschooler. *Child Care Quarterly*, 1979, *8*, 179–195.

Bagnato, S.J., Neisworth, J.T., & Eaves, R.C. A profile of perceived capabilities for the preschool child. *Child Care Quarterly*, 1978, *7*, 327–335.

Brassell, W.R., & Dunst, C.J. Fostering the object construct: Large scale intervention with handicapped infants. *American Journal of Mental Deficiency*, 1978, *82*, 507–510.

Conner, F.P., Williamson, G.G., & Sieppe, J.M. *Program guide for infants and toddlers with neuromotor and other developmental disabilities.* New York: Teacher's College Press, 1978.

Dickenson, D.J. Direct assessment of behavioral and emotional problems. *Psychology in the Schools*, 1978, *15*, 472–477.

Fenton, K.S., Yoshida, R.K., Maxwell, J.B., & Kauffman, M.J. Recognition of team goals: An essential step toward rational decision making. *Exceptional Children*, 1979, *45*, 638–644.

Fitzsimmons, R.M. Fostering productive interdisciplinary staff conferences. *Academic Therapy*, 1977, *12*, 281–287.

Haring, N., & Ridgway, R. Early identification of children with learning disabilities. *Exceptional Children*, 1967, *33*, 387–395.

Hayden, A.H., & Gotts, E.A. Multiple staffing patterns. In J.B. Jordan, A.H. Hayden, M.B. Karnes, & M.M. Wood (Eds.), *Early childhood education for exceptional children: A handbook of ideas and exemplary practices.* Reston Va.: Council for Exceptional Children, 1977.

Karnes, M.B., & Lee, R.C. *Early Childhood.* Reston Va.: Council for Exceptional Children, 1978.

Keogh, B.K. Early detection of learning problems: Questions, cautions, and guidelines. *Exceptional Children*, 1973, *40*, 5–11.

Kephart, W.B. Pre-kindergarten screening clinics. *Phi Delta Kappan*, 1974, *55*, 459.

Maher, C.A. COMPASS: A guide for delivering school-based special service programs. *Psychology in the Schools*, 1979, *16*, 230–234.

Maitland, S., Nadeau, B.E., & Nadeau, G. Early school screening practices. *Journal of Learning Disabilities*, 1974, *7*, 645–649.

Orlando, C.P., & Grund, W.E. Instruction vs. exclusion. *Phi Delta Kappan*, 1974, *56*, 148.

Sahin, S.T. Efficient preschool screening for educationally at-risk children. *Day Care and Early Education*, 1978, *5*, 42–45.

Yoshida, R.K., Fenton, K.S., Maxwell, J.P., & Kauffman, M.J. Ripple effect: Communication of planning team decisions to program implementation. *Journal of School Psychology*, 1978, *16*, 177–183.(a)

Yoshida, R.K., Fenton, K.S., Maxwell, J.P. & Kauffman, M.J. Group decision making in the planning team process: Myth or reality? *Journal of School Psychology*, 1978, *16*, 237–244.(b)

# Parental and Professional Agreement in Early Childhood Assessment

**Kathleen Gradel, Ed.D.**
*State University College at Buffalo*
*Buffalo, New York*

**Max S. Thompson, Ed.D.**
*Appalachian State University*
*Boone, North Carolina*

**Robert Sheehan, Ph.D.**
*Purdue University*
*West Lafayette, Indiana*

A RECENT emphasis in early childhood and special education has been the multidisciplinary evaluation of at-risk infants and handicapped children. The involvement of medical, psychological, and other health-related examiners, as well as of teachers and parents, has been supported as a means of improving information gathering (Cross, 1977; DuBose, Langley, & Stagg, 1977; Frankel, 1979; Honzik, 1976; Simeonsson, 1977; Simeonsson, Huntington, & Parse, 1980). There are obvious benefits of collecting child performance data across contexts and from multiple informed sources. More importantly, there is a strong possibility that corroboration between sources improves the credibility of these data (Irvin, Crowell, & Bellamy, 1979).

## MAJOR INFORMATION SOURCES

Typically there are three major sources of information on infants and preschoolers who are served in programs for developmentally delayed, at-risk, or handicapped children: the diagnostician, the teacher, and the parent. The trained diagnostician uses both standard-

30 ized instruments and less formal ones to substantiate clinical judgment. Teacher information usually includes a broad range of perceptions and expectations as well as developmental information summarized on formal and informal tests and checklists. Parent data are usually collected by the teacher, the diagnostician, or another service provider through interviews, questionnaires, and other inventories. These measures may be structured to assess parental attitudes, desires, and expectations; to measure satisfaction with instruction and services; or to obtain parents' estimates of their children's developmental functioning.

In practice, the relative assumed credibility of these data sources tends to dictate the extent to which they are considered in decisions about handicapped children. Parental input in particular is often minimized, or limited to information about child reinforcers and the child's home behavior (DuBose et al., 1977). More extensive data from parents are usually not sought by professionals on the assumption that parental estimates and expectations regarding child performance are likely to be inflated. At the other extreme, the diagnostician's view of child performance may be overrepresented in the data pool (Evans & Sparrow, 1976; Kiernan & DuBose, 1974), particularly in light of the possibility of a diagnostician's limited opportunity to become familiar with a child (Keogh, 1972). Teacher estimates tend to fall between the two extremes of assumed credibility, with formal and informal teacher assessments and observational data held to be of considerable value in intervention (DuBose et al., 1977; Moran, 1976), even if not highly regarded in wider diagnostic circles.

The extent to which these three most common sources of data can in fact be depended on to supply reliable assessment information has not been adequately determined. Research literature indicates differences in maternal and professional ratings of children, but no clear patterns of relationships between variables have been identified to account for these differences.

## PURPOSES OF THE RESEARCH

The research reported in this article investigated the relationship between mothers' estimations of the developmental performance of their handicapped infants and preschoolers and judgments of the same children by professional, more traditionally acceptable data sources—teachers and diagnosticians. The research had two primary purposes:

1. to determine the patterns of agreement and disagreement for test items and scale scores between alternate data sources on standardized instruments that have frequent use in the field; and
2. to investigate the relationship between child performance and overall agreement—or congruency—between data sources.

## METHOD

The sample in this research consisted of two subgroups: (1) 30 infants aged 3 to 24 months, their mothers, and their home-based teachers; and (2) 30 preschoolers aged 38 to 73 months, their mothers, and their center-based teachers. All children were enrolled in either a home- or center-based program (which type of program being primarily determined by their age). All mothers and children were Caucasian.

Child performance data were collected using three instruments: The *Alpern-Boll Developmental Profile* (Alpern & Boll, 1972), the *Bayley Scales of Infant Development* (Bayley, 1969), and the *McCarthy Scales of Children's Abilities* (McCarthy, 1972). Data were gathered via the Developmental Profile from each child's teacher and mother. The Bayley and the McCarthy Scales were used to collect data from the mother and the diagnos-

**Table 1.** Sources of data

| Child | Scale | Mother | Teacher |
|---|---|---|---|
| Infant | Bayley | 1. Developmental Profile<br>2. Modified Bayley Maternal Interview | Developmental Profile |
| Preschooler | McCarthy | 1. Developmental Profile<br>2. Modified McCarthy Maternal Interview | Developmental Profile |

tician. The Bayley was used for the infants, and the McCarthy was used for the preschool group. The Bayley and McCarthy were both modified into interview instruments by simplifying their vocabularies, converting them into a question format, and incorporating a demonstration into the presentation of each item. This adaptation was used only for the mother; the standard administration was completed for each child by a trained diagnostician. Table 1 summarizes the entire data collection procedure.

## RESULTS

The paramount issue of this research was congruency—the agreement between data sources on the assessment information. It was assumed that agreement between mothers and professionals on test items and scores validates input from the mother. Such an assumption is questionable in light of the study's results; nevertheless, it is one that is made by many diagnosticians in the field.

### Scale score congruency

*Bayley Scales.* Comparison of scores derived from the protocols of each data source yielded promising but somewhat varied relationships. On the Bayley Scales, significant correlations ($p < .05$) between diagnosticians' scores and mothers' scores were derived ($r =$ .686 for the Mental Development Index [MDI]; $r = .666$ for the Psychomotor Development Index [PDI]). In terms of the developmental age equivalents derived from the Bayley standard scores, the Bayley Scales demonstrated slightly higher predictive relationships between sources ($r = .845$ for the Mental Scale; $r = .710$ for the Motor Scale). The results also indicated, however, that there were significant differences between mothers and diagnosticians, with the professional assessors giving lower average assessments. (See Table 2.)

The highest agreement between mothers and the other data sources was obtained when the focus of the analysis was the children's developmental age (DA). This important finding is interpretable in light of the nature of the instrument in question and the severity of the handicapping conditions of the infants in the study. One difficulty with the Bayley Scales is

**Table 2.** Comparison of mothers' and diagnosticians' standard scores on the Bayley Scales

| | Mother | | Diagnostician | | Obtained | |
|---|---|---|---|---|---|---|
| Scale | $\overline{X}$ | SD | $\overline{X}$ | SD | $r$ | $t$ |
| MDI | 94.3 | 34.54 | 79.6 | 24.31 | .686 | 3.19* |
| PDI | 89.5 | 32.34 | 73.8 | 22.74 | .666 | 3.56* |

*$p < .05$ ($df = 29$)

32 that the lowest scale score obtainable is 50; children who have raw scores lower than this are all assigned a scale score of 50. Thus the lower correlations yielded by analyzing the standard scale scores were very likely influenced by the truncation which occurred with the 50-point cutoff. It is possible, however, to derive a developmental age score for these lower achieving children, which can go as low as 1 month.

*McCarthy Scales.* The congruency between the assessments made by preschoolers' mothers and diagnosticians on the McCarthy Scales was similar to that on the Bayley. Analyses of the four scale scores and the General Cognitive Index (GCI) of the McCarthy showed significant mother-diagnostician correlations ($p < .05$) ranging from .73 to .95 (see Table 3). As with mothers of handicapped infants, maternal score estimates were significantly higher than those resulting from professional judgment.

*Developmental Profile.* Correlations on the Developmental Profile between mothers of handicapped infants and their teachers ranged from .415 to .868; for the preschool group, mother-teacher correlations ranged from .95 to .98. Once again, there were significant differences ($p < .05$) between mothers and teachers, with all differences reflecting overestimation on the part of the mothers.

### Item congruency

An item-by-item comparison of maternal and professional responses verified the high percentage of agreement between mothers and diagnosticians. The mother and teacher agreed on an average of 91% on all the Developmental Profile items. On the McCarthy Scales, maternal and diagnostician agreement averaged 78% on the scored items. The percentage of agreement on the Bayley Mental and Motor Scales was 76% and 75%,

---

*An item-by-item comparison of maternal and professional responses verified the high percentage of agreement between mothers and diagnosticians.*

---

respectively. These results can be interpreted to mean that mothers are fairly accurate when estimating their children's current development.

But the primary purpose for analyzing agreement by item was to determine which items had high as compared to low agreement across cases, and whether a pattern existed. The study showed no pattern other than the scalar nature of the instruments (for the

**Table 3.** Comparison of mothers' and diagnosticians' standard scores on the McCarthy Scales

| Scale | Mother | | Diagnostician | | | Obtained |
| | $\overline{X}$ | SD | $\overline{X}$ | SD | r | t |
|---|---|---|---|---|---|---|
| Verbal | 40.33 | 7.15 | 35.83 | 6.67 | .87 | 7.02° |
| Perceptual | 35.20 | 12.08 | 31.23 | 10.05 | .95 | 5.60° |
| Quantitative | 38.40 | 10.16 | 3.67 | 7.79 | .73 | 2.37° |
| Memory | 37.10 | 9.45 | 34.27 | 8.69 | .86 | 3.23° |
| GCI | 76.80 | 16.31 | 68.93 | 14.67 | .88 | 5.65° |

°$p < .05$ ($df = 29$)

Developmental Profile and the Bayley) contributing to patterns of agreement across the items. In other words, as children reached their ceilings, they showed repeated failures on more difficult items. No specific content commonalities among items that had very high or very low agreement were identified for either the preschool or infant groups on the Developmental Profile and the Bayley Scales. The McCarthy showed no pattern—not even a scalar one—with respect to item congruency. This is to be expected since the McCarthy consists of 15 subtests, each containing relatively few ordinal items—as opposed to the other tests used in this research, which have fewer subtests but many more ordinal items.

### Overall congruency and child performance

The congruency scores derived for each case were correlated with the scores representing infant performance on each of the instruments (i.e., standard scores and derived age equivalents). Significant correlations ($p < .05$) were found only for the Bayley Mental and Motor Scale developmental age equivalents (Mental DA, $r = .653$; Motor DA, $r = .649$) and the IQE on the Developmental Profile ($r = .477$) for the infant group. In light of the large number of correlations computed, these findings are to be considered tentative pending replication.

### Congruency and demographic variables

One-way analyses of variance were computed on children's and infants' test scores and relevant demographic traits. Significant relationships ($p < .05$) existed for only the infant group between: (1) Developmental Profile IQE and prior assessment experience of the mothers, (2) Bayley PDI and levels of maternal education, and (3) Bayley Motor Scale developmental age and mothers' prior training in child development. The commonality in these demographic variables is obvious.

Additional analyses of variance were computed on the congruency scores in relation to specific maternal variables. Significant differences ($p < .05$) existed between groups when mothers' prior assessment experience was related to these scale scores: Bayley Mental Scale and the scores on the Developmental Profile Physical, Academic, and Communication Scales.

## DISCUSSION AND IMPLICATIONS

The results of the present research indicate that:

1. The developmental assessments of mothers of handicapped infants and children are highly correlated with alternate, more traditional data sources (teachers and trained diagnosticians).
2. Systematic differences exist between mothers and diagnosticians or teachers: mothers estimate their children's performance more highly than the professional data sources.
3. Mother-professional congruency is greater for the older preschool group than for the infant group.

Using three assessment instruments that have generally wide application in the field, systematic comparisons were made between data sources, based on completed protocols for each source, for each instrument. Analyses addressed a primary issue in assessment—the ability of a mother to describe her child's development in response to specific questions asked of her. This research compared maternal estimations with the most likely alternative of reference, the professional.

### Patterns of agreement and disagreement

Based on item-by-item comparisons, there was substantial agreement between professionals and mothers. Within the differences that occurred, mothers tended to overesti-

34 mate. However, it is important to note that there tended to be a measure of consistency across the scales within single instruments. For example, the percentage of mother-professional agreement on the Bayley Mental and Motor Scales was 75.7% and 75.9%, respectively. These figures demonstrate considerable consistency across the two scales, suggesting that agreement across scales followed a pattern, despite the differences implicit in item classification by scale. In other words, if mothers' ability to make judgments depended on the kind or content of items in each scale, a greater across-scales discrepancy between agreement figures might have been expected. This did not happen with any of the instruments or with either age group.

The data collected in this study support the general findings of other investigators (e.g., Frankenburg, Van Doorninck, Liddell, & Dick, 1976; Hunt & Paraskevopoulos, 1980; Knobloch, Gross, Holsapple, Lafave, Stevens, & Tate, 1973) that mothers tend to overestimate the developmental repertoires of their children. In the case of the present research, when an item disagreement occurred, it was usually in the direction of an overestimation on the part of the mother. However, these differences did not interfere with the significant positive correlations between mothers' and professionals' assessments on the three instruments, for both the younger and older groups.

### Professional "underestimation"

One way of looking at overestimation is to hypothesize that the trained examiner's view of the child *could* be substantially more narrow than that of the mother. In this light the professional data source would be considered to "underestimate" children's performance. This is more likely with the Bayley Scales and McCarthy Scales, which require highly trained examiners who typically assess

the child in only 1 to 3 sessions. Thus the opportunity that most diagnosticians have for repeated measurement or observation of the child is minimal or absent. As Haskett and Bell (1978) noted with respect to the Bayley Scales, "on any single administration of the scale . . . the examiner may not be able to secure a representative sample of an individual's behavior, and will, if anything, probably underestimate the repertoire" (p. 347).

### Maternal "overestimation"

If, in fact, typical clinical assessment limits the diagnostician's sampling of the child's developmental performance, the apparent overestimation by the mother makes sense. In other words, the repeated daily "assessments" available to the mother may give her a wider view of the child's acquired and evolving skills. This is even more plausible given the limited sensitivity of existing assessment approaches and instruments to: (1) the multiple presenting problems of these children (e.g., physical, motivational), (2) the absence or underpresentation of appropriate domains of behavior, and (3) the inherent variability of these children (Simeonsson et al., 1980).

The mandated inclusion of parents in the individualized education program (IEP) development phase can add crucial information about children's current levels of functioning. Elevating the credibility of the information provided by parents could decrease time spent by teachers at the outset of the instructional year doing gross assessment of children's skill repertoires. Additionally, by pairing their own natural assessment skills with more discrete means of collecting data (e.g., recording frequency or duration data), parents could provide teachers and other professionals with ongoing information about skill acquisition, maintenance, and generalization. This would be an attractive "bonus" for teachers, who are becoming increasingly accountable for teaching skills that have some current and projected impact on children's abilities to function in settings outside the school.

It is also worth noting that the concept of maternal overestimation originated with the early approaches to studying mothers' estimations of their children. The most frequently used procedure involved gross estimates by the parent of an IQ score or a developmental age equivalent (Ewert & Green, 1957; Heriot & Schmickel, 1967; Saxon, 1975; Schulman & Stern, 1959; Tew, Laurence, & Samuel, 1974; Wolfensberger & Kurtz, 1971). These must be regarded as extremely gross estimations of performance since they demand of parents a "guess" that focuses a complex array of frequent "assessments" into one abstract value. More recent studies investigating the ability of parents to define their children's behavior have used more precise methods (e.g., Field, Hallock, Dempsey, & Shuman, 1978; Hunt & Paraskevopoulos, 1980).

### Item and scale variation

The present research systematically accounted for variation occurring across items and scales. By coding agreement, underestimation, and overestimation for each item, it was possible to make discrete analyses relating to the ability of mothers to judge their infants' performances. In addition, the procedure of coding all items within the highest ceiling took into account all the possible scorable items for each infant, thus allowing the most realistic possible viewpoint of both overestimation and underestimation.

Similar procedures were employed by Hunt & Paraskevopoulos (1980) to assess the correlation between maternal estimates of nonhandicapped 5-year-olds and child performance. Their data provide another perspective on the overestimation question. Incorrect maternal estimates (as compared with diagnostician-rated child performance) were negatively correlated ($r = -.80$) with the number of items passed by the children. More specifically, most of the maternal differences were overestimates, with overestimations showing a negative correlation with the number of items the child passed ($r = -.77$). Hunt and Paraskevopoulos concluded that those mothers who had excessively high expectations of their children were providing less supportive developmental environments than mothers who were more accurate in their predictions. The extension of this is that mothers who have relatively accurate views of their children's development are more capable of providing them with appropriate learning situations. Generalizing these conclusions to the heterogeneous sample in this study, it can be assumed that mothers who are more accurate predictors of their children's performance can provide

*Mothers who are more accurate predictors of their children's performance can provide more realistic daily "teachable" moments to their handicapped children.*

more realistic daily "teachable" moments to their handicapped children. If, on the other hand, a mother's picture of her child's developmental repertoire were highly inflated, the tasks set up for the child to accomplish would tend to be too ambitious. This would likely result in fewer functional opportunities for the child to perform even the less advanced skills currently in his or her repertoire.

### Research directions

The present study and related research suggest several directions for future research. First, no comparisons have been made

36 between the types of professionals—diagnosticians and teachers—whose scores were used as the standards of comparison for maternal responses to test items. Comparisons across all common sources of data would make it possible to measure the reliability of each profession relative to the other profession and to the parent. A more definitive investigation of the relation of demographic variables to parental estimation should also be undertaken. Another critical issue continues to be overestimation. If it is true that parents may in fact be giving a more realistic, informally data-based perspective of the child, perhaps ongoing acquisition, maintenance, and generalization data could be measured across multiple, equally informed sources. Finally, the reliability of fathers as sources of assessment information on their children must be investigated. The research literature provides little information on the father as a contributor of assessment information, support, and instruction for the young handicapped child.

## Practice implications

The present study and related research also suggest some implications for practice. First, practitioners should not be surprised to discover that the use of multiple data sources yields a variety of perspectives on children's developmental performance. These perspectives will usually involve mothers "overestimating" or professionals "underestimating." Second, when a mother does provide data suggesting a developmental delay or problem, it particularly warrants investigation since the mother is likely to be describing the child's developmental performance at a higher level than any other observer. Third, disagreements between mothers and professionals are usually to be found with emergent items, those items close to a child's ceiling level of performance. Periodic reassessment is useful to ascertain whether performance on such items stabilizes and is exhibited on a more regular basis in standardized assessment situations.

## REFERENCES

Alpern, G.D., & Boll, T.J. *Developmental profile.* Indianapolis, Ind.: Psychological Development Publications, 1972.

Bayley, N. *Manual for the Bayley Scales of Infant Development.* New York: The Psychological Corporation, 1969.

Cross, L. Diagnosis. In L. Cross & K. Goin (Eds.), *Identifying handicapped children: A guide to casefinding, screening, diagnosis, assessment, and evaluation.* New York: Walker & Company, 1977.

DuBose, R.F., Langley, M.B., & Stagg, V. Assessing severely handicapped children. *Focus on Exceptional Children,* 1977, *9*(7), 1–13.

Evans, R., & Sparrow, M. Some new departures in the assessment of early childhood development. *Association of Educational Psychologists Journal,* 1976, *4*(1), 14–20.

Ewert, J.C., & Green, M.W. Conditions associated with the mother's estimate of the ability of her retarded child. *American Journal of Mental Deficiency,* 1957, *62*, 521–533.

Field, T.M., Hallock, N.F., Dempsey, J.R., & Shuman, H.H. Mothers' assessment of term and pre-term infants with Respiratory Distress Syndrome: Reliability and predictive validity. *Child Psychiatry and Human Development,* 1978, *9*(2), 75–85.

Frankel, R. Parents as evaluators of their retarded youngsters. *Mental Retardation,* 1979, *17*(1), 40–42.

Frankenburg, W.K., Van Doorninck, W.J., Liddell, T.N., & Dick, N.P. The Denver Prescreening Developmental Questionnaire. *Pediatrics,* 1976, *57*, 744–753.

Haskett, J., & Bell, J. Profound developmental retardation: Descriptive and theoretical utility of the Bayley Mental Scale. In C.E. Meyers (Ed.), *Quality of life in severely and profoundly mentally retarded people: Research foundations for improvement.* Washington, D.C.: American Association on Mental Deficiency, Monograph #3, 1978.

Heriot, J.T., & Schmickel, C.A. Maternal estimates of IQ in children evaluated for learning potential. *American Journal of Mental Deficiency,* 1967, *71*, 920–924.

Honzik, M.P. Value and limitations of infants tests: An overview. In M. Lewis (Ed.), *Origins of intelligence: Infancy and early childhood.* New York: Plenum, 1976.

Hunt, J.McV., & Paraskevopoulos, J. Children's psychological development as a function of the inaccuracy of their mothers' knowledge of their abilities. *The Journal of Genetic Psychology*, 1980, *136*, 285–298.

Irvin, L.K., Crowell, F.A., & Bellamy, G.T. Multiple assessment evaluation of programs for severely handicapped adults. *Mental Retardation*, 1979, *17*, 123–128.

Keogh, B.K. Psychological evaluation of exceptional children: Old hangups and new directions. *Journal of School Psychology*, 1972, *10*, 141–145.

Kiernan, D., & DuBose, R.F. Assessing the cognitive development of preschool deaf-blind children. *Education of the Visually Handicapped*, 1974, *6*, 103–105.

Knobloch, H., Gross, S., Holsapple, R., Lafave, H., Stevens, F., & Tate, J. Do mothers' answers to a questionnaire adequately evaluate the development of infants? *Journal of Pediatric Research*, 1973, *7*, 296.

McCarthy, D. *Manual for the McCarthy Scales of Children's Abilities*. New York: The Psychological Corporation, 1972.

Moran, M.R. The teacher's role in referral for testing and interpretation of reports. *Focus on Exceptional Children*, 1976, *8*, 1–16.

Saxon, S.A. Using mothers to screen for intelligence. *Pediatric Psychology*, 1975, *28*, 28–29.

Schulman, J.L., & Stern, S. Parents' estimates of the intelligence of retarded children. *American Journal of Mental Deficiency*, 1959, *63*, 696–698.

Simeonsson, R.J. Infant assessment and developmental handicaps. In B.M. Caldwell, D.J. Stedman, & K.W. Goin (Eds.), *Infant education: A guide for helping handicapped children in the first three years*. New York: Walker & Company, 1977.

Simeonsson, R.J., Huntington, G.S., & Parse, S.A. Assessment of children with severe handicaps: Multiple problems—multivariate goals. *Journal of the Association for the Severely Handicapped*, 1980, *5*(1), 55–72.

Tew, B., Laurence, K.M., & Samuel, P. Parental estimates of the intelligence of their physically handicapped child. *Developmental Medicine & Child Neurology*, 1974, *16*, 494–500.

Wolfensberger, W., & Kurtz, R.A. Measurement of parents' perceptions of their children's development. *Genetic Psychology Monographs*, 1971, *83*, 3–92.

# Administrative Issues in Evaluation of Exceptionality

**Carol McDanolds Bradley, Ph.D.**
*Iowa State Department of Public
    Instruction
Des Moines, Iowa*

**Clifford E. Howe, Ph.D.**
*University of Iowa
Iowa City, Iowa*

BEFORE THE MID-1960s, a special education administrator was expected to know theory and practice in special education and administration. Since then litigation, legislation, and negotiation have become additional areas of knowledge essential for one's survival in special education administration. Such knowledge is particularly critical in the evaluation of exceptionality.

## EFFECTS OF LITIGATION

Bersoff (1979) has convincingly detailed the use of testing in racial and ethnic discrimination in the schools following the *Brown v. Board of Education* decision, (347 U.S. 483 [1954]). He points out that for most people scores derived from psychometric instruments have historically been used for exclusionary purposes. In *Hobsen v. Hansen* (269 F. Supp. 401 [D.D.C. 1967]) the court ordered abolishment of a tracking system based

40 primarily on tests that were standardized for predominantly white, middle-class students. The court had found vastly disproportionate numbers of black children in the lower tracks and no evidence that they were receiving any compensatory education so that they might gain access to higher tracks.

## Administrator's Quandary

Diana v. California Department of Education (C.A. No. C-70 37 RFP) involved the identification of Mexican-American students as educable mentally retarded (EMR) and their subsequent placement in EMR classes. The plaintiffs contested the use of the Wechsler Intelligence Scale for Children (WISC) and Stanford-Binet tests in determining their ability to learn. The two parties entered into a consent decree. It stipulated that assessment prior to placement in EMR classes would involve an intelligence test, developmental history, educational evaluation, and adaptive behavior scale. This decree, the work of Mercer and others, and the position of the American Association on Mental Deficiency have resulted in most state definitions of mental retardation including a deficit in adaptive behavior component. Assessment of adaptive behavior is required, but so much controversy surrounds the issue that the administrator is in a quandary about which direction to take: (a) What instruments should be used (b) Are different instruments required for varied ethnic and social groups? (c) Do the best known current instruments discriminate against rural and suburban middle-class

students? (d) What type of diagnostic personnel are best trained to administer tests and interpret such assessment data?

## Slighting Adaptive Behavior

On the issue of adaptive behavior it is instructive to look at the work of Smith and Polloway (1979). They examined the subject selection procedures and subject descriptions in all research using mentally retarded persons published in the American Journal of Mental Deficiency from 1974 through 1978. They found that only 5.8% of the 374 research reports included measures of both intellectual functioning and adaptive behavior in subject descriptors. In an additional 3.7% of the studies, researchers reported some measure of adaptive behavior but did not always specify the instrument used. Smith and Polloway reported no marked increase over the five-year period in the number of research reports including both measures; each year a single measure of intelligence or mental age was the most common form of subject selection and description.

The major explanation for this finding is probably the increased time required for obtaining measures of adaptive behavior directly and the use by researchers of readily available data already collected by the schools. It seems to us, though, that researchers should lead the way for the practicing administrator in this endeavor.

## Scrutinizing Standardized Tests

More recently, in Larry P. v. Riles (343 F. Supp. 1306 [N.D. Cal. 1972] aff'd 502

F. 2d 963 [9th Cir. 1974]) the court ordered that the California Department of Education's chief administrator was "enjoined from utilizing, permitting the use of, or approving the use of any standardized intelligence tests for the identification of black EMR children or their placement into EMR classes, without securing prior approval by the court" (p. 104).

To obtain court approval, a written request must be submitted that details, among other items, that the tests are not racially or culturally discriminatory, will be administered in a manner that is nondiscriminatory in its effect on black children, and have been validated for the determination of EMR status or placement in EMR classes. The court also ordered the defendants to direct each school district to reevaluate every black child currently identified as an EMR pupil without using any standardized intelligence test that had not been approved by the court.

The court expressed reluctance to get involved but wrote in the introduction: "The history of this litigation has demonstrated the failure of legislators and administrative agencies to confront problems that clearly had to be faced, and it has revealed an all-too-typical willingness either to do nothing or to pass on issues to the court" (p. 2).

At this point the directions for administrators seem fairly obvious:

- Do not use standardized academic or intelligence tests if they may result in the placement of minority children in EMR classes or special "tracks" disproportionate to their number in the general school population.

*"The history of this litigation has revealed an all-too-typical willingness either to do nothing or to pass on issues to the Court." (quote from legal decision)*

- Use nonbiased assessment procedures that are culturally fair and valid for the purpose intended.
- Use multiple measures, including developmental history, educational evaluations, and adaptive behavior scales.
- Understand that assessment instruments and procedures are under the scrutiny of the court.

Before an administrator becomes too comfortable with these "directions," two other cases need to be reviewed.

### A Goal for the 1980s

In 1976 in *Frederick L. v. Thomas* (408 F. Supp. 832 [E.D. Pa. 1976]) the court interpreted "right to education" to include screening and evaluation for potentially learning disabled children. Part of the evidence in this case involved expert witness testimony for both sides that 3% was probably the prevalence of learning disabilities in the Philadelphia schools. This prevalence estimate would indicate approximately 7,900 learning disabled children, but only 1,300 were receiving special services.

The December 24, 1979, issue of *Education Daily* reported that a U.S. district court had ordered the New York City schools to evaluate and place 8,000 children *within 60 days*. The order applied to 2,000 children who had been referred for evaluation and another 6,000 handicapped students awaiting placement in special education programs.

Administrators face a series of questions, if not dilemmas, in reconciling the "directions" with these two cases, including:

1. How is it possible to evaluate 2,000 children appropriately in 60 days and meet the culture-fair, nondiscriminatory, valid, multiple-measure criteria?

2. How does one screen for potential learning disabilities without using standardized tests when teacher referral as a source has been exhausted?

3. How does one evaluate for suspected learning disabilities without using standardized intelligence tests when an essential criterion in determining learning disability is a significant discrepancy between ability and achievement (remember the 60 days)?

4. Is it permissible to use data from standardized academic and intelligence tests to support a finding of "nonhandicapped"?

It is easy to understand why some special education administrators believe the solution is to eliminate the need for classification by handicapping condition, describe children in terms of their unique needs, and presumably develop multiple alternatives to deliver appropriate education to all.

While these are worthy goals, special education administrators need to be certain their motivation is in behalf of children and not an embarrassed reaction to scrutiny of practices in special education that have been less than professional, a fear of being sued, or a wish to shift the total responsibility to the general education administrator now that accountability is a watchword. Eliminating the necessity of determining that students are handicapped in obtaining an education could also eliminate children's hard-won rights to education under the law. A more reasonable approach is to work diligently to see that rights afforded the handicapped minority are extended to the majority of students in America's schools. If all students and their parents had the right by law to be involved in decisions regarding evaluation and selection of appropriate educational alternatives, the need for "special" or "protected" classifications would be eliminated.

It remains to be seen whether society at large will make this type of investment in the education of its youth. Such an investment seems doubtful in a time of high inflation, taxpayer revolt, and energy and defense crises. It is a worthy goal for the 1980s—one special education administrators should diligently pursue.

## EFFECTS OF LEGISLATION

The protection of PL 94-142 accrues only to students "suspected" of being

---

*If all students and their parents had the right by law to be involved in decisions regarding evaluation and selection of appropriate educational alternatives, the need for "special" or "protected" classifications would be eliminated.*

---

handicapped and those who have been determined to be handicapped and in need of special education and related services. This statute and accompanying regulations require that pupils be identified by the familiar categories. The regulations go on to define these categories. Clearly, such classification and eligibility criteria were spelled out for the purpose of narrowing the potential number of clients and thus controlling associated costs.

Similar criteria exist at the state level. Because local school district budgets have been so strapped recently, many states have accepted the responsibility of developing legislation that provides most of the excess costs of educating handicapped students. Legislators ask and expect answers to questions about who these handicapped children are, how many there are, and what their appropriate education will cost. They expect some consistency and uniformity across a state, usually calling for definitions and procedures to be well detailed.

## Grasping the Need for Improvement

It seems, then, that an immediate effect of this legislation is an understanding that practices in evaluation of exceptionality or potential exceptionality must be greatly improved. In the near future, practicing administrators, who daily face questions about measurement of exceptionality— questions that have no answers—should be the greatest supporters of research and evaluation in this area.

## New Safeguards, New Questions

Because of reported abuses in the evaluation process, Congress wrote into PL 94-142 a number of procedural safeguards regarding testing and evaluation. Most notably, each child suspected of being handicapped is to receive a full and individual evaluation. This was augmented by regulations adopted by the Office for Special Education and Rehabilitative Services (formerly Bureau of Education for the Handicapped), which delineated specific evaluation procedures that must be met. Included were requirements that test and evaluation materials (a) be provided and administered in the child's native language or other mode of communication, if feasible; (b) be valid for the purpose for which they are used; (c) be given in a standardized way by properly trained personnel; (d) include those tailored to assess specific areas of educational need rather than just those providing a single, general intelligence quotient; (e) be ones that accurately reflect the factors that the tests claim they measure. Regulations specify that the evaluation is to be made by a multidisciplinary team and not by a single examiner. Also, handicapped students are to be reevaluated at least every three years according to the same requirements.

These regulations immediately raised and continue to provoke tough questions for the practicing administrator:

- How do I locate diagnosticians who speak languages other than English when I need them?
- Is an interpreter for those doing the

44

assessment sufficient to meet the requirements of the law?

- What instruments and procedures are "valid enough?"
- How can I ensure that assessments are done in a standardized way? No short forms? No extrapolation?
- Who are the "properly trained" personnel? Every specialty area believes that *its* professionals are best trained.
- What constitutes a multidisciplinary team? How many disciplines? Each discipline believes that it is essential.
- If the child is still "obviously" handicapped, must the reevaluation be so comprehensive, especially in light of data already available in the annual review of the individualized education program?

Jones (1978) argues that these regulations apply to group testing programs as well as to individual evaluations. This assertion rests on the premise that group testing programs and individual testing procedures are interrelated in the sense that results from group testing are sometimes the first level of identification of children who may need specialized services. Also, any composite educational picture of an individual pupil includes group test results.

## Inappropriate Labeling of Minorities

These rather restrictive regulations stemmed from a history of inappropriate labeling of some children as handicapped, principally Mexican and black students. Ysseldyke (1978) recently reviewed this issue of bias in assessment and concluded that the concerns were much broader than just fairness of tests used with minority groups. Various abuses or misuses of assessment data throughout the whole process of making decisions about pupils are of concern. He summarized these abuses as including (a) use of tests for purposes other than those for which they were designed, (b) comparison of students with others who differ systematically in several characteristics, (c) use of technically inadequate tests, and (d) making inferences that go beyond the data (p. 159).

Administrators and teachers are frustrated by their additional responsibilities. At the same time, appropriations have fallen far short of the accelerating funding schedule authorized by Congress in the original bill. There is some suggestion that school officials are not actively identifying additional children who may be handicapped and in need of special education because of the attendant time and dollar costs as well as the prospect of parental disagreement and due-process proceedings (see Magliocca & Stephens, 1980). The time-honored practice of putting children on waiting lists creates all types of legal problems today.

To retain sanity and stay in the business, administrators must strike a reasonable balance between the fear of being sued and of protecting the rights of handicapped pupils in relation to evaluation and identification under the provisions of PL 94-142 (see also Bateman & Herr, in press; Ysseldyke & Shinn, in press).

## Satisfying "Irrelevant Demands"

As funds become more scarce, the amount of personnel time (thus money) spent on identification practices aimed at determining eligibility for additional public funding becomes more questionable. Larsen (1977) points out, "evaluation is all too often undertaken to satisfy generally irrelevant administrative demands that are extraneous to the main purpose of teaching" (p. 123).

While there may be differences of opinion about the relevance of procedural safeguards and adequate financing, we would certainly not argue that much current practice in evaluation is not focused on the teaching and learning process. Assessment procedures must be developed, used, and evaluated that can, whenever possible, serve the dual purpose of identification and instructional program planning. Data from these procedures need to be of use whether or not the pupil is found to be handicapped. Without doubt, much of the assessment data must come from extensive observations of students in natural settings and less from formal tests given in isolated settings. This will require diagnosticians to have broad mastery of the education field; they will not be able to rely on skills acquired only in narrow specialty-area training programs. The need for assessment data to serve the purposes of identification and instructional program planning and the competition for scarce fiscal resources will provide momentum for the well-trained special educator to serve also as a primary diagnostician (see articles by Meyen & Lehr, and Poplin & Gray, this volume).

## Problems for Administrators

Administrators face problems relating to staffing patterns, new personnel selection, and the need for retraining existing diagnostic personnel. There will not be a role in the future for school psychologists, who give only WISC and Stanford-Binet tests, speech clinicians, who rely on Wepmans and the Illinois Test of Psycholinguistic Abilities, or educational diagnosticians who depend on Wide-Range Achievement Test and Peabody Individual Achievement Test to assess present levels of educational functioning.

## PERSONNEL DECISIONS

Administrators must make decisions about what type of personnel are necessary to the evaluation process and how many of each type are needed. These decisions must be made in partial ignorance; administrators are not and cannot be experts in all aspects of evaluation. Various educational professions cannot be relied on to help with this decision. The members of each discipline seem to believe the solution lies in employing more people just like them! Furthermore, one cannot discount the self-serving interests of groups to protect their own employment status.

Once administrators decide how many and what types of diagnostic personnel to employ, they must decide how to deploy them. To whom a referral is first made can significantly contribute to the eventual disposition of the case. Some administrators have set up referral processing teams to guard against the "gatekeeper" phenomenon by one discipline as well as to preclude unnecessary and routinized evaluation by a host of varying specialists in all cases.

### ACHIEVING UNIFORMITY IN EVALUATIONS

Another perplexity involves achieving a reasonable degree of uniformity or consistency in evaluation practices across districts or even buildings within a single district. Those who have spent considerable time in the public schools know that a pupil who is viewed as a candidate for referral for evaluation of a suspected disability in one building or district might well not be viewed in that way by the staff of another school. There seems also to be a tendency for the faculty of an individual building or small district to view pupils' suspected disabilities in terms of the types of programs they have available for children. This is seen in referrals that state "evaluation needed for learning disabilities program" or "evaluate for resource room program." Students are too often labeled to conform to local building programs rather than evaluated for problems that could involve transportation to a more appropriate program 20 miles away.

### ALTERNATIVES TO RELOCATION

These "at home" solutions are appropriate in some individual circumstances. Some schools have developed alternatives within general education in which mildly handicapped pupils particularly are appropriately included. Some teachers can and do adjust their expectations, curriculum, and instructional strategies to accommodate a wide range of individual differences. Other faculty understand their students so well that they can accurately predict suspected disabilities and know which program options would be appropriate. Special education administrators need to reinforce and encourage such practices.

However, it would be a mistake to assume that low referral rates necessarily indicate positive attitudes and appropriate education for the potentially handicapped of a given building or district. There are too many instances of social promotion and even graduation without students' having acquired essential survival skills to believe that all children are being properly educated. Dropout rates in many areas are increasing. Youth unemployment rates, particularly for the black and poor, have reached alarming proportions. Absenteeism, tardiness, and truancy are often highest in schools with generally lower-than-average achievement levels, possibly the very same schools with lower referral rates.

### MORE QUESTIONS

A number of questions about locating the potentially handicapped under such conditions must be addressed:

- Should more reliance be placed on screening programs and less on teacher referral?
- If so, what screening procedures can be developed that are time and cost efficient and do not yield large numbers of false positives?
- Would a "child find" media campaign aimed at student self-referral be more productive and less costly?
- Should a far more active campaign be launched to reach parents who are not easy to reach, such as those who do not belong to PTA, advocacy groups, Lions, or Rotary?

- Is more in-service training the answer?
- Is a building-based special education teacher the best person to screen potentially handicapped individuals?

The reverse of low referrals occurs when districts, schools, or teachers view all students not at grade level as potentially handicapped and therefore refer many of their students for evaluation. This problem should lessen as the least-restrictive-environment concept becomes fully implemented. There is increasingly less chance that such referrals will result in total removal of mildly handicapped pupils from the classroom, building, or district. This should remove the motivation to make such wholesale referrals on the hope that the "problem child" will leave or at least be someone else's responsibility. Admittedly, there is no magical cutoff point separating the handicapped from the so-called normal child. The greatest conflicts appear with youngsters in the borderline areas.

ENVIRONMENTAL FACTORS

A major shortcoming of educational evaluation has been "the tendency to ignore the significant variables of the student's immediate environment in causing and maintaining academic and/or social problems" (Larsen, 1977, p. 130). In addition to the benefits of an ecological assessment model as enumerated by Larsen, this type of assessment is absolutely essential in helping to determine who is *not* handicapped. Assessment data taken across environments, persons, curricular areas, and instructional conditions can identify system defects or personnel problems that need remediation instead of a child who needs special education. Again, the primary purpose of evaluation should be to aid in instructional programing, not to "sort" who qualifies for additional monies.

EFFECTS OF NEGOTIATION

Negotiation is broadly defined here to mean conferring, discussing, or bargaining to reach agreements. It includes concepts such as group process, shared decision making, and participative management, as well as the formal collective bargaining process.

Many, if not most, currently practicing administrators were trained to function in bureaucratic organizations under a hierarchical authority model (Herda, 1980). Within school systems, special education administrators often operated independently of general education administrators; in effect, dual systems were in place. Further, there tended to be a distinct separation between special education and other public and private agencies serving the handicapped. Special education administrators typically were not trained for nor had much experience in sharing responsibility or authority with staff or peers. They were not prepared to negotiate—to confer, discuss, or bargain to reach agreements. Administrators did not understand that one positive way to influence others is to share power. Events of the last 10 years have demanded that special education administrators quickly come to terms with these requirements for competent performance.

48

### The Team Approach

PL 94-142 requires a multidisciplinary evaluation team; presumably a "team" will confer, discuss, and reach agreements that are better than a single individual's judgment. This outcome (better decisions) is not guaranteed just because a group of people are involved. A team implies something more than—and successful functioning as a team member requires an additional set of skills beyond—technical adequacy in evaluation processes.

Administrators' new responsibility is to recruit and employ diagnostic personnel who have the additional group process and communication skills necessary to function effectively as a team. Provisions will have to be made for in-service or continuing education programs for currently employed personnel. Administrators need to develop and implement personnel evaluation systems that attend to these factors for use in contract renewal, salary, promotion, and termination decisions.

### New Skills and Attitudes

The administrator is not exempt from needing to quickly acquire these new

---

*The administrator's new responsibility is to recruit and employ diagnostic personnel who have the additional group process and communication skills necessary to function effectively as a team.*

---

skills and attitudes. Implementation of effective and cost-efficient referral and evaluation mechanisms is a system wide responsibility. To accomplish this, the special education administrator must give up independent decision making and work with general education administrators on a co-equal basis.

The special education administrator must learn that working with disgruntled parents and their advocates does not have to be adversarial. Generally, there is more than one solution to every problem; by conferring, discussing, and even bargaining, a compromise position can be reached that is appropriate for the child and satisfactory to the school and the parents.

As access to special education has broadened to include children from age 3 (birth, in some states) to 21, the special education administrator will be working increasingly with other agencies that serve the handicapped. Inevitably problems of "turfmanship" will surface. The only way to solve these problems is by joint decision making, probably prefaced by long hours of discourse. Particular examples of issues administrators will face relative to evaluation include:

- Accepting another agency's determination of disability;
- Avoiding duplication of screening efforts, particularly with infants and young children;
- Varying criteria for determination of disability—for example, mental health authorities, vocational rehabilitation;
- Assessing potentially handicapped youth in correctional facilities.

*Results of Collective Bargaining*

Most states now have laws permitting or requiring collective bargaining for public employees. Attitudes of special education administrators toward collective bargaining seem to run the gamut from the "chicken little" pessimistic outlook to those who see this new era as an opportunity to develop a more humane and fair system of participatory decision making. Following are examples of items that have been included in collective bargaining negotiations that can affect the evaluation of exceptionality:

- The setting of class size limitations that double count handicapped students integrated into regular classrooms. This could affect teachers' willingness to refer and their subsequent identification of pupils as handicapped.
- Determining what is to be included in in-service training programs and setting limits in terms of time, frequency, and length of faculty meetings. How does one find adequate time to provide in-service programs on evaluation procedures?
- Limiting parent conferences in terms of frequency, purpose, and time. What happens when the parents can meet only after 5 p.m. and the contract day ends at 4:15 p.m.?
- Mandating referrals of students to other personnel. To the degree that

the item negotiated involves the degree and amount of aberrant behavior to be tolerated in a regular classroom, operational definitions of "handicap" and "requiring special education" could be affected.

- Determining the ratio of supportive personnel to teaching staff or dictating their modes of operation within the school. Each of these areas traditionally has been an administrative prerogative.

Of course, items cannot be negotiated that are contrary to state and federal law. Nevertheless, the special education administrator must quickly acquire understandings and skills in the negotiation process so as not to be bewildered and ineffectual through the 1980s.

## SUMMARY

This article has attempted to examine the effects of three relatively new phenomena in education—litigation, legislation, and negotiation—on the evaluation of exceptionality from an administrative view. We have raised more questions than we have answered. The questions must be answered in the decade ahead. This decade will not be a comfortable one for many administrators. It will not be for the faint hearted. It will be an exciting one.

## 50    REFERENCES

Bateman, B., & Herr, C. Law and special education. In J. M. Kauffman & D. P. Hallahan (Eds.), *Handbook of special education.* Englewood Cliffs, N.J.: Prentice-Hall, in press.

Bersoff, N. Regarding psychologists testily: Legal regulations of psychological assessment in the public schools. In B. Sales & M. Novick (Eds.), *Perspectives in law and psychology,* Vol. III: *Testing and evaluation.* New York: Plenum, 1979.

*Education Daily,* 12(245) Washington, D.C.: Capitol Publications, 1979.

Herda, E. A. Aspects of general education governance and PL 94-142 implementation. *Focus on Exceptional Children,* 1980, 12(5).

Jones, R. J. Protection in evaluation procedures: criteria and recommendations. In *Developing criteria for the evaluation of protection in evaluation procedures provisions.* Washington, D.C.: United States Office of Education, 1978.

Larsen, S. C. The educational evaluation of handicapped students. In R. Kneedler & S. Tarver (Eds.), *Changing perspectives in special education.* Columbus, Ohio: Charles E. Merrill, 1977.

Magliocca, L. A., & Stephens, T. M. Child identification or child inventory? A critique of the federal design of child-identification systems implemented under PL 94-142. *Journal of Special Education,* 1980, *14,* 23-36.

Smith, J. D., & Polloway, E. The dimension of adaptive behavior in mental retardation research: An analysis of recent practices. *American Journal of Mental Deficiency,* 1979, *84,* 203-206.

Ysseldyke, J. E. Implementing the "protection in evaluation procedures" provisions of Public Law 94-142. In *Developing criteria for the evaluation of protection in evaluation procedures provisions.* Washington, D.C.: United States Office of Education, 1978.

Ysseldyke, J., & Shinn, M. Psychoeducational diagnosis. In J.M. Kauffman & D. P. Hallahan (Eds.), *Handbook of special education.* Englewood Cliffs, N.J.: Prentice-Hall, in press.

# PART II:
# THEORY, MODELS, AND APPROACHES

# A Conceptual Framework for Assessment of Curriculum and Student Progress

*Mary Poplin, Ph.D.*
*Claremont Graduate School*
*Claremont, California*

*Richard Gray, Ph.D.*
*Private Consultant*
*Austin, Texas*

WORDS AND PHRASES certain to arouse rounds of applause and nods of agreement from today's educators include *individualization, assessment for instruction,* and *specially designed programs to meet unique needs,* among others of similar meaning to special educators. Of less certainty, especially in actual practice, are answers to questions such as (a) Who should be responsible for the assessment? (b) Who is best suited to conduct the assessment and design of individualized programs? and (c) How can one be assured that both the assessment and the educational program resulting from that assessment are appropriate and meaningful?

The authors contend that classroom teachers are best suited to assess students' progress because (a) they have unequaled knowledge of the student and the goals most necessary to his or her life, (b) they have continual contact with the child in

54    the classroom, and (c) student progress is ultimately their primary concern. Therefore teachers, rather than diagnostic, psychometric, or supervisory personnel, should have the primary responsibility for assessment of student needs and progress. The authors also believe that many, if not most, teachers now perform the informal assessments that are the most relevant, regardless of the edicts of school district policy or state and federal regulations.

The following discussion of assessment is directed to the special teachers and, to a lesser extent, to school administrators and other decision makers who design systems for assessment of student progress in the schools. The intent is to discuss a conceptual framework that will facilitate appropriate, meaningful, and efficient educational instruction and assessment of student progress toward meeting life-related goals and objectives. Because good informal classroom assessment activities are virtually synonymous with good classroom instruction, the stages presented apply to instruction as well as to the design and implementation of efficient informal assessments.

Assessment is the key to appropriate instruction. For classroom purposes, assessment performed for any other reason is without meaning (Wallace & Larsen, 1978). Regardless of fine phrases such as "instruction designed to meet unique needs," assessment of a student is based on the assessor's perceptions of what is important and on predetermined curricula imposed by school systems, publishers, and "experts." Effectiveness in instruction and assessment is directly related to the teacher's intuitive or learned understanding of the following: (a) functional, life-related needs and goals for the education of each individual; (b) instructional content that best incorporates those goals; (c) development of curriculum designed to achieve these goals; and (d) instructional strategies used to systematically teach and assess student progress. Combined, these elements are the guiding force in both instruction and the assessment of student progress.

The implication is this: the appropriateness of any curriculum depends on the effectiveness of a teacher in meeting its objectives, and meaningful assessment of student progress depends on appropriate use of the curriculum. The most appropriate curriculum is that curriculum designed by the teacher(s) responsible for its implementation with individual students. Therefore an important teaching skill is the teacher's willingness and ability to design and continuously evaluate the curriculum as it is being implemented in the classroom. Only when the curriculum is continuously evaluated can any direct student assessment be considered valid.

## STAGES OF ASSESSMENT

Two stages are necessary for teachers to conduct effective assessment: *stage 1*—continuous evaluation or assessment of the curriculum being implemented to help students achieve life-related goals; and *stage 2*—direct assessment of student performance within that curriculum through the careful structuring and observation of instructional strategies.

*Stage 1: Teacher Assessment of Educational Curricula*

Informal assessment or evaluation of curricula for exceptional learners accomplishes several purposes. First, and perhaps most important, it allows teachers to continually design, select, modify, and change goals and objectives for individual students on the basis of their best professional judgment rather than on the edicts of the school administration, the latest educational fads, or the latest commercially produced curriculum materials. Second, it gives teachers a greater awareness of, as well as a greater control over, what is happening to students whose education is their responsibility. Third, through continuous design, redesign, and evaluation of a curriculum one obtains greater flexibility in applying information obtained from direct assessment of students in the classroom to other educational environments; that is, instructional objectives and strategies can be selected on the basis of knowledge of the student's previous educational background and present life circumstances. Figure 1 presents a model to facilitate the evaluation of curriculum from the teacher's perspective.

**Figure 1. Stage of Informal Assessment: A Model for the Classification of Educational Curriculum**

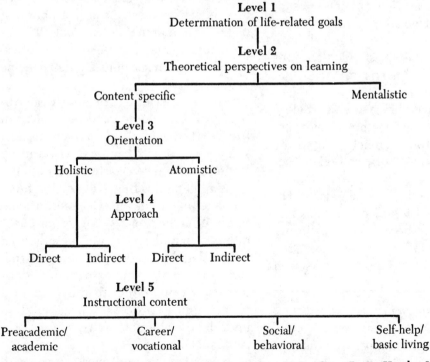

**Level 1**
Determination of life-related goals

**Level 2**
Theoretical perspectives on learning

Content specific          Mentalistic

**Level 3**
Orientation

Holistic          Atomistic

**Level 4**
Approach

Direct   Indirect   Direct   Indirect

**Level 5**
Instructional content

Preacademic/   Career/   Social/   Self-help/
academic       vocational  behavioral  basic living

Adapted from Hammill, D. D., Brown, L. L., Brown, V. L., Gray, R. A., Hresko, W. P., Larsen, S. C., McNutt, G., Poplin, M. S., Reid, D. K., & Wiederholt, J. L. A model for classifying instructional strategies. Unpublished manuscript, University of Oklahoma, 1979.

## LEVEL 1: DETERMINATION OF LIFE-RELATED GOALS

The danger of using a predetermined curriculum as the basis for assessment and instructional programming, no matter how sound its rationale, is that the curriculum becomes the master; the child's needs are seen only in terms of what the curriculum has to offer. The only content suitable as a basis for effective assessment and instruction results from a comparison of the child's present abilities and the abilities and understanding necessary for a satisfying, self-fulfilling life.

The most meaningful long-range life goals include independent functioning in adult society—that is, the ability to (a) interact effectively and appropriately with family, friends, and coworkers; (b) support oneself financially; (c) find satisfaction in both work and leisure; and (d) have options and make satisfying decisions regarding career, marriage, social life, and civic participation.

More immediate life goals, albeit often less meaningful ones to the student, are those skills that allow functioning in the social system imposed by the school environment—for example, to stay in one's chair, perform well on worksheets, wait or walk in line, and follow other rules and conventions of the classroom. Being closest to the individual student, the teacher is the most important person in

---

*The danger of using a predetermined curriculum as the basis for assessment and instructional programming . . . is that the curriculum becomes the master.*

---

determining these life-related goals and thus in structuring curricula to fill these needs. Often, special educators are aware of the differences in what is required for successful adult functioning and what is demanded for successful school functioning. This awareness, painful as it often is, requires teachers to juggle lifelong and school-related goals into an amalgamated curriculum. The current trend in mainstreaming the handicapped child into the regular classroom has made this task of combining long-range and immediate life goals an even more arduous one.

## LEVEL 2: THEORETICAL PERSPECTIVES ON LEARNING

Once teachers have determined life-related goals, they must clarify their own theoretical perspectives on learning that will be apparent in their curricula. Teachers can take one of two major theoretical perspectives on learning: content specific or mentalistic.

Content-specific curriculum deals directly with instruction and assessment of life-related goals. All activities and knowledge directed to or discovered by students should be clearly relevant to the skills and abilities they will need to function adequately in life. Reading instruction will center on reading experiences rather than underlying processes thought to be related to reading. Writing instruction will center on expressing ideas through writing rather than hypothetical psychological processes presumed to underlie the ability to write, such as perceptual skills.

In an adaptation of a working paper to propose a model for classifying and analyzing approaches to instruction, Hammill, Brown, Brown, Gray, Hresko, Larsen, McNutt, Poplin, Reid, and Wiederholt (1979) suggested two major approaches to education: the educational content approach (as described previously) and the mentalistic process approach, in which presumed psychological prerequisite functions are trained to facilitate content and skill acquisition. The authors point out that research does not support such a mentalistic process approach at this time. We agree with this observation and have chosen not to deal further with mentalistic process curriculum, as indicated by Figure 1 (see Mann, 1980, for further discussion of process training).

LEVEL 3: ORIENTATION TO EDUCATION

At a third level, teachers must evaluate whether the orientation to their curriculum is holistic or atomistic. The holistic orientation assumes that instruction involves structuring the educational environment to provide students with experiences that will allow them to purposefully assimilate new meanings, skills, relationships, and insights into their present knowledge. This assimilation will, in the context of a relevant instructional environment, develop into systems of useful skills and information. Children learn through practical, self-selected experiences in a carefully arranged and structured environment. For a more extensive review of this approach the reader is referred to Eisner (1979), Eisner and Vallance (1974), Reid and Hresko (1981), and Smith (1973, 1978, 1981).

The atomistic orientation, in contrast, assumes that the steps for learning skills and content areas are known or can be adequately developed, that rules must be taught, and that systematic presentation of the steps and rules will add up to mastery of the specific whole—the skill or specific content area. In this orientation, content, steps, and sequence are predetermined and imposed. Children learn through direct instruction in specific component skills. Competency-based education and assessment is an example of atomistic orientation to learning.

The authors believe that the most appropriate orientation generally is holistic; however, it is necessary for teachers to have a full understanding of the skills involved in any content area to facilitate student progress in meeting the chosen life-related goals. We also recognize the possibility that some educational goals or objectives may be most efficiently met through an atomistic approach or that atomistic learning may sometimes precede holistic assimilation (see Vygotsky's 1962 discussion of the development of spontaneous versus scientific concepts). Currently, the education and assessment of exceptional learners is almost entirely approached from an atomistic perspective, a trend that is unwise.

LEVEL 4: APPROACH TO INSTRUCTION

Teachers who design and assess curriculum are also aware of the various approaches possible to the instruction of content-specific material. Some curricula are designed to instruct students specifically in the life-related goals. These curricula use the direct approach. Other curricula are generated to teach strategies or skills that hopefully will transfer and generalize so that life-related skills are more easily attainable. These curricula take the indirect approach.

However, both of these approaches deal with educational *content* as opposed to mentalistic *processes*. For example, curricula that are designed to teach students study skills from an indirect approach deemphasize the content of the social studies or science materials being used. The assumption is that students who have acquired certain study skills or strategies will be able to more efficiently learn and understand the social studies or science materials. Teachers using a direct instructional approach design curriculum that contains the specific content to be learned by the students. The differences between these two approaches result in considerable variations in curricula.

### LEVEL 5: INSTRUCTIONAL CONTENT

As indicated in Figure 1, the content of life-related goals is clustered under four headings: preacademic/academic, career/vocational, social/behavioral, and self-help/basic living skills. It is at this level that teaching strategies are important in the curriculum and that decisions made at previous levels are put into operation.

### IMPORTANCE OF CURRICULUM ASSESSMENT

The importance of teachers' informally assessing their own curricula during the first stage of pupil assessment cannot be overstated. Unless teachers intuitively understand and are free to choose and change their kinds of curriculum, they are merely automatons of some large system that dictates their teaching. In addition,

unless teachers understand their own curriculum perspectives, direct pupil assessment will be vague and without meaning.

The first stage of pupil assessment must therefore be assessment of the educational curriculum with attention given to the determination or designation of life-related goals (level 1), the theoretical perspective on learning held by individual teachers (content specific or mentalistic, level 2), the general orientation to education (holistic or atomistic, level 3), the approach to instruction considered most viable (direct or indirect, level 4), and the content of instruction (level 5). Unfortunately, with the exception of level 2, there is little research that clearly guides the choices of teachers of handicapped individuals. Once the life-related curriculum has been established and clarified, teachers can begin the direct informal assessment of student progress in meeting educational goals and objectives (stage 2).

## Stage 2: Direct Assessment of Student Progress

The second stage of informal assessment requires a more specific model, one that examines actual classroom *instructional strategies* and allows the teacher to assess student progress within the curriculum. This stage is closely related to level 5 of the model for classification of educational curriculum (Figure 1). Instructional strategies are defined as the interaction between educational objectives and classroom activities. This fusion of educational objectives and classroom activities fills virtually every instructional day and produces what are commonly called "instructional objectives." The model presented here is an attempt to provide a simple, efficient framework from which teachers can assess student progress in meeting various educational objectives within the context of classroom activities. The model also provides a way of explaining, examining, and structuring curriculum.

A model that allows for specific inspection of instructional strategies (i.e., educational objectives and classroom activities) accomplishes several purposes. First—and most critical to this discussion—is that the model of curriculum allows educators to develop appropriate means or activities for informally assessing student performance in given educational objectives. Inherent in this purpose is the advantage of being able to consciously designate a particular activity as representing mastery of that objective. Second, it allows teachers to evaluate classroom activities in terms of the objective(s) to be met. Thus teachers using this model are also stimulated to make conscientious decisions regarding classroom activities based on the awareness of alternatives and the even more acute awareness of which activities constitute mastery of specified goals. Third, both models or stages can guide and stimulate the much-needed research into the acquisition of knowledge by providing a classification structure for the various kinds of classroom activities that are presently planned.

Figure 2 is designed to provide structure for the above purposes; however, central to this discussion is that the model will direct teachers in the development and execution of informal assessments of student progress toward the mastery of educational objectives. The two-dimensional model depicts the interaction

**Figure 2. A Model of Instructional Strategies for the Informal Assessment of Student Progress**

| | | EDUCATIONAL OBJECTIVE | |
|---|---|---|---|
| | | Mechanical | Conceptual |
| CLASSROOM ACTIVITY | Natural | | |
| | Synthetic | | |

60

between classroom activities and educational objectives (i.e., the level of the curriculum that is used to assess students' progress).

## CLASSROOM ACTIVITIES

Classroom activities have been categorized into two distinct types of actions: *natural* and *synthetic* (created purely for instructional purposes). To determine whether an assessment activity is synthetic or natural, one must consider the goal or activity that would constitute mastery. For example, if the ultimate goal or mastery of the activity is that a student use the appropriate punctuation marks at the ends of sentences, but the assessment activity requires that the student rewrite a given sentence correctly, circle errors, or punctuate given sentences, then the activity is synthetic. The activity has been synthetically created and artificially imposed on the student for instructional purposes. In contrast, if the student writes a composition and the teacher notes end-mark punctuation errors and abilities, the assessment activity would be considered natural. Teachers conduct natural assessments by observing the student in the actual activity required for mastery of the objective. Synthetic assessment activities are manufactured within a highly structured, artificial setting.

The advantage of synthetic activities is that observation or assessment is made uniform across students and situations and thus is simplified. Standardized instruments are almost exclusively synthetic because of the necessity to standardize (make reliable and valid) and

*Synthetic activities . . . do not provide students the chance to practice, nor teachers the opportunity to observe, mastery of a given educational objective in a real-life situation.*

simplify scoring and to sample large numbers of educational objectives in relatively short periods of time. Synthetic activities, including both formal and informal assessment activities, are far more common than natural activities in most school curricula.

The disadvantage of synthetic activities is that they do not provide students the chance to practice, nor teachers the opportunity to observe, mastery of a given educational objective in a real-life situation. Unfortunately there is also a serious lack of research that answers such questions as whether (or to what degree) synthetic activities promote mastery of given educational objectives in natural settings.

Natural activities and assessment are more life-related activities and offer a different set of advantages. The most obvious advantage is, of course, that they allow the student an opportunity to apply and practice certain skills or objectives within their natural context. Thus there is little or no question that the objective can be accomplished when and where needed. A concomitant advantage is that generalization to other settings (e.g., the use of appropriate end marks in letter writing and social studies reports) would be more likely to occur.

The disadvantages of natural activities are the primary reason for the scarcity of such activities and assessments in today's classrooms. By the nature of such activities, assessment must be conducted through careful observation. This observation often involves both observation of the process or operation while the student performs the activity, and careful analysis of the resultant product. Products of natural activities are highly individual rather than uniform, making the analysis even more difficult. Of course, the time and adaptability of the teacher required for natural assessments and activities are tremendous.

These added burdens obviously are discouraging to teachers of handicapped children who are already inundated with individual differences, not to mention the paperwork demands of special education today (see Katzen, 1980). However, natural activities and assessments may be even more important for students with problems than for ordinary students. The "normal" student may make rapid generalizations from synthetic activities and transfer these skills to other settings much more readily than handicapped learners. Regardless, both synthetic and natural activities and assessments comprise one dimension of instructional strategies, that is, classroom activities.

EDUCATIONAL OBJECTIVES

The second dimension of the model of instructional strategies represents the two primary types of educational objectives: *mechanical* and *conceptual*. Mechanical objectives are those objectives or skills that require learning by rote facts, rules, or principles, the sequential operation of a series of related tasks, or the systematic application of these skills within the con-

texts of certain situations. The addition of two three-digit numerals is a skill that can be acquired mechanically and applied in several settings, as can the appropriate use of end-mark punctuation.

While these mechanical skills can often be generalized or transferred to other settings through specific instruction, generalization and transfer abilities are far more uncertain than with conceptual objectives. However, an educational objective that is conceptual demands that the student understand intuitively the reasons behind various mechanical performances, allowing for more flexibility, generalization, and transfer to occur. The student who has acquired the conceptual objective of three-digit addition understands the principles of place value, set union, and numerosity, among others. A student may, however, intuitively understand the *concept* of place value and not know the mechanics of reciting the rules or even the label for such a principle.

Another example of the differences between conceptual and mechanical objectives is apparent in spoken language differences. A student from one cultural background may not use the plural *s* at the end of words. This in no way indicates that the child imagines only one animal when he or she says "Three dog got in a fight." Another student with more conceptual language disorders may be taught the mechanics of adding *s* to nouns following certain numbers of objects but may not actually understand the concept of "more than one."

Many educational objectives stated or observed in the classroom are mechanical rather than conceptual. Mechanical

61

62   objectives (i.e., the production of rote rules, facts, and principles or the sequential production of certain motions) involve activities that are more easily designed, instituted, and assessed. In addition, teachers find mechanical objectives easy to define into readily observed tasks, thus more conducive to assessments using behavioral technology. True conceptual objectives are not so readily taught or assessed by using a task analysis and reinforcement technology because they are not easily broken into individual tasks and subtasks and require both integration and assimilation by students. Providing students with a multitude of concrete experiences such as those discussed by Piagetian and Brunerian scholars seems the most appropriate means for both the instruction and observation of those objectives. Progress toward conceptual objectives must be assessed through a long series of fairly complex and often subjective observations of the students interacting within their various environments. Conceptual as well as mechanical objectives are necessary in all good classroom curricula; both must be assessed in thorough, informal evaluations of student progress.

INSTRUCTIONAL STRATEGIES IN ASSESSMENT

The instructional strategies that result from the interaction of educational objectives and classroom activities provide the structure for designing appropriate informal assessment activities. To demonstrate the dynamics of this interaction as it relates to classroom assessment, several examples are offered. Educational objectives from the areas of math computation, written expression-punctuation, math

concepts, and self-help skills are used in the following comparisons.

Figure 3 illustrates instructional strategies that might be used to assess student progress in selected general objectives. Of particular note is the manner in which each objective is assessed with the use of both synthetic and natural activities. The following objectives are used as examples in Figure 3:

- Addition of decimal numerals;
- End-mark punctuation;
- Sight word vocabulary (level N Dolch);
- Concept of bigger, larger, smaller, greater than, less than; and
- Drinking from cup.

By their nature, some general objectives will be either mechanical or conceptual. For example, "end-mark punctuation" is a mechanical skill, while "greater than, less than" is a conceptual objective. Therefore not every general objective can be assessed conceptually and mechanically. However, together the conceptual objectives involved in sentence construction and the mechanical skills of punctuation result in a major step toward the goal of natural and independent written expression.

Research does not indicate whether worksheet decimal addition in any way aids or enhances the learning of the concept of the decimal system and its application to addition (see discussion by Cawley, Fitzmaurice, Shaw, Kahn, & Bates, 1978). It is probably true that the closer one is to the natural mechanics and conceptual activities, the closer one is to achieving the ultimate goal or objective. It appears from the examples that perhaps

**Figure 3.  Examples of Instructional Strategies Used for Informal Assessment of Objectives**          63

| CLASSROOM ACTIVITIES | | EDUCATIONAL OBJECTIVES | |
|---|---|---|---|
| | | Mechanical | Conceptual |
| Natural | | Adds own lunch bill without aids. | Shows addition of decimals by estimating and summing amounts owed or received. |
| | | Uses appropriate end-mark punctuation in originally composed sentences. | |
| | | Reads aloud level N Dolch words when presented in contextual reading materials. | Silently reads a selection containing Dolch words and summarizes contents of selection. |
| | | | Chooses the larger or smaller group of objects when needed. |
| | | Asks for "cup" when thirsty. | Uses "cups" of all dimensions when thirsty. |
| Synthetic | | Adds decimal numbers on a worksheet. | Solves story problems involving the addition of decimal numbers. |
| | | Rewrites a given sentence and supplies missing end-mark punctuation. | |
| | | Names aloud level N Dolch words when shown in isolation. | Chooses correct Dolch words from a multiple-choice format to complete a given sentence. |
| | | | Places "greater than" and "less than" signs in a list of digit pairs (< >). |
| | | Says "cup" when presented a picture or object. | Selects all containers that could be cups from a picture or set of objects. |

64     the least valuable or most questionable are those synthetic conceptual activities. These appear to be far removed from the mechanical or conceptual abilities that are ultimately the goal, although they certainly are expedient classroom activities.

These are but a few examples of the ways in which teachers can design and implement informed assessment activities using this model. The model also provides teachers with a way of monitoring instructional and assessment strategies taking place in their classrooms, allowing them once again to make conscientious and informed decisions.

•   •   •

Both stages of assessment—teachers' assessment of their own curriculum theories, orientations, and approaches, and direct assessment of students through use of strategies that incorporate both mechanical and conceptual objectives in natural or synthetic settings—are necessary for the efficient assessment of student progress. Both stages involve assessment that can be done efficiently only by the special teacher who is daily responsible for the handicapped learner's program.

## REFERENCES

Cawley, J. F., Fitzmaurice, A. M., Shaw, R. A., Kahn, H., & Bates, H. Mathematics and learning disabled youth: The upper grade levels. *Learning Disabilities Quarterly*, 1978, *1*, 37-52.

Eisner, E. *The educational imagination.* New York: Macmillan, 1979.

Eisner, E. & Vallance, E. (Eds). *Conflicting conceptions of curriculum.* Berkeley, Calif., McCutchan, 1974.

Hammill, D. D., Brown, L. L., Brown, V. L., Gray, R. A., Hresko, W. P., Larsen, S. C., McNutt, G., Poplin, M. S., Reid, D. K., & Wiederholt, J. L. A model for classifying instructional strategies. Unpublished manuscript, University of Oklahoma, 1979.

Katzen, K. To the editor: An open letter to CEC. *Exceptional Children*, 1980, *46*, 582.

Mann, L. *On the trail of process: A historical perspective on cognitive processes and their training.* New York: Grune & Stratton, 1980.

Reid, D.K. & Hresko, W.P. *A cognitive approach to learning disabilities.* New York: McGraw-Hill, 1981.

Smith, F. *Psycholinguistics and reading.* New York: Holt, Rinehart & Winston, 1973.

Smith, F. *Comprehension and learning.* New York: Holt, Rinehart & Winston, 1978.

Smith, F. *Writing and the writer.* New York: Holt, Rinehart & Winston, 1981.

Vygotsky, L. S. *Thought and language.* Cambridge, Mass.: The MIT Press, 1962.

Wallace, G. & Larsen, S. C. *Educational assessment of learning problems.* Boston: Allyn & Bacon, 1978.

# Thinking About Thinking About It in That Way: Test Data and Instruction

**D. Kim Reid, Ph.D.**
*University of Texas*
*Dallas, Texas*

**Wayne P. Hresko, Ph.D.**
*North Texas State University*
*Denton, Texas*

THE MANDATES of PL 94-142 have been double-edged. While they have sought to improve current testing practices, they have also served to promote testing as the sacred cow of educational decision making. Both norm-referenced and criterion-referenced tests have proliferated. (We are using the term *test* to refer to the use of formal or informal instruments and not to any systematic data collection that occurs under predetermined conditions.) Developers of norm-referenced tests have given considerable attention to statistical issues, although few tests used in special education meet the standards set for them (Salvia & Ysseldyke, 1978). Criterion-referenced tests have been designed to directly and absolutely assess whether students have acquired specific knowledge. These occurrences have led to increased willingness to rely on the results of testing as the primary basis for both diagnosis and teaching.

66

We do not take issue with the use of norm-referenced tests for the purposes for which they were intended: to compare children's performances and to make judgments about their past rates of learning. Neither do we argue with the use of criterion-referenced tests for exploring children's performances vis-a-vis specific curriculum objectives. However, we assert that testing should *not* become the basis for curriculum design. (For detailed accounts of some reasons behind such an argument see Salvia & Ysseldyke, 1978; Tyron, 1979.) An extension of that objection—and this will constitute the thrust of the discussion presented here—is that tests inappropriately constitute the major data source for making assertions about what children know and do not know for the purpose of teaching.

## IF AN ANSWER IS WRONG

It is not unusual to hear an educator declare that Mary does not know certain information because she did not answer a question or a series of questions on a test—often a norm-referenced or criterion-referenced test on which the child's performance was analyzed item by item. That kind of analysis assumes that individuals always have access to everything they know—under all or nearly all circumstances. Although no exhaustive review of research has been attempted, we will give examples from research in developmental psychology, developmental psycholinguistics, and education to question the validity of such an assumption. Knowledge is not immutable (Das, Kirby, & Jarman, 1975). For example,

Mary's knowing a fact may not be sufficient to ensure that she will be able to recall it when a question designed to elicit that fact is presented. The same potential problems would exist if Mary were asked to define a word, to use a word in a sentence, or to apply a rule.

Of course, some levels of knowledge are more susceptible to problems of demonstration than others. Knowledge of facts, terms, rules, and principles, for example, may be easier to measure with assurance than knowledge of procedures, translations, or applications. However, even measures of direct recall are potentially misleading because forgetting is often rapid and even information in long-term storage is altered by experiences that follow its acquisition (Loftus & Loftus, 1980). Furthermore, unless test items are measures of direct recall, they are themselves problems of application. Bloom, Hastings, and Madaus (1971, p. 120) defined application as requiring the recognition of the essential aspects of the problem; determining the rules, principles, and generalizations that are relevant; and then using those ideas to solve a problem that has not been previously encountered. Although there is undoubtedly some information that may have no application (e.g., a state capital or the color of a dress), most of the objectives of schooling (especially reading, writing, and arithmetic) have validity only if they can be applied. Whatever the child's knowledge or level of functioning at the time of testing, however, the child may or may not think of bringing those abilities into play. Children may not "think of thinking about it in that way" (Duck-

---

*Most of the objectives of schooling (especially reading, writing, and arithmetic) have validity only when they can be applied.*

---

worth, 1979, p. 304). Therefore the question for educators is: Under what circumstances can the child bring knowledge into play? Answers may well be more closely related to one or more of the following considerations than to abstract "knowledge of the fact."

The complications that "thinking about thinking about it in that way" have on the interpretation of test data for educational planning are not limited to young or handicapped children. Duckworth (1979) described intelligent, adult students who experimented with floating and sinking objects for seven sessions before one of them thought about thinking that floating depends on weight and volume. Walter (cited in Duckworth) noted the amazement of an adult student trained in mathematics when she realized that moving one point of a rubber band to different points on the same row of a geoboard did not change the area of a triangle she had formed. She was so excited about her discovery that she shared it with the rest of the group, who also held degrees in mathematics. It was only after considerable discussion that they realized she had rediscovered a fact all of them had "known" since elementary school, namely, that the area of a triangle is half the base times the height. By moving only the apex of the triangle to another peg on the same row, she had maintained the area. Kuhn (1979) reported a similar

phenomenon in her work with a variety of persons ranging from preadolescent to elderly. Although many were unable to solve the problems she gave them, strategies appropriate to a successful problem solution were within their capacity, but for some reason they failed to use them.

## Knowing How to Know

It is likely that what is measured by tests is as much a function of children's knowing how to know (Brown, 1975, 1978; Flavell, 1970, 1971, 1977; Flavell, Beach, & Chinsky, 1966; Flavell & Wellman, 1976); that is, the way they approach the task, as it is an estimate of what they in fact know. In the field of learning disabilities, for example, there is a body of literature accumulating that is impressive in regard to the consistency of its findings: learning disabled children (a) tend to approach problems with strategies characteristic of younger, normally achieving children; and (b) this delay in the spontaneous application of strategies appears to be approximately 2 years (Hallahan, 1975; Hallahan, Gajar, Cohen, & Tarver, 1978; Hallahan, Kauffman, & Ball, 1973; Hallahan, Tarver, Kauffman, & Graybeal, 1978; Tarver, Hallahan, Cohen, & Kauffman, 1977; Tarver, Hallahan, Kauffman, & Ball, 1976; Torgesen, 1977).

Wong's (1979) study of story comprehension in learning disabled and normally achieving children is illustrative. She first determined empirically what idea units (Brown & Smiley, 1977) were most important to the theme of a story. That story was then read to small groups of children as they read along. For the children in the

68 questions condition (half of each group), questions related to the thematically important idea units were embedded in the text prior to the paragraph in which the answer was contained. After the story was read to the children, they were asked to recall as much of it as possible. The number of units recalled provided a score.

As expected, normally achieving children in the no-question condition significantly outscored the learning disabled children in the same condition. However, a significant interaction effect indicated that in the question condition the learning disabled performed as well as the normally achieving children. The performance of normally achieving children did not improve as a result of having the questions available. Wong's explanation is that the normally achieving children were already using appropriate strategies in the recall task, so the use of questions did not help them. The learning disabled children, in contrast, appeared not to use strategies as effective as those used by the normally achieving children. Hence they benefited from the presence of the questions. Wong posited that "because the learning disabled children [in the question condition] read to answer the given questions, they ceased to be what Torgesen (1977) terms the inactive learner who typically does not participate in his/her learning" (p. 46).

However, the question arises whether the learning disabled children were "inactive" in the sense that they were not strategizing or whether they were using inferior, inefficient, or immature strategies. Work by a variety of professionals suggests the latter is true. Hallahan and colleagues (see Hallahan, 1975; Hallahan et al., 1978; Tarver et al., 1977) have found, for example, that learning disabled children exhibit immature strategies in both memory and attention tasks. Kershner (1975) and Reid and her colleagues (see Reid, 1980; Reid & Knight-Arest, 1980; Reid, Knight-Arest, & Hresko, 1980) have found that children with reading problems tend to continue the use of perceptually dominated strategies well after their agemates have shifted to more efficient, more cognitively oriented approaches to learning.

Some describe this problem as a production deficiency (Hall, 1980; Hallahan & Kneedler, 1979). A production deficiency occurs when children fail to use a strategy they are capable of using (Brown, 1975). One critical aspect of a production deficiency is that the child is able to use the ability when instructed to do so. For example, Spache (1976) reported that learning disabled children who had mastered phonics skills did not use them spontaneously while reading. However, they could use them when teachers instructed them to do so.

## An Invalid Assumption

Making judgments about what children know for the purpose of teaching is therefore a complex chore. If teachers were interested in assessing children's knowledge of certain content, would it be more appropriate to consider their knowledge that which they can recall with questions or without them? If teachers are interested in teaching them to read, perhaps the decision would be different. Do children who use phonic analysis only when specifically instructed to do so really "know" phonics? What is the validity of teaching a curriculum to mastery on test performance when the only real purpose for such instruction is to enable children to use those skills whenever they need them to assist in reading? Assuming that what children demonstrate they can do by taking a test reflects their knowledge clearly is not an adequate basis for instructional planning.

## IF THE ANSWER IS RIGHT

The complementary issue in the interpretation of test data for instructional purposes is this: Can one be assured that a child who answers a question or set of questions correctly on a test does in fact know the material? The answer may be yes—or it may be that the child was able to succeed by guessing or by using information contained in the questions themselves to decipher an appropriate answer. De Villiers and de Villiers (1978, p. 99), for example, asked a child, "Is it upside-down, hm?" The child responded, "It upaside-down." That certainly appeared to be a correct response. But further questioning led to a different assessment of the child's competence. When the adult asked "What kind of truck is it, Billy?" the child answered, "It's a kind of truck." He had learned that something in the question had something to do with the answer he should give. The strategy he adopted was, at least in some instances, successful and gave the appearance that he had abilities that he had not in fact mastered. These are obvious problems of

which educators tend to be aware and which are minimal when well-constructed, individually administered tests are used.

Following are two other points important to consider if one is planning to teach a child: (a) that the child may have learned a verbal rule but does not really understand the concept behind it and (b) that giving a correct response does not tell the examiner whether a child can use that knowledge.

### Verbal Rule Learning

Knight-Arest and Reid (1980) conducted a study in which learning disabled and normally achieving children were invited to a party in groups of three (always classmates together). One child—previously determined to be the only one of the three children who was a nonconserver—was asked to pour juice for his two friends. The nonconserver and one of the other children had short, wide glasses. The second conserver had a tall, thin glass. The children were instructed not to drink the juice until all had agreed that the pouring was fair. Of course, once the nonconserver poured the juice in the tall, thin glass only up to the level of the juice in the short, wide glasses, the conservers began arguing for a fairer apportionment. The investigator did not intervene, but only recorded the arguments the conservers used to convince the nonconserver that the child with the tall, thin glass deserved more juice. After the children agreed that the pouring was fair, the party was held. Within a day, a comparable conservation-of-liquids task was administered to the children who had been nonconservers, and the reasons they gave to support their decisions were recorded.

Statistically there was no difference in the number of normally achieving or learning disabled children who could conserve on the posttest. However, there were striking differences in their reasons. The normally achieving children were able to give reasons for their conservation responses that were not offered by their peers during the party (a phenomenon that has also been documented by Doise & Perret-Clermont, 1975). Although the learning disabled children were also giving conservation responses, their reasons were limited to those they had heard from their peers. On a delayed posttest (2 weeks later), a very high percentage of the normally achieving children had maintained the conservation response. However, there were significantly fewer learning disabled children who continued to give conservation responses. It appears that the learning disabled children had acquired a verbal rule without understanding. They were able to give correct answers shortly after the learning experience, but once the advantage of recency was lost, the learning disabled children were no longer able to remember or apply the rule.

Another well-known example of the same problem is Engelmann's (1971) teaching conservation-of-volume responses using a verbal rule strategy to a group of young children. Engelmann was free to instruct the group of students until he was satisfied that they had reached criterion performance. At that point, Kamii and Derman (1971) reexamined the children, pressing them to explain their answers. They concluded that the children had learned only a rote application of the rule.

Because the children can give a rule, it appears that they have understood the rule. But in fact they may only have memorized it. They may be repeating empty words. Many times the right answer may be given on Monday, but the child fails the same item if he or she is retested a few days later. Perhaps memorizing without understanding accounts in some measure for learning disabled and retarded children's inability to retain what they have learned.

## Functional Language

The study of pragmatics in developmental psycholinguistics raises similar questions about reliance on test data for instructional planning. Pragmatics refers to the functional use of language in interpersonal communication. Basic to using language is being able to ask questions when you need to know something: it is important to know what you do not know. Also important are understanding and responding to the other participants' needs in the interaction, and knowing how to say the "right thing in the right way at the right time and place. . . ." (Ervin-Tripp, 1971, p. 37).

*Because the children can give a rule, it appears that they have understood the rule. But in fact they may only have memorized it.*

Passing test items measuring vocabulary, sentence repetition, inflectional endings, and the like does not ensure that children are effective language users. Bloom and Lahey (1978, p. 290) noted that children with language disorders or disabilities "may have learned something about the world and something about the conventional code, but are unable to *use* the code in speaking or understanding in certain contexts or for certain purposes." They indicate that the effect of language impairment in some children is that they do not verbalize. Yet when these same children are prodded into verbalization during testing, they do well. They have the code, but do not understand its use. This impairment in the ability to *use* language is noted in the literature related to the mentally retarded and the emotionally disturbed (Bloom & Lahey, 1978).

In research with learning disabled children, *use* problems have been identified by a number of independent investigators. Use problems have been related to fillers (Wiig & Semel, 1976), lack of verbal fluency (Bryan, 1974), overuse of a limited, concrete vocabulary (Wiig & Semel, 1976), use of pronouns without antecedents (Reid & Knight-Arest, 1980), and giving misinformation or failing to clarify correct information (Bryan & Pflaum, 1978). However, prior testing had revealed that the children were capable of defining vocabulary words and had knowledge of pronouns. Performance in a game requiring give and take of information with hyperactive children indicated less efficient language use with respect to answering and asking questions and giving and using feedback (Whalen, Henker,

Collins, McAuliffe, & Vaux, 1979). Knowing something about vocabulary or syntax does not guarantee competent language use. Most tests of language used with exceptional children do not include any measure of *how* children use their language knowledge. Muma (1978) suggested that in a test setting, examination of language usage probably cannot be accomplished.

In summary, if a child's answer on a test is correct, that does not necessarily mean that the child knows the correct answer. It means that he or she knows under those circumstances. Similarly, children who succeed on test items often fail to use that knowledge in the day-to-day situations in which its use would be appropriate. If educators are comparing children's standing with that of their peers or are screening them for curriculum placements, testing (norm-referenced and criterion-referenced) makes good sense. But if the aim is to teach children, teachers cannot take for granted that children know what the tests indicate they know.

## DEPTH OF KNOWLEDGE

There is one additional consideration to note in regard to the interpretation of test answers. It is often important to teachers to know *how* an answer was formulated. Examples will be taken from the research on analogical reasoning and metaphorical language, since they are both curriculum objectives and familiar question types.

A number of researchers have shown that young children can both understand and produce metaphors (Billow, 1975) but require the complex reasoning abilities

71

not developed until adolescence to appreciate the figurative meaning (Gallagher & Wright, 1977; Ortony, 1979). Hillman's (1980) research with adolescents' analogical reasoning highlighted this distinction. She argued that answers to analogy problems reflect experiences children have with the content of the analogies, general intelligence, and facility with language. If the purpose of testing is comparison to a normative group, those factors do not necessarily hinder interpretation of the child's performance. However, if the purpose of testing is to plan to teach children analogies or metaphorical language, one would need to know *why* the response was given. Hillman reported that one of the adolescents she tested gave the response mare to the analogy Horse is to _____ as cow is to calf (p. 94). Asked to explain her answer, the child replied, "Because a mare is a baby horse as a calf is a baby cow" (p. 64). The response was incorrect, because the child was not familiar with the vocabulary—not because the child did not understand the structure of analogies. (Of course, it was recognition of such problems that led Piaget to conduct his early research.) This difference would not be important in norm-referenced testing, but it would be important to make such a distinction if criterion-referenced tests were being used. Although their major function is to provide data relevant to instruction, few criterion-referenced tests are designed to reveal the nature of the error.

## CONCLUSIONS

It is frequently argued that valid and reliable norm-referenced tests provide teachers with considerable information useful to teaching. Writing of this article was motivated by recent experiences in four states in two separate sections of the country in which teachers, school psychologists, and educational diagnosticians relied heavily on the results of standardized testing for both diagnostic evaluations and the development of individualized education programs (IEPs). Some of the professionals with whom we worked acknowledged that tests measuring pervasive cognitive and psychomotor abilities contribute relatively little to the development of the IEP once a diagnosis has been made.

However, nearly all of them maintained that achievement tests—either norm-referenced or criterion-referenced—that provide information about a child's performance on particular items or objectives were useful in IEP development. Most of these individuals were firmly convinced that children's performance on a criterion-referenced test characterized the state of their knowledge. Educational planning was based on the accomplishment of objectives derived from testing. Long-range goals were set for a full year and short-term objectives devised for several months. Often the periodic review of the IEP and its revisions was based on additional testing, especially criterion-referenced tests.

There is no difficulty in this approach if school professionals recognize test performances as samples of behavior that do not necessarily reflect a child's state of knowledge. Lawler (cited in Zivian, 1977) noted that test items that most children pass (or fail) are not included in standardized tests. Test scores may therefore obscure what children know. But tests and test scores tend to be both seductive and viewed as accurate. When the results of instruction do not match anticipated outcomes, instead of considering that a child may have performed well on a test or poorly on a test for reasons such as those presented above, school personnel tend to be surprised that the child learned so easily or forgot so rapidly.

Even more important, reliance on tests as indicators of children's progress diverts attention from the only true evaluation that can be accomplished: ongoing daily appraisal. Many teachers who use test data regularly do not keep careful records of children's responses to questions or ap-

---

*Reliance on tests as indicators of children's progress diverts attention from the only true evaluation that can be accomplished: ongoing appraisal day by day.*

---

proaches to learning. Instead tests are given at the end of units or lessons—after the child has already succeeded or failed—and children are either advanced to new objectives or are left to repeat the old ones.

We agree with Wallace and Larsen (1978) that testing for teaching must be continuous. But we would go one step beyond their recommendations by suggesting that it is also necessary to test the test results. Only through continuing dialogue with students and continued observation, probing, and record keeping can teachers determine what strategies children use to approach tasks, whether they have learned only to verbalize a rule or whether they really understand, whether they can *use* the information they have learned, and what depth of understanding they have attained. Knowledge of all of these outcomes is necessary for educational planning, but test data do not provide these observations.

## REFERENCES

Billow, R. M. A cognitive developmental study of metaphor comprehension. *Developmental Psychology*, 1975, *11*, 415-423.

Bloom, B. S., Hastings, J. T., & Madaus, G. S. *Handbook on formative and summative evaluation of student learning.* New York: McGraw-Hill, 1971.

Bloom, L., & Lahey, L. *Language development and language disorders.* New York: John Wiley & Sons, 1978.

Brown, A. L. The development of memory: Knowing, knowing about knowing, knowing how to know. In H. W. Reese (Ed.), *Advances in child development and behavior* (Vol. 10). New York: Academic Press, 1975.

Brown, A. L. Knowing when, where, and how to remember: A problem of metacognition. In R. Glaser (Ed.), *Advances in instructional psychology.* Hillsdale, N.J.: Lawrence Erlbaum Associates, 1978.

Brown, A. L., & Smiley, S. S. Rating the importance of structural units of prose passages: A problem of metacognitive development. *Child Development*, 1977, *48*, 1-8.

Bryan, T. Peer popularity of learning-disabled children. *Journal of Learning Disabilities*, 1974, *7*, 261-268.

Bryan, T., & Pflaum, S. Social interactions of learning disabled children: A linguistic, social, and cognitive analysis. *Learning Disabilities Quarterly*, 1978, *1*, 70-79.

Das, J. P., Kirby, J., & Jarman, R. F. Simultaneous and successive syntheses: An alternative model for cognitive abilities. *Psychological Bulletin*, 1975, *82*, 87-103.

de Villiers, J. G., & de Villiers, P. A. *Language acquisition.* Cambridge, Mass.: Harvard University Press, 1978.

**74**

Doise, W., & Perret-Clermont, A. W. Social interaction and the development of cognitive operations. *European Journal of Social Psychology*, 1975, *5*, 367-383.

Duckworth, E. Either we're too early and they can't learn it or we're too late and they know it already: The dilemma of "Applying Piaget." *Harvard Educational Review*, 1979, *49*, 297-312.

Engelmann, S. E. Does the Piagetian approach imply instruction? In D. R. Green, M. P. Ford, & G. P. Flamer (Eds.), *Measurement and Piaget*. New York: McGraw-Hill, 1971.

Ervin-Tripp, S. Social backgrounds and verbal skills. In R. Huxley & E. Ingram (Eds.), *Language acquisition: Models and methods*. New York: Academic Press, 1971.

Flavell, J. H. Developmental studies of mediated memory. In H. W. Reese & L. P. Lipsitt (Eds.), *Advances in child development and behavior, Vol. 5*. New York: Academic Press, 1970.

Flavell, J. H. First discussant's comments: What is memory development the development of? *Human Development*, 1971, *14*, 272-278.

Flavell, J. H. *Cognitive development*. Englewood Cliffs, N.J.: Prentice-Hall, 1977.

Flavell, J. H., Beach, D. H., & Chinsky, J. M. Spontaneous verbal rehearsal in a memory task as a function of age. *Child Development*, 1966, *37*, 283-299.

Flavell, J. H., & Wellman, H. M. Metamemory. In R. V. Kail & J. W. Hagen (Eds.), *Memory in cognitive development*. Hillsdale, N.J.: Lawrence Erlbaum Associates, 1976.

Gallagher, J. M., & Wright, R. J. Children's solution of verbal analogies: Extension of Piaget's concept of reflexive abstraction. Paper presented in the symposium "Thinking with the left hand: Children's understanding of analogy and metaphor." Society for Research in Child Development, New Orleans, 1977.

Hall, R. J. Cognitive behavior modification and information processing skills of exceptional children. *Exceptional Education Quarterly*, 1980, *1*(1), 9-15.

Hallahan, D. P. Distractibility in the learning disabled child. In W. M. Cruickshank & D. P. Hallahan (Eds.), *Perceptual and learning disabilities in children, Vol. 2: Research and theory*. Syracuse, N.Y.: Syracuse University Press, 1975.

Hallahan, D. P., Gajar, A. H., Cohen, S. B., & Tarver, S. G. Selective attention and locus of control in learning disabled and normal children. *Journal of Learning Disabilities*, 1978, *11*, 231-236.

Hallahan, D. P., Kauffman, J. M., & Ball, D. W. Selective attention and cognitive tempo of low achieving and high achieving sixth grade males. *Perceptual and Motor Skills*, 1973, *36*, 579-583.

Hallahan, D. P., & Kneedler, R. D. Strategy deficits in the information processing of learning disabled children. Technical Report No. 6, University of Virginia Learning Disabilities Research Institute, Charlottesville, 1979.

Hallahan, D. P., Tarver, S. G., Kauffman, J. M., & Graybeal, N. L. A comparison of the effects of reinforcement and response cost on the selective attention of learning disabled children. *Journal of Learning Disabilities*, 1978, *11*, 430-438.

Hillman, I. D. A developmental study of sex, aspiration and the onset of formal operations. Unpublished doctoral dissertation, New York University, 1980.

Kamii, C., & Derman, L. Comments on Engelmann's paper. In D. R. Greene, M. P. Ford, & G. P. Flamer (Eds.), *Measurement and Piaget*. New York: McGraw-Hill, 1971.

Kershner, J. R. Visual-spatial organization and reading: Support for a cognitive developmental interpretation. *Journal of Learning Disabilities*, 1975, *8*, 30-36.

Knight-Arest, I., & Reid, D. K. Peer interaction as a catalyst for conservation acquisition in normal and learning disabled children. *Proceedings of the Ninth Interdisciplinary International Conference on Piagetian Theory and the Helping Professions*, Los Angeles, 1980.

Kuhn, D. The application of Piaget's theory of cognitive development to education. *Harvard Educational Review*, 1979, *49*, 340-360.

Loftus, E. S., & Loftus, G. R. On the permanence of stored information in the human brain. *American Psychologist*, 1980, *35*, 409-420.

Muma, J. R. *Language handbook: Concepts, assessment, intervention*. Englewood Cliffs, N.J.: Prentice-Hall, 1978.

Ortony, A. Beyond literal similarity. *Psychological Review*, 1979, *86*, 161-182.

Reid, D. K. Learning from a Piagetian perspective: The exceptional child. In I. E. Sigel, R. M. Golinkoff, & D. Brodzinsky (Eds.), *Piagetian theory and research: New directions and applications*. Hillsdale, N.J.: Lawrence Erlbaum Associates, 1980.

Reid, D. K., & Knight-Arest, I. Cognitive processing in normally achieving and learning disabled boys. In M. Freidman (Ed.), *Intelligence and learning*. New York: Plenum, 1980.

Reid, D. K., Knight-Arest, I., & Hresko, W. P. The development of cognition in learning disabled children. In J. Gottlieb & S. S. Strichart (Eds.), *Developmental theories and research in learning disabilities*. Baltimore: University Park Press, 1980.

Salvia, J., & Ysseldyke, J. E. *Assessment in special and remedial education*. Dallas: Houghton Mifflin Co., 1978.

Spache, G. D. *Diagnosing and correcting reading disabil-ities.* Boston: Allyn and Bacon, 1976.

Tarver, S. G., Hallahan, D. P., Cohen, S. B., & Kauff-man, J. M. The development of visual selective atten-tion and verbal rehearsal on learning disabled boys. *Journal of Learning Disabilities,* 1977, *10,* 491-500.

Tarver, S. G., Hallahan, D. P., Kauffman, J. M., & Ball, D. W. Verbal rehearsal and selective attention in chil-dren with learning disabilities: A developmental lag. *Journal of Experimental Child Psychology,* 1976, *22,* 375-385.

Torgesen, J. K. The role of nonspecific factors in the task performance of learning disabled children: A theoreti-cal assessment. *Journal of Learning Disabilities,* 1977, *10,* 27-34.

Torgesen, J. K., & Goldman, T. Verbal rehearsal and short-term memory in reading-disabled children. *Child Development,* 1977, *48,* 56-60.

Torgesen, J. K., Murphy, H. A., & Ivey, C. The influence of an orienting task on the memory performance of children with reading problems. *Journal of Learning Disabilities,* 1979, *12,* 396-401.

Tyron, W. W. The test-trait fallacy. *American Psy-chologist,* 1979, *34,* 402-406.

Wallace, G., & Larsen, S. C. *Educational assessment of learning problems: Testing for teaching.* Boston: Allyn and Bacon, 1978.

Whalen, C. K., Henker, B., Collins, B. E., McAuliffe, S., & Vaux, A. Peer interaction in a structured communi-cation task: Comparisons of normal and hyperactive boys and of methylphenidate (Ritalin) and placebo effects. *Child Development,* 1979, *50,* 388-401.

Wiig, E. H., & Semel, E. M. *Language disabilities in children and adolescents.* Columbus, Ohio: Charles E. Merrill, 1976.

Wong, B. Y. L. Increasing retention of main ideas through questioning strategies. *Learning Disabilities Quarterly,* 1979, *2,* 42-47.

Zivian, N. T. Dialectics: Paradigms for the social sciences. *Human Development,* 1977, *20,* 249-252.

# Significant Discrepancies in the Classification of Pupils: Differentiating the Concept

*John Salvia, Ed.D.*
*Roland Good III, M.S.*
*Pennsylvania State University*
*University Park, Pennsylvania*

**D**IFFERENCES in scores that an individual earns on various tests have assumed increased importance. From simply worrying about under-achievement (or overachievement), educators have assumed that "significant" discrepancies indicate underlying pathology. Nowhere is this type of thinking clearer than in the learning disabilities literature. The very definitions of learning disability stress differences and deficits (cf. Hallahan & Kauffman, 1976).

The assumption behind this conceptualization is clear. Unequal scores reflect unequal development; unequal development is undesirable. Some number is arbitrarily selected as an indicator of underlying pathology and then is used to explain the pathology—somehow the symptom becomes the cause through simple renaming. The selection of the arbitrary number is based on *conjectural significance* (i.e., "I think an 8-point difference is significant") and is used to classify an individual as abnormal. One searches in vain for an empirical rationale for any discrepancy levels in the literature or in governmental regulations.

The significance of discrepancies is not too complicated empirically. There are three elements to the definition of significant discrepancy: (1) reliable discrepancy, (2) unusual discrepancy, and (3) meaningful discrepancy. The concepts are unidirectional and hierarchical; that is, meaningful discrepancies presume unusual and reliable discrepancies, and unusual discrepancies presume reliable discrepancies. However, reliable differences may be neither unusual nor meaningful, and unusual differences may not be meaningful.

## SIGNIFICANCE OF DISCREPANCIES: RELIABLE DIFFERENCES

The first step in evaluating a difference score is to ascertain the likelihood that it could occur by chance. A person's true abilities as measured by two tests may be the same. However, obtained scores fluctuate because of error.

The error fluctuation of any score $(x)$ that is known as the standard error of measurement $(SE_x)$ is a function of the standard deviations of the score $(SD_x)$ and the reliability of the score $(r_x)$:

$$SE_x = SD_x \ \sqrt{1 - r_x} \ . \qquad (1)$$

Difference scores are notoriously prone to error; many introductory texts on measurement and evaluation warn the novice about this. However, educators'

reliance on difference scores for classification of pupils suggests that these warnings have gone unheeded.

Two similar methods of evaluating the reliability of differences between two scores for any individual have been suggested. One, described by Thorndike in 1963 and recently advocated in part by Shepard (1980), uses a regression model to evaluate the difference between scholastic aptitude and achievement. Here, aptitude or intelligence is assumed to be causally related to achievement; differences in achievement are believed to be caused in part by differences in aptitude. When a pupil's predicted achievement $(\hat{y})$, based on the correlation between achievement and aptitude $(r_{xy})$, does not correspond to actual achievement $(y)$, a discrepancy from prediction $(Dp)$ exists:

$$Dp = \hat{y} - y. \qquad (2)$$

The reliability of $Dp$ $(r_{Dp})$ is a function of the reliability of the predictor $(r_x)$, the reliability of the criterion $(r_y)$, and the correlation between them $(r_{xy})$:

$$r_{Dp} = \frac{r_y + r_x \ r_{xy}^2 - 2r_{xy}^2}{1 - r_{xy}^2} . \qquad (3)$$

The standard deviation of $Dp$ $(SD_{Dp})$, also known as the standard error of estimate, is a function of the standard deviation of the criterion $(SD_y)$ and $r_{xy}$:

$$SD_{Dp} = SD_y \ \sqrt{1 - r_{xy}^2} \ . \qquad (4)$$

By substituting into Equation 1, the standard error of the discrepancy from prediction $(SE_{Dp})$ is obtained:

$$SE_{Dp} = SD_y \sqrt{1 + r_{xy}{}^2 - r_y - r_x r_{xy}{}^2} \quad . \quad (5)$$

A second way of evaluating the reliability of differences was proposed by Stake and Wardrop (1971). They considered the difference $(Di)$ between the scores $(x, y)$ on each measure:

$$Di = x - y. \quad (6)$$

Their procedure does not presume that one variable causes the other, but it does require that the two measures be expressed in the same units of measurement (e.g., standard scores). Because there is unreliability associated with each score on which the difference is based, there is error variability in the difference scores. The reliability of the difference score $(r_{Di})$ is a function of the reliability of each score $(r_x$ and $r_y)$ and the correlation between them $(r_{xy})$:

$$r_{Di} = \frac{\frac{1}{2}(r_x + r_y) - r_{xy}}{1 - r_{xy}}. \quad (7)$$

The standard deviation of the difference scores $(SD_{Di})$ is a function of the standard deviation of each score $(SD_x$ and $SD_y)$ and $r_{xy}$:

$$SD_{Di} = \sqrt{SD^2{}_x + SD^2{}_y - 2r_{xy} SD_x SD_y} \quad . \quad (8)$$

The standard error of the difference $SE_{Di}$ is then obtained by again substituting into Equation 1:

$$SE_{Di} = \frac{\sqrt{SD^2{}_x + SD^2{}_y - 2r_{xy} SD_x SD_y}}{\sqrt{1 - \dfrac{\frac{1}{2}(r_x + r_y) - r_{xy}}{1 - r_{xy}}}} \quad . \quad (9)$$

Both of these approaches allow the construction of confidence intervals $(CI)$ about an obtained difference:

$$95\% \; CI_D = D \pm 1.96 \, (SE_D), \quad (10)$$

where $D$ may be either $Dp$ or $Di$. The sizes of the obtained confidence intervals differ somewhat between the two approaches.

## SIGNIFICANCE OF DISCREPANCIES: ATYPICAL DIFFERENCES

Although a discrepancy may be reliable (and therefore real), it may also be commonplace. Casual observations tell us that humans vary markedly in abilities. Characteristics shared by most individuals are seldom considered significant; only rare or atypical differences are useful for diagnosis and classification.

Differences between people are absolute or relative. Absolute differences have nonoverlapping distributions; membership in one group precludes membership in another group. For example, the perception of color is physiologically determined by the presence of photosensitive enzymes in the cones of the eyes. The enzymes are either present or absent. Anomaloscopic evaluation of individuals with normal color vision, protanopes, and deuteranopes reveals three discrete distributions, as shown in Figure 1. Each distribution is separated by sev-

80

eral standard deviations, and there are genetically based differences among the groups.

Relative differences occur when individuals are classified on a trait or ability that varies continuously. For example, individuals are classified as mentally retarded primarily on the basis of measured intelligence. However, the distribution of intelligence contains no sharp breaks, that is, areas of discontinuity. Therefore, classifications of intelligence are arbitrary. The lowest level of "normal" intelligence may be set at $-1.0\,SD$, $-1.3\,SD$, or $-2.0\,SD$, depending on what standard is used. The person classified as having abnormally low intelligence is only slow relative to others. The point that separates normal and retarded intelligence is arbitrary.

Scores on tests of psychological and educational constructs provide continuous distributions that are usually normal; thus differences between individuals within the distribution are *relative*. A general rule of thumb is that scores obtained by the median 50% of the population are "average," and scores obtained by the median 90% of the population are "normal." Thus "significant" discrepancies should be unusual (i.e., not average) or abnormal. There is little evidence that the rarity of discrepancies is considered in educational theory or practice. However, there are some notable exceptions.

Paraskevopoulos and Kirk (1969) provided tables, based on the performance of the standardization sample used in the revised edition of the Illinois Test of Psycholinguistic Abilities (ITPA), that assign percentile ranks to average deviations (scatter) on the ITPA. Thus the unevenness of a child's profile can be compared with the variability of performances of average children. Presumably, if there is unusual scatter, something may be wrong with the child: "The larger the deviation, the more discrepant the child's growth, and the more likely it is that the child will have learning disabilities" (Paraskevopoulos & Kirk, 1969, p. 142).

Kaufman (1979) examined verbal-performance discrepancies in the standardization sample of the Wechsler Intelligence Scale for Children-Revised. He found that "about half of the children . . . had discrepancies of 9 or more points, about one third had discrepancies of 12 or more, and about one fourth had discrepancies of 15 or more IQ points" (p. 741). If the median 90% is the limit of normality, a person would need to manifest a 20-point difference between verbal and performance IQs to be considered abnormal, although a 12-point difference

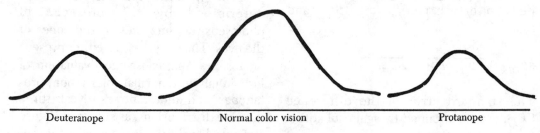

Figure 1. Discrete distributions for absolute differences.

is reliable (using a 95% confidence interval).

Calculations of the reliability of the difference also yield the information necessary to evaluate the rarity of the difference. The percentage of area of a normal curve more extreme than $z_d$ corresponds to the percentage of people obtaining discrepancies more severe than the discrepancy examined:

$$z_d = \frac{D}{SD_D}, \qquad (11)$$

where $D$ may be either $Di$ or $Dp$.

## SIGNIFICANCE OF DISCREPANCIES: MEANINGFUL DIFFERENCES

Although a discrepancy may be reliable and unusual, it may have little social or psychological meaning. When individuals who manifest the discrepancy behave in a qualitatively different manner because of the discrepancy, that discrepancy is meaningful.

Examples of qualitative differences between scores from intelligence tests (as opposed to quantitative discrepancies between scores from two tests) are fairly rare, but they do exist. Jensen (1980, p. 114) identified four thresholds that are socially and personally important:
- attendance in regular school (IQ = 50);
- mastery of the traditional elementary school curriculum (IQ = 75);
- graduation from a college preparatory high school (IQ = 105);
- graduation from an accredited 4-year college with grades good enough to get into a professional school.

Zeaman (1965) found little documentation for learning sets among moderately retarded persons. Ellis (1970) noted that retarded individuals may not spontaneously rehearse material to be recalled. Thus significantly low IQs are psychologically meaningful.

Investigations of the consequences of *intra*personal discrepancies are far more complicated than are investigations of *inter*personal differences on single scores. Two factors must be considered. First, the psychological and social consequences must be attributable to the discrepancy rather than to an unusually low score on either test on which the discrepancy is based. For example, severely limited knowledge of social studies in a 12-year-old child with normal intelligence and first-grade reading ability could be attributed to poor reading skills that hinder acquisition of social studies information as well as to some underlying pathology that produced the IQ-reading discrepancy. To paraphrase Occam, pathologies should not be multiplied without necessity. The more parsimonious explanation (e.g., poor reading) should be used unless we can show otherwise (e.g., gifted individuals with average reading ability who manifested severely limited knowledge of social studies).

Thus the important effect on the underlying constructs of the two tests is the *interaction* between the two tests (or their underlying constructs): an effect solely attributable to the discrepancy between the tests and not accounted for by each test individually. Most studies to date have compared children of average

82 intelligence and low achievement with peers of average intelligence and average achievement. Only a few studies have compared children with low achievement and average intelligence with children of low achievement and low intelligence. There are apparently no published studies that examine discrepancies per se while controlling for low scores on both tests.

The second factor that complicates investigations of discrepancies is that the psychological and social consequences should be qualitatively affected by the marked or significant discrepancy. This could happen in several ways: Individuals with severe discrepancies may seldom gain employment in technical fields in which their scores (taken individually) would qualify them; individuals with severe discrepancies may fail to develop adequate self-concepts, and so forth. Apparently no published studies have determined the point at which discrepancies produce qualitative differences in psychological and social variables.

## DISCUSSION

For a discrepancy to be significant it must be reliable, unusual, and meaningful. The treatment of discrepancy within the educational system has been simplistically undifferentiated. Confidence intervals for discrepancies are rarely determined; normative data on the rarity of discrepancies between IQ and achievement are seldom reported in the literature. No systematic evaluations of the consequences of severe discrepancies (those that are rare and reliable) are reported. "Significance" has been defined more pragmatically. Whoever wields the most power, whoever can muster the most votes gets to decide what is significant.

Research in this area is needed. In the field of learning disabilities, much time, effort, and money has been devoted to ameliorating the effects of a discrepancy between intelligence and achievement. Yet no study has sought to identify the effects of a discrepancy while controlling for the scores on the individual tests.

## REFERENCES

Ellis, N. Memory processes in retardates and normals. In N. Ellis (Ed.), *International review of research in mental retardation.* New York: Academic Press, 1970.

Hallahan, D., & Kauffman, J. *Exceptional children.* Englewood Cliffs, N.J.: Prentice-Hall, 1976.

Jensen, A. *Bias in mental testing.* New York: Free Press, 1980.

Kaufman, A. *Intelligent testing with the W.I.S.C.-R.* New York: Wiley, 1979.

Paraskevopoulos, J., & Kirk, S. *The development and psychometric characteristics of the revised Illinois Test of Psycholinguistic Abilities.* Urbana: University of Illinois Press, 1969.

Shepard, L. An evaluation of the regression discrepancy method for identifying children with learning disabilities. *Journal of Special Education,* 1980, *14*(1), 79-91.

Stake, R., & Wardrop, J. Gain score errors in performance contracting. *Research in the teaching of English,* 1971, *5*, 226-229.

Thorndike, R. *The concepts of over- and underachievement.* New York: Columbia University Press, 1963.

Zeaman, D. Learning processes in the mentally retarded. In S. Osler & R. Cooke (Eds.), *The biosocial basis of mental retardation.* Baltimore, Md.: Johns Hopkins University Press, 1965.

# Educational Assessment Using Direct, Continuous Data

*Michael S. Rosenberg, Ph.D.*
*Paul T. Sindelar, Ed.D.*
*Pennsylvania State University*
*University Park, Pennsylvania*

**P**HYSICIANS RELY on the measurement of vital signs to determine the health of their patient and the effectiveness of their prescribed treatment. When an individual is ill, the individual's temperature, heart rate, respiratory rate, and blood pressure are affected. Physicians use these direct and sometimes continuous measures of these bodily functions to diagnose problems and assess treatment. These measures are also sensitive to change, so that in the course of treatment, the physicians expect to observe change in temperature and the other vital signs as the patient improves.

Deno and Mirkin (1977) likened the physician's need for direct, continuous measures to the educator's need for such measures. Educational assessment has no analogous system of measurement. There is no thermometer that educators can use to measure reliably and continuously the vital signs of learning. However, some educational measurement practices pro-

84

vide more direct, continuous, and sensitive data than others. In this article, measurement practices are evaluated against these three criteria. Data-based methods, it is demonstrated, most closely meet the criteria for effective assessment.

## LEARNING DISABILITIES: AN ILLUSTRATIVE EXAMPLE

All definitions of learning disabilities have two common elements: normal intelligence and underachievement. These elements are clearly associated with familiar measurement practices: intelligence and achievement testing. Information from achievement tests obviously has the most relevance for teachers. Achievement is a direct measure of the problem of learning disabilities. However, measurement in the area of learning disabilities is not limited to achievement testing. On the contrary, measurement procedures abound. Some measure underlying processes or abilities that are presumed to be related to achievement; others repeatedly assess performance on highly specific instructional objectives (i.e., data-based teaching). Ability testing is less direct than achievement testing; the measurement of performance on specific instructional objectives is more direct than achievement testing. In this article, these three assessment procedures are evaluated according to the criteria of directness, continuousness, and sensitivity.

### Ability testing

Many theorists and practitioners in the field of learning disabilities believe that deficiencies in underlying processes are responsible for learning problems. For example, Kirk and Kirk (1971) argued that deficiencies in psycholinguistic abilities are responsible for problems in learning academic content. Frostig (1972), on the other hand, posited that deficiencies in visual perception may cause problems some children face in school learning. Although these two examples do not exhaust the kinds of explanations experts have developed for learning problems, they are illustrative and familiar to almost everyone in the field.

The assessment of these abilities is clearly less direct than the assessment of achievement. Tests developed to measure these abilities—for example, the Illinois Test of Psycholinguistic Abilities (ITPA) and the Developmental Test of Visual Perception (DTVP)—measure hypothetical constructs that are only presumed to relate to achievement. The logic involved in the measurement of abilities involves: (1) measuring abilities reliably and identifying strengths and weaknesses, (2) training the abilities that have been shown to be weak, (3) retesting to determine if the training has been effective, and (4) observing the effects of improved abilities on achievement. However, the effectiveness of this logic has not been clearly demonstrated.

First, with regard to the reliability, Salvia and Ysseldyke (1981) noted that for the DTVP the subtests are not sufficiently reliable for the purposes of differential diagnosis. Thus for this instrument it is not clear that scores on the subtests are sufficiently reliable to identify strengths and weaknesses in visual perception. Consequently, treatment plans based on these scores may or may not be appropriate for a particular child. Salvia and Ysseldyke also argued that the subtests of the ITPA are, with some exceptions, not reliable enough for use in differential diagnosis. Neither of these instruments meets rigorous criteria for use in diagnosing strengths and weaknesses. This conclusion does not imply that with further development the instruments could not be improved or that other measures of other underlying abilities cannot be used reliably to identify strengths and weaknesses. Consequently, the second of the steps in the logic underlying ability testing should be considered.

Previous literature reviews (e.g., Hammill & Larsen, 1978) disputed the efficacy of psycholinguistic training. In response, Kavale (1981) conducted a meta-analysis of these studies. Kavale concluded that the average effect size of psycholinguistic training was .4 standard deviation and that certain subtests of the ITPA (Verbal Expression and Manual Expression) were found to have average effect sizes in excess of the average. Ignoring the problems associated with the use of meta-analyses (Horan, 1980), we conclude that Kavale demonstrated that psycholinguistic abilities are trainable and that the subtests of the ITPA are sufficiently sensitive to measure the effects of training. Similarly, Kavale and Matson (cited in Glass, 1981) conducted a meta-analysis of perceptual motor training approaches, including training based on Frostig's (1972) DTVP training model. However, the average effect size in studies investigating this program was .096 standard deviation, a figure small

enough to lead Glass (1981) to conclude that all perceptual motor training programs, including the Frostig "show up equally bad" (p. 11).

The question that remains is whether improvement on psycholinguistic abilities is related to improvement in achievement, and neither Kavale's (1981) nor Glass's (1981) analysis addresses this issue. In terms of meeting the criterion for directness of measurement, this issue is critical: If achievement is independent of improvement in underlying abilities, then the measurement and training of abilities are of questionable value. If improved abilities do lead to increased achievement, then although the measure is indirect, its relationship to the defining characteristic of learning disabilities is clear. At this point, the question is moot (Arter & Jenkins, 1979), and the lack of directness in measuring abilities is a failing that practitioners must address.

## Achievement testing

Achievement testing is generally agreed to be a more direct measure. However, under the heading of achievement testing, there are two approaches that vary in directness: norm-referenced and criterion-referenced testing. In norm-referenced testing, an individual's performance is compared with the performance of his or her peers, and mastery of content is expressed only in relation to the performance of other individuals. The information obtained in norm-referenced testing is typically expressed as grade equivalent or percentile scores. Consequently, little information is available to

86    the teacher concerning placement within a curriculum.

In criterion-referenced testing, on the other hand, individual performance is measured against an absolute criterion of mastery. Information from criterion-referenced tests identifies the skills children have and have not mastered and helps the teacher plan instruction, especially when the test is linked to a curriculum or a series of instructional objectives.

In a sense, then, criterion-referenced testing is more direct than norm-referenced testing: The information is more specific and more useful for instructional planning, and in some cases the information is more directly linked to an instructional curriculum or sequence of objectives. Both types of achievement measures are sensitive to improvement due to instructional programming. However, because criterion-referenced tests may be linked to specific curricula and norm-referenced tests usually are not, the former may be more consistently sensitive than the latter (Jenkins & Pany, 1978). However, neither can be used repeatedly to obtain continuous measures of the effectiveness of an instructional program; both require a considerable amount of time to administer, and the effects of repeated administration on the technical properties of the instruments are unknown. Neither type of achievement measure satisfactorily meets all three criteria.

### Data-based teaching

To solve the problems outlined above, technologies have been developed that allow for repeated assessment of performance. Among the most notable of these efforts are precision teaching (White & Haring, 1980) and data-based teaching (Deno & Mirkin, 1977). The assessment procedures associated with these two approaches are direct (in that performance on specific instructional objectives is measured), sensitive to improvement, and, most importantly, continuous.

### NEED FOR A BEHAVIORAL DATA-BASED ASSESSMENT PROGRAM

Several factors underscore the need for a functional data-based assessment methodology in the classroom. Both the diagnostic-prescriptive and direct instruction models of teaching require data-based assessment methodology. In the diagnostic-prescriptive teaching model, teaching involves the identification of the most effective instructional strategies for an individual student. It is believed that each child responds differently to different instructional programs and approaches. Although one child may successfully respond to a particular instructional strategy, another child may require either a new or modified instructional design.

A diagnostic-prescriptive approach to teaching assumes several conditions. Ysseldyke and Salvia (1974) grouped these conditions into four critical factors that form the cornerstone for effective diagnostic and prescriptive teaching:

1. Teachers believe that children enter an instructional situation with specific strengths and weaknesses.
2. These strengths and weaknesses are

linked to the skill level each child has achieved.

3. Specific strengths and weaknesses can be reliably and validly assessed.
4. Identifiable relationships exist between each child's pattern of strengths and weaknesses and the level of instructional effectiveness.

These four assumptions have suggested the use of a task or component analysis as part of an overall assessment and instructional process. Terminal objectives are broken down into teachable subtasks that are arranged in an appropriate sequence. The sequence is used as a hierarchy or continuum of subskills a child achieves on the way to a terminal goal. Therefore, assessment is geared toward determining a child's strengths and weaknesses on the skill hierarchy. Directive teaching then begins on the specific subskills that are needed for progress toward the terminal goal.

Directive teaching relies heavily on observable, measurable, and logically sequenced instructional subtasks. As specific behavioral objectives, the tasks reflect the conditions as well as the criteria for learning (Wheeler & Fox, 1971). In addition, when the subtasks are arranged in the proper sequence, the successful completion of one objective or subtask can be viewed as a prerequisite for moving on to the next objective. The student is more likely to be successful because the teacher can plan more efficiently and effectively and can closely monitor the student's progress (Reith, Polsgrove, & Semmel, 1981).

To determine where a student is on a particular skill hierarchy or continuum,

teachers use a variety of formal and informal assessment techniques. As noted earlier, the use of standardized instruments often does not address the specific terminal goals or component subskills projected for an individual student. However, the most valid individual assessment devices can be characterized as "teacher made." The kinds of devices vary from informal criterion-referenced skill inventories to simple, direct observation. Nonetheless, it is clear that student performance data are crucial for assessing a student's placement in a skill hierarchy.

The need for student performance data in assessment and instructional decision making is readily acknowledged, but many do question the frequency with which data should be collected. A number of educators (Haring & Gentry, 1976; White & Liberty, 1976) have stressed the need for continuous student performance data to allow for accurate and timely adaptations in a student's educational program. Several continuous and direct evaluative frameworks, best labeled as *data based*, have been developed to meet this need.

## WHAT IS DATA-BASED ASSESSMENT?

Data-based assessment combines four distinct concepts: (1) the use of instructional pinpointing, (2) direct continuous measurement, (3) charting, and (4) data interpretation and utilization.

### Instructional pinpointing

Educators frequently characterize the academic performance and classroom be-

88 havior of students in general terms (e.g., dyslexic, hyperactive, etc.). For these descriptions educators usually rely heavily on standardized tests and formal rating scales from which specific behavior is only implied. That is, only general academic or social behavior is sampled; specific academic or social behaviors are not directly assessed. General descriptions of behavior are often referred to as trait labels because they presumably portray overall patterns of student functioning. Still, although most professionals use trait labels, the labels serve only as a nebulous indicator of a problem's existence. In addition, trait labels imply that problems are pervasive and that problem behavior may occur in any environment. This implication contradicts the established principle of situational specificity: that behaviors occur under certain environmental conditions but not under others.

What is needed is specific and precise information about the functioning or characteristics of individual behaviors. Within a behavioral framework, this information is obtained by operationalizing or pinpointing a general problem area, that is, breaking down a skill into discrete measurable components. Trait labels and inferential constructs are avoided, and only overt and observable movements are specified. The goal is valid and reliable data on student performance.

### Direct continuous measurement

Data-based procedures directly measure instructional pinpoints. This concept is based on the notion that what is taught should be measured. With direct measurement, test validity is not questioned; the behavior of concern has been directly recorded (Lindsley, 1964). For example, a child being taught multiplication facts should be tested on those same multiplication facts. "Thus, the child's specific academic behaviors themselves, not abilities supposedly revealed by a sampling of related performances, are the concern of behavior modifiers" (Kauffman, 1975, p. 399).

Van Etten and Van Etten (1976) outlined two direct measurement procedures that require objective specification of what is being taught. Direct and noncontinuous measurement, like the achievement testing described earlier, is used most often. After a given interval, students are tested on what they have been taught (e.g., the Friday spelling posttest). Other types include unit mastery tests and time-ruled checklists.

Direct, continuous measurement is a more sensitive method of assessment. The teacher records the progress, performance, and acquisition of a student on a continuous basis. Usually, a daily reading of correct and incorrect responses is obtained and a chart or table constructed to reflect the results. In the case of spelling, students would practice spelling their words daily. If a word is spelled correctly for a specified number of consecutive days, the word would be considered mastered and replaced with a new unmastered word. Students would not have to wait until Friday in order to exhibit successful performance. The time saved would most likely result in more efficient learning because the youngster would not spend time on words already mastered.

Thus direct, continuous assessment of performance allows teachers to make changes in instructional programming more rapidly than traditional direct and noncontinuous methods. Several investigators (Bannatyne, 1974; Douglas, 1975; Jenkins & Mayhall, 1976) have reported that academic performance improves faster when daily recorded or charted measurements are used rather than noncontinuous measures. The continuous assessment of performance allows teachers to make changes in instructional programs when they are of the greatest benefit to the pupil (Rosenberg & Sindelar, 1981).

### Charting

The direct, continuous assessment data that have been collected should be presented in an easily interpreted form. This is best accomplished with charts or graphs that indicate the rate at which a child is learning and help determine whether instructional strategies should be modified. Several authors have provided step-by-step guidelines for the preparation of various data-based charts (e.g., Deno & Mirkin, 1977; Rosenberg, in press; White & Haring, 1980).

### Data interpretation and utilization

Along with the specification of instructional pinpoints and their direct, continuous measurement, data-based assessment helps teachers use the information most effectively. By using expected progress lines teachers can project a rate of growth toward the accomplishment of a pinpointed goal. The student accomplishes daily aims leading toward a goal within a specified time period. The expected progress line helps a teacher evaluate an instructional intervention. As long as a child's performance is consistently above the expected progress line, the existing instructional program is presumed to be adequate (Sindelar, 1981). When a student's performance consistently falls below the progress line, the instructional program should be changed. A child may eventually master the goal even if the program is not changed, but a more efficient, more effective, and less frustrating method might have been discovered.

When constructing expected progress lines, teachers may consider any one of several alternatives, such as normative data guidelines, peer samples, previous performance guidelines, and an adult-to-child proportion formula. In addition, White and Liberty (1976) suggested minimum change coefficients for either accelerating or decelerating rates of behavior. Whatever method of construction is used, the completed estimated progress line serves as a continuous comparative measure to determine whether a specific instructional intervention was effective in either reducing or increasing a pinpointed behavior. For more information on the construction of estimated progress lines see Deno and Mirkin (1977), Rosenberg (in press), or Sindelar (1981).

## DATA-BASED BENEFITS FOR BOTH TEACHERS AND STUDENTS

The benefits of a data-based methodology fall under three major categories: educational accountability, instructional methods verification, and efficacy.

90

## Educational accountability

Perhaps the greatest benefit of a functional data-based system is educational accountability. Public Law 94-142 (Education for All Handicapped Children Act, November 29, 1975) requires that special education teachers evaluate the effectiveness of their instruction. With instructional pinpoints, direct and continuous measurement, charting, and data utilization, teachers have objective means of assessing their students' performance as well as evaluating their instructional interventions. The graphic representation of instructional gains cannot be overemphasized. With graphic representations teachers can monitor the success of their instruction and present an understandable skill-by-skill report to parents of student progress through a specific skill hierarchy. Parents as well as educational professionals can easily compare a child's performance in relation to the projected goals. Parents are usually overwhelmed with psychoeducational jargon; telling parents that their son or daughter has mastered addition of two, two-digit numbers conveys more information than sharing scaled IQ scores or achievement test percentiles.

Data-based targeted skills can also help special education professionals place students in the least restrictive environment. Sindelar (1981) outlined a method by which expected progress lines can be developed through the use of peer samples within a least restrictive environment. Goals are set according to normative data; movements to less restrictive environments are signaled when students achieve normative performance on critical behaviors. Deno and Mirkin (1979) developed a structured data-based approach for developing individual educational programs (IEP). Such an approach, they claimed, results in both procedural and substantive compliance with the requirements of Public Law 94-142. Thus data-based assessment techniques embody the spirit of both the IEP guidelines and the least restrictive concept.

## Instructional methods verification

When dealing with children who have problem behaviors (be they academic or social), teachers can evaluate the success of their instructional strategies. Deno and Mirkin (1977) accurately asserted that at the present time we are unable to prescribe with certainty specific and effective changes in instruction for individual students. Instructional programming consists of hypotheses that need empirical verification of their efficacy for individual students. Thus if a particular instructional program is helping a student reach academic or social goals, teachers should continue using that intervention. If not, the instructional program should be changed.

Although standardized achievement tests often assist in determining whether a student has learned certain curricular objectives, they are often too late for remedial efforts or a modification in instruction. Frequent if not daily information about a child's growth is needed in order to make timely decisions about the effects of instruction. The "instruction as hypothesis" view of a data-based methodology allows for the continuous evaluation of teaching tactics and results in a general improvement of those teachers through the careful evaluation of student performance. Thus, as Jenkins (1979) asserted, "There is less likelihood of short and long duration errors since teachers cannot persist with ineffective interventions" (p. 100).

## Efficacy

Another major benefit of a data-based methodology is that it results in greater student achievement. Several researchers have reported significant student academic and social gains as a result of data-based techniques. Component analyses of data-based techniques indicate that charting and data decision rules are the active ingredients of such programs (Bohannon, 1975; Deno & Mirkin, 1979; Jenkins, Mayhall, Peschka, & Townsend, 1974). Students are frequently motivated by the continuous feedback to reach terminal goals. When students are not motivated or are unable to perform under a particular instructional style or method, the data reflect the need for a program change. The modified instructional method is often close to the best style for the student; improved performance is the result.

## REFERENCES

Arter, J.A., & Jenkins, J.R. Differential diagnostic-prescriptive teaching: A critical appraisal. *Review of Educational Research*, 1979, *49*, 517-555.

Bannatyne, A. Programs, materials, and techniques. *Journal of Learning Disabilities*, 1974, *7*, 597-604.

Bohannon, R. *Direct and daily measurement procedures on the identification and treatment of reading behaviors of children in special education.* Unpublished doctoral dissertation, University of Washington, 1975.

Deno, S.L., & Mirkin, P.K. *Data-based program modification: A manual.* Reston, Va.: Council for Exceptional Children, 1977.

Deno, S.L., & Mirkin, P.K. *Data-based IEP development: An approach to substantive compliance* (Monograph No. 13). Minneapolis: University of Minnesota, Institute for Research on Learning Disabilities, 1979.

Douglas, S. Precision teaching of visually impaired students. *Education of the Visually Impaired*, 1975, *7*, 48-52.

Frostig, M. Visual perception, integrative function, and academic learning. *Journal of Learning Disabilities*, 1972, *5*, 1-15.

Glass, G.V. *Effectiveness of special education.* Paper presented at the Working Conference of Social Policy and Educational Leaders to Develop Strategies for Special Education in the 1980's, Racine, Wisconsin, September, 1981.

Hammill, D.D., & Larsen, S.C. The effectiveness of psycholinguistic training: A reaffirmation of position. *Exceptional Children*, 1978, *44*, 402-414.

Haring, N.G., & Gentry, N.D. Direct and individualized instructional procedures. In N.G. Haring & R.L. Schiefelbusch (Eds.), *Teaching special children*. New York: McGraw-Hill, 1976.

Horan, J.J. *Experimentation in counseling and psychotherapy: New and renewed mythologies.* Paper presented at the meeting of the American Educational Research Association, Boston, April 1980.

Jenkins, J. Behavioral research methodology: A reaction. In J.E. Ysseldyke & P.K. Mirkin (Eds.), *Proceedings of the Minnesota Roundtable Conference on Assessment of Learning Disabled Children*. Minneapolis: University of Minnesota, Institute for Research on Learning Disabilities, 1979.

Jenkins, J.R., & Mayhall, W.F. Development and evaluation of a resource teacher program. *Exceptional Children*, 1976, *43*, 21-29.

Jenkins, J.R., Mayhall, W.F., Peschka, C., & Townsend, M.A. Using direct and daily measures to increase learning. *Journal of Learning Disabilities*, 1974, *10*, 604-608.

Jenkins, J.R., & Pany, D. Standardized achievement tests: How useful for special education? *Exceptional Children*, 1978, *44*, 448-453.

Kauffman, S.M. Behavior modification. In W.M. Cruickshank & P.P. Hallahan (Eds.), *Perceptual and learning*

92

*disabilities in children* (Vol. 2). Syracuse, N.Y.: Syracuse University Press, 1975.

Kavale, K. Functions of the Illinois Test of Psycholinguistic Abilities (ITPA): Are they trainable? *Exceptional Children*, 1981, *47*, 496-510.

Kirk, S.A., & Kirk, W.D. *Psycholinguistic learning disabilities: Diagnosis and remediation.* Urbana: University of Illinois Press, 1971.

Lindsley, O.R. Direct measurement and prosthesis of retarded behavior. *Journal of Education*, 1964, *147*, 62-81.

Reith, H.J., Polsgrove, L., & Semmel, M.I. Instructional variables that make a difference: Attention to task and beyond. *Exceptional Education Quarterly*, 1981, *2*, 61-72.

Rosenberg, M.S. The use of direct observation and decision rules for assessment. In R.M. Smith & J.T. Neisworth (Eds.), *Teacher diagnosis of educational difficulties* (2nd ed.). New York: Houghton-Mifflin, in press.

Rosenberg, M.S., & Sindelar, P.T. Computer-assisted data management of instructional programming. *Education Unlimited*, 1981, *3*, 37-40.

Salvia, J., & Ysseldyke, J.E. *Assessment in special and remedial education* (2nd ed.). Dallas, Tex.: Houghton-Mifflin, 1981.

Sindelar, P.T. Operationalizing the concept of the least restrictive environment. *Education and Treatment of Children*, 1981, *4*, 279-290.

Van Etten, C., & Van Etten, G. The measurement of pupil progress and selecting instructional materials. *Journal of Learning Disabilities*, 1976, *9*, 469-480.

Wheeler, A.H., & Fox, W.L. *Behavior modification: A teacher's guide to writing instructional objectives.* Lawrence, Kan.: H&H Enterprises, 1971.

White, O.R., & Haring, N.G. *Exceptional teaching* (2nd ed.). Columbus, Ohio: Merrill, 1980.

White, O.R., & Liberty, K.A. Behavioral assessment and precise educational measurement. In N.G. Haring & R.L. Schiefelbusch (Eds.), *Teaching special children.* New York: McGraw-Hill, 1976.

Ysseldyke, J.E., & Salvia, J. Diagnostic-prescriptive teaching: Two models. *Exceptional Children*, 1974, *41*, 181-185.

# Evolving Practices in Assessment and Intervention for Mildly Handicapped Adolescents: The Case for Intensive Instruction

*Edward L. Meyen, Ph.D.*
*Donna H. Lehr, Ph.D.*
*University of Kansas*
*Lawrence, Kansas*

IN MAKING instructional decisions for mildly handicapped adolescents, increased attention should be given to their educational histories. Special emphasis should be placed on their responses to intensive instruction. Merely knowing the level at which a 16-year-old mildly handicapped youth is currently functioning is an insufficient basis on which to make instructional decisions. In this article we attempt to place in perspective the evolution of curriculum or instructional programs for the mildly handicapped adolescent and to identify several major influences on current practices. These current practices are briefly reviewed before we examine the assumptions underlying assessment and intervention in the context of what we refer to as "intensive instruction."

Presumably the current professional literature provides a reference point for resolving the learning and behavioral problems characteristic of mildly handi-

93

94

capped students. However, the literature represents several independent and circumscribed perspectives: assessment of current strengths and weaknesses, determination of learning styles, choice of intervention strategies, construction of curriculum content alternatives, design or adaptation of materials, and selection of placement options. On one hand, these perspectives in the literature are reasonable and explainable, considering the interests of researchers and expertise of practitioners. However, learning is a consequence of interactions that are difficult, if not impossible, to sort. To continue studying the mildly handicapped adolescent from these perspectives alone will lead to refinement, but it may further delay the development of an instructional environment having maximum benefit for the student.

## THE MILDLY HANDICAPPED ADOLESCENT

The most common characteristic of mildly handicapped adolescents is their history of poor school performance. Their learning profiles may show relative strengths and weaknesses, but throughout their school attendance they have failed to achieve at the expected level. Varied interventions may have had limited impact in remediating their learning disabilities. Some mildly handicapped adolescents have developed strategies that compensate for their deficiencies; most have continued to experience the frustrations of failure. Specially designed curricula can result in such students meeting minimal school requirements. In real-

ity, however, these special curricula greatly restrict their opportunities. Special curricula may satisfy the needs of school officials to grant students diplomas, but they work to the disadvantage of mildly handicapped youth who, as adults, need demonstrated skills and knowledge even more than credentials.

Most mildly handicapped students who were given special instruction at the elementary school level continue to have learning problems as adolescents. This may partly be accounted for by the slowness of the public schools to respond to these students' needs as they progressed through the grades. It may also be due to the lack of validated instructional interventions appropriate for the secondary school level. *Learning problems are persistent, and it is this persistence that should attract the attention of special educators involved in the design of curriculum or instructional strategies.*

## HISTORY AND CURRENT DIRECTIONS OF EDUCATING THE MILDLY HANDICAPPED

A review of the history of education for mildly handicapped youth reveals two parallel courses of development for children categorized as either mildly men-

---

*Most mildly handicapped students given specialized instruction at the elementary level continue to have learning problems as adolescents.*

---

tally retarded or learning disabled (LD). We believe this parallel is inappropriate and counterproductive in the search for more powerful interventions and instructional environments that are commensurate with the varied needs of mildly handicapped students.

The pattern of education for mildly mentally retarded and LD children has been somewhat similar. The following applies to mildly mentally retarded students:

- Programs began at the elementary school level.
- Students who were identified as mildly mentally retarded exhibited a general pattern of low academic performance.
- Poor performance generally described the students' social behavior in school.
- Though achievement in school-related activities was the focus of concern, as a group they presented a wide range of troublesome behaviors.
- All intervention strategies promulgated lacked sufficient power to correct the learning deficits.
- Programs shifted from self-contained classes to part-time special class placement equivalent to resource rooms.
- Learning problems persisted as elementary-age students became secondary-age students.
- Eventually the need for secondary programs became evident.
- The failure of intervention strategies at the elementary school level resulted in movement to a functional

curriculum, with an emphasis on coping skills and options for work-study or on-the-job placement.
- Follow-up studies of the mildly mentally retarded populations suggested that, once they escaped the demands of the school curriculum and settings with similar demands, they performed reasonably well.

In examining the relatively short history of programs for LD students, we observed a similar pattern in spite of presumed significant difference in learning characteristics.

- Students demonstrated a varied profile of deficits.
- The initial program focused on the elementary school level.
- Educators placed strong emphasis on instructional models designed for remediation.
- Secondary level programs developed slowly.
- The learning disabled performed reasonably well in nonschool settings.
- The current trend is toward functional or coping skills curriculum.
- As adolescents, LD students continued to demonstrate learning problems similar to those experienced in elementary school.

The history of programs for mildly mentally retarded students is significantly longer than that of programs for LD youth. Yet this longer history of educational programming for mildly mentally retarded students has not resulted in powerful interventions or even a sound basis for curriculum development at the secondary school level.

96

Currently programs for mildly mentally retarded youth are being dissolved as students are assigned to (presumably) less restrictive placements. This emphasis on less restriction appears to reflect concern for the student's immediate social needs and may not be in the best interest of the mildly handicapped student from the perspective of instruction and life-long needs. The selection of the least restrictive environment for mildly handicapped children should be based on knowledge of conditions that offer the highest probability for remediating academic performance deficits and not conditions that are merely socially least restrictive (Meyen & Lehr, 1980). Many of the required instructional conditions are currently unlikely to occur in the typical regular classroom setting; and because of the absence of these conditions, the regular class is actually highly restrictive (Meyen & Lehr, 1980). The integration of mildly handicapped children into regular classrooms for social benefits or "value" enrichment for nonhandicapped peers is not sufficient compensation for ineffectual instruction.

Lowrey, Deshler, and Alley (1979) identified five options in current learning disabilities programs: the remediation, tutorial, learning strategies, functional curriculum, and work-study models. The functional and work-study models closely approximate curriculum for mildly mentally retarded students. Both have face validity and are receiving considerable attention in the public schools. The functional curriculum model aims to develop skills that will enable students to function independently in society. Consumer information, career education, financial

management, grooming, and homemaking skills are emphasized. Users of this approach assume (a) that the LD adolescent requires direct instruction in this area to function adequately in society, (b) the student cannot benefit maximally from a traditional curriculum, and (c) a specific set of skills can be identified that can be taught to enable independent functioning. The work-study model directly provides instruction to the student in job- and career-related skills. Frequently students spend half the day in an instructional setting where they are presented with job-related information and the other half of the day in a job setting. This model assumes that providing specific training to the student in job-related skills is necessary.

This movement toward an applied coping-functional curriculum for the LD student may be necessary for some adolescents, but the assumption underlying these procedures is that the learner is not capable of further academic skill development. Thus increased use of the coping skills curriculum can prevent the development of new powerful remediation interventions. Additionally, the coping skills orientation places responsibility for nonachievement on the learner and ignores the previous history of the student's school interaction that failed to produce sufficient results. Continued use of these procedures may cause the trend to become institutionalized. This appears to have already occurred with mildly mentally retarded students.

Furthermore, the use of the applied coping-functional curriculum assumes that LD adolescents share the same instructional and educational histories. That students have been in school for 8 to 10 years and subjected to various educational programs because of their learning problems does not in itself offer much evidence regarding the intensity of instruction experienced by the students; nor does it indicate their incapacity to profit from instruction. Despite the array of programs or number of years in school, in reality the individual may not have received intensive instruction over a sustained period. *The key factor warranting investigation may be the intensity of instruction over time, not simply the amount of time in instruction.*

## IMPLICATIONS FOR ASSESSMENT AND INTERVENTION

In reviewing the history and current status of program development for mildly handicapped and LD students, we have noted what appears to be a subtle or at least unvoiced commitment to assuring a level of comfort for the mildly handicapped learner. Much of what is done instructionally for the handicapped occurs in a context of protectiveness. This is not to suggest that mildly handicapped children live in a sheltered and protected environment; but there is a tendency in placement and instructional programming to be unduly sensitive to exposing the handicapped learner to pressure or high expectations. The consequences of this protection from pressure and expectation may account for the current failure of curricula and interventions. The personal costs of living a life inhibited by marginal performance are great. Cur-

riculum development and instructional planning for mildly handicapped youth should be guided by the results (within reason) of instruction and not restricted by the assumed demands placed on the learner. *We must learn to accept the personal costs of remediation.* This applies to the learner and parent as well as the professional.

In this context of the personal costs of remediation we advocate intensive instruction. Intensive instruction is defined as a set of circumstances that have an impact on the actual interaction of the learner in the instructional situation. Many researchers (Anderson, 1973; Bloom, 1974; Cahen & Filby, 1979; Carnine, 1976; Carrol, 1963) have examined various aspects of these circumstances. The following discussion of intensive instruction is based on our previous work (Meyen & Lehr, 1980).

Intensive instruction can be characterized by the following:

1. Consistency and duration of time on task;

2. Timing, frequency, and nature of feedback to the student based on the student's immediate performance and cumulative progress;

3. Regular and frequent communication by the teacher to the student of his or her expectancy that this student will master the task and demonstrate continuous progress; and

4. A pattern of pupil-teacher interaction in which the teacher responds to student initiatives and uses consequences appropriate to the responses of the student.

98

A student's history of interaction with these circumstances, related to intensity of instruction, is important in determining the most appropriate educational setting for that student. The exclusive emphasis given to the current functioning level, as determined by achievement tests and other cognitive instruments, limits the student. A more useful approach, in addition to establishing the student's level of performance, is to determine the intensity of the instruction per unit of time that contributed to the student's current level of functioning. We recognize that though this is a researchable hypothesis and perhaps practical as an approach in the future (see Gerber & Kauffman, 1980; Kauffman & Hallahan, 1975), it presents problems in reconstructing evidence of past instruction. The emphasis in educational programs for the mildly handicapped must be placed on the intensity of instruction, not merely elapsed time. For mildly handicapped students placed in regular classes, a higher proportion of their time is spent in the context of elapsed time rather than the context of instructional time; and, consequently, the remediation environment becomes restrictive. At least such a context inhibits rather than enhances the student's performance.

Several conditions must be met if intensive instruction is to occur. These conditions include low pupil-teacher ratios,

*The emphasis in educational programs for the mildly handicapped must be placed on the intensity of instruction, not merely elapsed time.*

teachers capable of implementing the features of intensive instruction, instructional materials allowing for individualization, use of instructional management practices that incorporate specific objectives and careful monitoring of pupil progress, and flexible scheduling that enables instruction to occur within varied time frames.

Current conditions in the typical classroom also are not conducive to intensive instruction. Decisions on least restrictive placements for the mildly handicapped should be based on a determination of settings that offer the highest probability that intensive instruction appropriate to the students' needs will occur. The degree to which such conditions are met will depend to a great extent on reorienting those responsible for educational assessment and decision making. Examples of options worth exploring include the following:

1. In making placement decisions on mildly handicapped adolescents, evaluators should consider the nature of the student's educational history and, to the degree possible, determine the intensity of the instruction that contributed to the student's current level of functioning.

2. If a student is not identified as mildly handicapped until junior or senior high school, consideration should be given to placing the student in a highly intensive instructional program for two to three months until the effectiveness of the remediation has been substantiated. Then begin to increase par-

ticipation in the regular classroom setting. During this time, determine the conditions necessary for the student to be maximally responsive to both academic and vocational instruction.

3. The pupil-teacher ratio in mainstreamed classrooms should be reduced to 15:1 or lower. If it is not economically feasible to do this for a full day, a half-day program might be beneficial.

4. Teachers of mainstream classrooms should be trained to use techniques related to intensive instruction; for example, feedback to students, maintenance of on-task behavior, and individual instruction.

5. Continuous instruction should be provided. Summer school remedial programs should be held during the time in which students are progressing toward a performance level that would enhance their participation in a regular classroom.

6. Peer-tutor programs could occur in the mainstreamed classrooms. Nonhandicapped students could be partly responsible for instructing handicapped peers.

7. Increased attention should be given to the development of postsecondary and extended secondary programs to allow students to attain needed academic and vocational skills.

## SUMMARY

Mildly handicapped adolescents share a number of common behavioral and learning characteristics, but they vary significantly in instructional needs. In comparing the developmental history of programs for mildly mentally retarded and LD adolescents, we observed a trend toward a functional, nonacademic curriculum for both groups. We believe that a nonacademic approach is acceptable for some mildly handicapped youth, but that a significant number of adolescents could still profit from intensive academic remediation. The rationale for this argument stems from the perspective that throughout their educational histories many, if not most, mildly handicapped students have not been subjected to intensive instruction, although they have been recipients of special educational services. Therefore they have attained their current level of functioning without much effort. Given exposure to intensive instruction, they may respond. The need to assess the functional performance of mildly handicapped adolescents from the perspective of their educational histories is emphasized. We caution those responsible for the education of the mildly handicapped adolescent not to be too quick in moving to a work- or application-oriented curriculum and to recognize that continuing the academic education of the mildly handicapped adolescent into young adulthood may not only be desirable but essential.

## 100 REFERENCES

Anderson, L. W. *Time and school learning.* Unpublished doctoral dissertation, University of Chicago, 1973.

Bloom, B. S. Time and learning. *American Psychologist,* 1974, *29,*682-688.

Cahen, L. S., & Filby, N. N. The class size/achievement issue: New evidence and a research plan. *Phi Delta Kappan,* 1979, *60,* 492-495.

Carnine, D. W. Effects of two teacher-presentation rates on off-task behavior, answering correctly, and participation. *Journal of Applied Behavioral Analysis,* 1976, *9,* 199-206.

Carrol, J. B. A model of school learning. *Teachers College Record,* 1963, *64,* 723-733.

Gerber, M., & Kauffman, J. M. Production functions in special education: Microanalysis and behavioral technology. *Journal of Special Education Technology,* 1980, *4,* 25-28.

Kauffman, J. M., & Hallahan, D. P. Evaluation of teaching performance. In W. M. Cruickshank & D. P. Hallahan (Eds.), *Perceptual and learning disabilities in children. Vol. 1. Psychoeducational practices.* Syracuse, N.Y.: Syracuse University Press, 1975.

Lowrey, N., Deshler, D., & Alley, G. Programming alternatives for learning disabled adolescents: A nationwide survey. *Academic Therapy,* 1979, *14,* 389-397.

Meyen, E. L. & Lehr, D. H. Perspectives on instructionally least restrictive environments: Instructional implications. *Focus on Exceptional Children,* 1980, *12,* 1-8.

# Measurement of Functional Competencies and the Handicapped: Constructs, Assessments, and Recommendations

**J. Lee Wiederholt, Ed.D.**
*University of Texas*
*Austin, Texas*

**Mary E. Cronin, M.S.Ed.**
*University of Texas*
*Austin, Texas*

**Virginia Stubbs, M.Ed.**
*Texas Association for Children*
  *with Learning Disabilities*
*Austin, Texas*

IN RECENT YEARS, parents and professionals have voiced growing concern over the competencies of youngsters. As a result a majority of states have recently initiated and passed legislation mandating assessment of the functional competencies of high school students. This article addresses the assessment of competencies in regard to the handicapped student. The first part discusses the construct of functional competencies. The second part contains an overview of current assessment practices. The final part makes recommendations on the handicapped and the measurement of their competencies.

## THE CONSTRUCT OF FUNCTIONAL COMPETENCY

Kerlinger (1979) defines a *construct* as a concept with a specified meaning given to it by individuals. To adequately address

101

102

the topic of functional competencies, it is essential that the term be understood. Therefore this part presents a brief overview of the historical development of the concept of functional competency and the terminology associated with this construct.

### History

Functional competency was first referred to as "literacy." Before the 1870s a literate person was one who could leave one's "mark" (signature) on stone, wood, or paper. During the 1870s and 1880s the ability to read a simple passage as well as the ability to write one's name became the indicator of a literate person. By 1890, society required additional writing of a literate person, such as personal correspondence and record keeping (Grattan, 1959).

World War I recruits were considered literate by the federal government if they could read, write, and comprehend a 2,800-word vocabulary. In addition, a reading speed of 150 words per minute was also necessary to demonstrate literacy (Cook, 1977).

After World War II the United Nations Education, Scientific, and Cultural Organization (UNESCO) developed a definition of literacy to be used worldwide. The official UNESCO definition stated that literacy was the ability to read and write a short simple statement of everyday life with understanding. In 1965 the U.S. Office of Education (USOE) established a national norm for literacy. The USOE norm coupled satisfactory achievement of four years of elementary

school with the ability to function in society. Functional literacy included math, reading, and writing ability as well as a general understanding of everyday life—for example, banking, working, maintaining a home.

As can be seen, the historical progression of the construct of functional competency has moved from the most rudimentary form of signing one's name to a more complex concept. Today functional competency appears to be viewed by large governmental agencies as the ability to live independently, through use of skills in reading, writing, and math.

### Terminology

The term *functional competency* in this article describes the construct of basic skills or independent living. Schools sometimes add the word *minimal* to this term. The term *minimal functional competencies* appears to refer to those skills that are presumed to be the most basic within the construct. While the latter term is most associated with this construct in schools today, other terms have frequently been used to describe basic skills or independent living. Table 1 lists related terms, the person(s) suggesting them, and their definitions.

An analysis of the terms reveals relationships in their specific areas of focus,

*The historical progression of the construct of functional competencies has moved from the most rudimentary form of signing one's name to a much more complex concept.*

## Table 1
### Terminology Related to Functional Competency

| Terminology | Author/Date | Definition |
|---|---|---|
| Literacy | Bormuth, 1975 | Ability to respond competently to real world tasks. |
| | Davis, 1977 | The level of one's functioning in any skill area that is generally considered necessary in today's society. |
| | Dauzat & Dauzat, 1977 | Defined by its properties: (a) economic value, (b) personal-social value, and (c) political value. |
| | Elgin, 1978 | Ability to read with sufficient pleasure and write with sufficient ease so that both activities become a part of one's daily life that one would be unwilling to give up. |
| | Wiemann, 1978 | Reading, writing, speaking, and listening. |
| Basic literacy | Powell, 1977 | Ability to use correspondence of visual shapes to spoken words in order to decode written material and translate into oral language. |
| Functional literacy | Miller, 1973 | Ability to read (decode and comprehend) materials needed to perform everyday vocational tasks. |
| | Buchanan, 1975 | Rudimentary social literacy—that is, those skills required by a prospective employer or institution that a student is deemed likely to encounter in adult life. |
| | Sticht, 1975 | Possession of those skills needed to successfully perform some reading task imposed by an external agent between reader and a goal the reader wishes to obtain based on demand of reading task, not skill level. |
| Civilized literacy | Buchanan, 1975 | Skills and knowledge derived from reading that provide guides to the exercise of power, reason, and virtue. |
| Survival skills | Norton, 1979 | Competence needed for personal growth for successful existence as citizens, consumers, job holders, taxpayers, and members of families. |
| Basic skills | Lieb-Brilhart, 1977 | Areas of listening, speaking, reading, writing, and arithmetic represent areas fundamental to literacy. |
| Competence | Murphy, 1975 | Reading skills suitable for adequate functioning in normal day-to-day life. |
| Communicative competence | Larson, 1978 | Ability to demonstrate a knowledge of the socially appropriate communicative behaviors in a given situation. |
| Functional illiteracy | Cook, 1977 | Cannot read or write to survive everyday tasks. |
| | Smith, 1977 | Cannot function effectively in their particular occupation, their community, or society. |
| Illiteracy | Harman, 1970 | Inability to read and write a simple message either in English or any other language. |

104

which cluster around the following five areas:

1. *Vocational or job related competency:* Buchanan (1975), Miller (1973), and Smith (1977);
2. *Daily adult life:* Bormuth (1975), Cook (1977), Davis (1977), Elgin (1978), Larson (1978), Murphy (1975) and Norton (1979);
3. *Skills in reading, writing, speaking, listening, and math:* Harman (1970), Lieb-Brilhart (1977), Powell (1977), Sticht (1975), and Wiemann (1978);
4. *Philosophical competency:* Buchanan (1975); and
5. *Ability to attain goals:* Dauzat and Dauzat (1977).

Authors also may use the same term but define it somewhat differently. For example, both Bormuth (1975) and Davis (1977) use the term *literacy*, but Bormuth defines it as the ability to respond competently to real-world tasks. Davis, in contrast, defines it as the level of one's functioning in any skill area that is generally considered necessary in today's society. Both definitions are obviously related or have a similar focus. However, when one compares the definitions of *functional literacy*, one can note some obvious differences in focus. For example, Sticht (1975) limits functional literacy to reading, while Buchanan (1975) focuses on social behaviors.

Other authorities avoided using only one term when defining the construct of functional competency and instead focused on graduated levels of the concept. In other words, they might distinguish between preliteracy and functional literacy. The graduated levels and definitions

for each level suggested by four writers are shown in Table 2.

Robinson (1963) outlined what he called a "stairway of [reading] literacy" consisting of five levels. These levels ranged from complete illiteracy (unable to read English at all) to complete literacy (ability to read effectively, adjusting rate and approach to purpose and difficulty of material). Miller (1973) divided literacy into three categories: basic literacy, comprehension literacy, and functional or practical literacy. He postulated that decoding and comprehension are necessary before a person can read the materials required to perform everyday vocational tasks.

The adult performance level (APL) (Northcutt, 1975) divided functional competency into three levels, of which income, education, and job status were the criteria. The lower a person's income, education, and job status, the lower his or her performance level. The APL project outlined four aspects of a general theory instead of a definition of adult functional competency.

First, functional competency was seen as a construct that is meaningful only in a specific societal context. For example, the person who is functionally competent in one society may be incompetent in another. Also, as the technology of the society changes, the requirements for competency change. Second, functional competency was seen as two-dimensional and was described as the application of a set of skills (reading, writing, etc.) to a set of general knowledge areas (occupational knowledge, health, etc.). Third, a person was viewed as functionally competent

## Table 2
## Levels of Functional Competencies

| Terms | Author/Date | Definition |
|---|---|---|
| 1. Complete illiteracy | Robinson, 1963 | 1. Unable to read English at all. |
| 2. Low-level literacy | | 2. Able to read at grade levels 1-4. Barely able to contend with the adult reading material available. |
| 3. Partial literacy | | 3. Able to read at grade levels 5-6. Just able to read essential information for daily living and working at low levels. |
| 4. Variable literacy | | 4. Able to read many kinds of materials at a variety of levels. |
| 5. Complete literacy | | 5. Able to read effectively, suiting reading rate and approach to purposes and difficulty of material. |
| 1. Basic literacy | Miller, 1973 | 1. Ability to use correspondences of visual shapes to spoken sounds in order to decode written materials and translate into oral language. |
| 2. Comprehension literacy | | 2. Ability to understand the meaning of verbal materials. |
| 3. Functional or practical literacy | | 3. Ability to read (decode and comprehend) materials needed to perform everyday vocational needs. |
| Level 1 | Northcutt, 1975 | 1. Adults who function with difficulty (income poverty level or less, 8 years of school or fewer, and unemployment or low-status jobs). |
| Level 2 | | 2. Functional adults (income above poverty level but no discretionary income, education of 9 to 11 years of school, and menial-job-status occupations). |
| Level 3 | | 3. Proficient adults (high levels of income, 12 years of school or more, and high levels of job status). |
| Preliteracy level Basic literacy level Functional or career literacy level | Powell, 1977 | Sees literacy as the universe and the general indicator levels as subsystems in an ongoing process with each level developing out of previous levels. |

106     only to the extent that he or she could meet the requirements extant at a given time. Functional competency was seen as a dynamic rather than a static state. Fourth, functional competency was viewed as directly related to success in adult life. More competent adults were expected to be more successful.

Finally, Powell (1977) saw literacy as the universe and the general indicator levels as subsystems. He suggested three subsets designated as the preliteracy level, the basic literacy level, and the functional (practical) or career literacy level. At the preliteracy level the person is just beginning to obtain knowledge and use of language as well as the computational processes essential for literacy. Skills are considered unstable at this level. At the basic literacy level the skills are believed to become permanent, automatic, and generative. They can be used on demand and develop without formal instruction. The career literacy level that Powell suggested was not as stable nor as generative as the previous level but depended on the knowledge base of the preliteracy and basic literacy levels. Powell believed that because demands and tasks vary with every occupation, specialized requirements and the level of knowledge and skill would also vary accordingly.

The apparent lack of agreement regarding the construct of functional competency is probably directly related to the lack of research. Few reliable data concerning what makes one group of people competent and another group incompetent are available. Because the construct is often defined in an encompassing and general manner (i.e., the ability to function independently in life), a person undoubtedly requires several skills and abilities before he or she can achieve this independence. Until empirical data are available, it is likely that the construct of functional competency will continue to be ill defined and incompletely understood.

Despite the lack of agreement among scholars about what functional competency is, many school personnel are now legally required to assess their students' skills and abilities in this area. This is a difficult task because a universally accepted definition of the construct is not available. How professionals in the nation's schools approach this task is the problem discussed next.

## CURRENT ASSESSMENT PRACTICES

Although the construct is defined in many different ways, most states require that their students be tested for functional competency. Pipho (1979) recently compiled an extensive list of state activities regarding competency testing. The data the authors found most relevant to the topic of this article (the areas to be tested by the 38 states that require competency testing) are shown in Table 3.

*Until empirical data are available, it is likely that the construct of functional competencies will continue to be ill defined and incompletely understood.*

Some states indicate assessment of general skill areas (basic skills, life skills, basic communication skills, etc.). Others measure specific skills areas (reading, writing, and math) as an indicator of a functionally competent person. Reading is the testing area with the highest percentage (74%) followed by math (68%) and writing (45%). Some skill areas probably overlap—for example, reading and reading comprehension, as well as math and computation, as used in California. The meaning of the specific differentiation between mathematics and computation or the distinctions among any other overlapping skill areas are unclear, partly because the tests are difficult to obtain for inspection. Elgin (1978, p. 10) has stated this problem well:

You may not have had the opportunity to examine the literacy tests lately. They are not easy to look at. Even someone like myself, armed with all the required academic credentials and legitimately funded for research on the question, requires something approaching an Act of Congress to obtain access to them.

Obviously, one reason the tests are difficult to obtain is the fear that if they are made widely available, then the tests will be taught to students. However, the authors cannot help wondering about the rationale for selection of items and tests, the standardization data on these measures, and the reliability and validity of the results.

Table 3 provides an overall picture of the variability in competency testing throughout the United States for non-handicapped students. Another survey was recently completed by the National Association of State Directors of Special Education (NASDSE). This survey determined the extent of competency testing and the awarding of diplomas for the handicapped population (Linde, 1979). Table 4 provides a summary of some of the data in the NASDSE survey. Of the 54 states and territories surveyed, 17 have established some form of competency testing for the handicapped. Two of these states, Tennessee and Hawaii, will require competency testing in 1982 and 1983, respectively. Idaho leaves the decision regarding testing to the local school boards.

Six states require handicapped students to take the competency tests. Florida requires that only the speech and language impaired, visually impaired, and orthopedically impaired be tested. Massachussetts designates evaluation teams to decide on an individual basis whether handicapped students should be included in the testing program. New York requires all but the retarded to participate in competency testing. California, Maryland, and Vermont require that all handicapped students take the competency tests.

A total of seven states are either providing or are in the process of developing special testing procedures for the handicapped population. California, Florida, Nebraska, and New York are implementing special procedures for administering competency tests to the handicapped population. Hawaii, Massachusetts, and Vermont are currently studying or developing special testing procedures for handicapped students.

**Table 3**

**Skill Areas Assessed by States***

| State | Setting of standards† | Reading | Reading comprehension | Application of reading | Mathematics | Computation | Consumer economics | Government/economics | Language arts | Grammar | Spelling | Writing | Application of writing | Composition | Basic communication skills | Listening skills | Speaking skills | Career development | Personal development | Cultural arts | Basic skill areas | Functional literacy | Life skills | Survival skills | Local district option | CED | APL | To be determined |
|---|---|---|---|---|---|---|---|---|---|---|---|---|---|---|---|---|---|---|---|---|---|---|---|---|---|---|---|---|
| | | | | | | | | | | | | | | | | | | | | | | | | | Other options | | | |
| Alabama | SDE | • | | | • | | | | | | | • | | | | | | | | | | | | | | | | |
| Arizona | Both | • | | | | • | | | | | | • | | | | | | | | | | | | | | | | |
| Arkansas | SBE | • | | | • | | | | | | | | | | | | | | | | | | | | | | | |
| California | Both | • | • | | • | • | • | | | | | • | | | | | | | | | | | | | | | | |
| Colorado | LB | | | | | | | | | | | | | | | | | | | | | | | | | | | |
| Connecticut | Both | • | | | • | | | | • | | | | | | | | | | | | | | | | • | • | • | |
| Delaware | SDE | | | | • | | | | | | | | | | | | | | | | | | | | | | | |
| Florida | Both | | | • | | | | | | | | | • | | | | | • | | | • | • | | | | | | |
| Georgia | SDE/SBE | • | | | • | | | | | | • | • | | | | | | | | | | | | | • | | | |
| Idaho | SBE | • | | | • | | | | | | • | | | | | | | | | | | | | | | | | |
| Illinois | Both | | | | | | | | | | | | | | | | | | | | | | | | | | | |
| Indiana | LB | | | | | | | | | | | | | | | | | | | | | | | | | | | |
| Kansas | SDE/SBE | • | | | • | | | | | | • | • | | | • | | | | | | | | | | | | | |
| Kentucky | SDE | • | | | • | | | | • | | • | | | | | | | | | | | | • | | | | | |
| Louisiana | SSS | • | | | | | | | | | | | | | | | | | | | | | | | | | | |
| Maine | SDE | • | | | • | | | | | | | • | | | | | | | | | | | | | | | | |
| Maryland | SBE | • | | | • | • | | | | | | | | | | | | | | | | | | | | | | |
| Massachusetts | LB | | | | • | | | | | | | | | • | • | | | | | | | | • | | | | | |
| Michigan | SDE | • | | | • | | | | | | | | | | | | | | | | | | | | | | | |
| Missouri | SDE | | | • | • | | | • | | | | | | | | | | | | | | | | | | | | |
| Nebraska | LB | | | | • | | | | | | | | | | • | • | • | | | | | | | | | | | |
| Nevada | SBE | • | | | • | | | | | | | • | | | • | | | | | | | | | | | | | |
| New Hampshire | SDE | | | | • | | | | | | | • | | | | | | | | | | | | | | | | |
| New Jersey | SDE/SBE | • | | | • | | | | | | | • | | | | | | | | | | | • | | | | | |

## Table 3 (Continued)
## Skill Areas Assessed by States*

| State | Setting of standards† | Reading | Reading comprehension | Application of reading | Mathematics | Computation | Consumer economics | Government/economics | Language arts | Grammar | Spelling | Writing | Application of writing | Composition | Basic communication skills | Listening skills | Speaking skills | Career development | Personal development | Cultural arts | Basic skill areas | Functional literacy | Life skills | Survival skills | Local district option | CED | APL | To be determined |
|---|---|---|---|---|---|---|---|---|---|---|---|---|---|---|---|---|---|---|---|---|---|---|---|---|---|---|---|---|
| New Mexico | SDE | ● | | | | | | | | | | ● | | | | | | | | | | | | | | | | ● |
| New York | SBR | | | | ● | | | | | | | ● | | | | | | | | | | | | | | | | |
| North Carolina | ●● | ● | | | | | | | | | | | | | | | | | | | | | | | | | | ● |
| Oklahoma | None | | | | | | | | | | | | | | | | | | | | | | | ● | | | | |
| Oregon | LB | ● | | | ● | ● | | | | | | ● | | | | | | | | | | | | | | | | |
| Rhode Island | SSC/SBR | ● | | | ● | | | | ● | | | ● | | | | | | ● | ● | ● | | | ● | | | | | |
| South Carolina | SBE | ● | | | ● | | | | | ● | ● | | | | | | | | | | | | | | | | | |
| Tennessee | Both | ● | | | ● | | | | ● | | | ● | | | | | | | | | | | | | | | | |
| Texas | State | ● | | | ● | | ● | ● | | | | | | | | | | | | | | | | | | | | |
| Utah | LB | ● | | | ● | | | | | | | ● | | | | ● | ● | | | | | | | | | | | |
| Vermont | SBE | ● | | | ● | | | | | | | ● | | | | ● | ● | | | | | | | | | | | |
| Virginia | Both | ● | | | ● | | | | | | | | | | ● | | | | | | | | ● | | | | | |
| Washington | LB | ● | | | ● | | | | ● | | | | | | | | | | | | | | | | | | | |
| Wyoming | LB | ● | | | | ● | | ● | | | | ● | | | | | | | | | | | | | | | | |
| No. of states | | 28 | 1 | 2 | 26 | 5 | 2 | 3 | 5 | 1 | 4 | 17 | 1 | 1 | 4 | 3 | 3 | 2 | 1 | 1 | 1 | 1 | 4 | 1 | 2 | 1 | 2 | 1 |
| Percentage of states (of 38) | | 74 | 3 | 5 | 68 | 13 | 5 | 8 | 13 | 3 | 11 | 45 | 3 | 3 | 11 | 8 | 8 | 5 | 3 | 3 | 3 | 3 | 11 | 3 | 5 | 3 | 5 | 3 |

*Data compiled from information presented by Chris Pipho, Education Commission of the States, July 1979 (grant no. NIE-G-79-0033).

†LB, Local board decision; SBE, state board of education decision; SDE, state department of education decision; Both, state and local decision; SSS, state superintendent of schools; ●●, Competency test commission; SSC, state standards council; SBR, state board of regents.

## Table 4
## Summary of NASDSE Survey*
## on Competency Testing of Handicapped Children

| State | Mandatory competency test for graduation | Handicaps required for student to take test | | | | | | | | | Special procedures | Regular diplomas | Special diplomas | Certificate of attendance |
|---|---|---|---|---|---|---|---|---|---|---|---|---|---|---|
| | | EMR | TMR | LD | SP/Lang | ED | VI | HI | IO | MH | | | | |
| Alabama | No | | | | | | | | | | | Yes | | |
| Alaska | No | | | | | | | | | | | LB | | No |
| Am. Samoa | No | | | | | | | | | | | Yes | | No |
| Arizona | No | | | | | | | | | | | LB | LB | No |
| Arkansas | No | | | | | | | | | | | LB | | |
| California | Yes | • | • | • | • | • | • | • | • | • | Yes | LB | | LB |
| Colorado | No | | | | | | | | | | | LB | | LB |
| Connecticut | Yes | | | | | | | | | | | LB | LB | LB |
| Delaware | Yes | | | | | | | | | | | LB | | No |
| Dist. Col. | No | | | | | | | | | | | Yes | | Yes |
| Florida | Yes | | | | • | | • | | • | | Yes | Yes | Yes | Yes |
| Georgia | No | | | | | | | | | | | LB | LB | LB |
| Guam | No | | | | | | | | | | | Yes | | No |
| Hawaii | Yes 1983 | | | | | | | | | | Yes 1983 | Yes | | Yes |
| Idaho | LB | | | | | | | | | | | Yes | | No |
| Illinois | No | | | | | | | | | | | Yes | | |
| Indiana | No | | | | | | | | | | | Yes | | LB |
| Iowa | No | | | | | | | | | | | Yes | | |
| Kansas | No | | | | | | | | | | | | | |
| Kentucky | No | | | | | | | | | | | Yes | | Yes |
| Louisiana | No† | | | | | | | | | | | Yes | | No† |
| Maine | No | | | | | | | | | | | LB | | LB |
| Maryland | Yes | | | • | • | • | • | • | • | • | | Yes | | No |
| Massachusetts | No | Evaluation team decision | | | | | | | | | | Yes | Pilot Study | Yes |
| Michigan | No | | | | | | | | | | | Yes | | No |
| Minnesota | No | | | | | | | | | | | Yes | | |
| Mississippi | No | | | | | | | | | | | No | LB | |
| Missouri | Yes | | | | | | | | | | | Yes | LB | LB |
| Montana | No | | | | | | | | | | | LB | LB | LB |

**Table 4 (Continued)**
**Summary of NASDSE Survey***
**on Competency Testing of Handicapped Children**

| State | Mandatory competency test for graduation | EMR | TMR | LD | SP/Lang | ED | VI | HI | OI | MH | Special procedures | Regular diplomas | Special diplomas | Certificate of attendance |
|---|---|---|---|---|---|---|---|---|---|---|---|---|---|---|
| | | Handicaps required for student to take test | | | | | | | | | | | | |
| Nebraska | Yes | | | | | | | | | | Yes | LB | LB | No |
| Nevada | No | | | | | | | | | | | LB | LB | LB |
| New Hampshire | Yes | | | | | | | | | | | LB | | Yes |
| New Jersey | No | | | | | | | | | | | Yes | | No |
| New Mexico | Yes | | | | | | | | | | | LB | LB | LB |
| New York | Yes | ● | | ● | ● | ● | ● | ● | ● | ● | Yes | Yes | | No |
| N. Carolina | Yes | | | | | | | | | | | Yes | | Yes |
| N. Dakota | No | | | | | | | | | | | | | LB |
| Ohio | No | | | | | | | | | | | Yes | | No |
| Oklahoma | No | | | | | | | | | | | Yes | | Yes |
| Oregon | No | | | | | | | | | | | Yes | | Yes |
| Pennsylvania | No | | | | | | | | | | | Yes | LB | No |
| Puerto Rico | No | | | | | | | | | | | Yes | | |
| Rhode Island | No | | | | | | | | | | | Yes | LB | |
| S. Carolina | Yes | | | | | | | | | | | | | |
| S. Dakota | No | | | | | | | | | | | LB | LB | LB |
| Tennessee | Yes 1982† | | | | | | | | | | | LB | LB | LB |
| Texas | No | | | | | | | | | | | Yes | | No |
| Utah | Yes | | | | | | | | | | | Yes | LB | LB |
| Vermont | Yes | ● | | ● | ● | ● | ● | ● | ● | ● | Developing | Yes | | No |
| Virginia | Yes | | | | | | | | | | | LB | LB | LB |
| Washington | No | | | | | | | | | | | Yes | | No |
| W. Virginia | No | | | | | | | | | | | | | |
| Wisconsin | No | | | | | | | | | | | LB | LB | LB |

*LB, Local board decision; EMR, educable mentally retarded; TMR, trainable mentally retarded; LD, learning disabled; SP/Lang, speech/language; ED, emotionally disturbed; VI, visually impaired; HI, hearing impaired; OI, orthopedically impaired; MH, multihandicapped.
†Local board decision in Orleans parish only.

112

The issuance of regular diplomas also varies among states. Thirty-one states issue regular diplomas to handicapped students. Seventeen states reported that the decision to issue regular diplomas is left to the local school board's discretion. Mississippi did not issue regular diplomas to handicapped students. Special diplomas are issued to handicapped students in Florida. Twelve states reported that they did not issue special diplomas to handicapped students. In 15 states, local school boards decide whether to issue special diplomas.

As indicated in Table 4, certificates of attendance for the handicapped are issued by the District of Columbia and eight states (Florida, Hawaii in 1983, Kentucky, Massachusetts, New Hampshire, North Carolina, Pennsylvania, and Oregon). Certificates of attendance were not issued to the handicapped in 18 states. In 17 states the local board decides whether to issue certificates of attendance to handicapped high school students.

Two additional points need to be made regarding this overview. First, the data presented in Tables 3 and 4 are the most recent available. However, several states have had legislative sessions since the compilation of these data. Some of these legislative bodies have introduced, studied, or changed the policy regarding competency testing in their individual states. Consequently, while these data represent current practices, the situation is probably somewhat different in some states at the time of publication of this article. Second, while some states have not mandated competency testing, individual local education agencies (LEAs)

have made it a policy of their district. For example, Texas does not (at this time) require competency testing. However, the LEA of Austin, Texas, requires that students be assessed for competency. This is probably also true of some of the other school districts throughout the United States.

Although the data presented are not the exact current practices of the states, and some LEA's have their own policies regarding testing, some conclusions can be made. First, there is no consistency regarding the assessment of functional competency throughout the United States. In addition, how the handicapped participate (if at all) in this process also varies considerably. It appears that decisions on these matters are being made more on the basis of local or state philosophy than on any consistent framework for the measurement of functional competency. This should be of considerable concern to parents, educators, and legislators throughout the nation.

## LEGAL AND EDUCATIONAL ISSUES

As states began mandating competency testing, two important federal laws also were passed. These laws provided a free appropriate public education in the least restrictive environment for the handicapped student (PL 94-142) and

*An inherent conflict exists between competency testing requirements and the recent federal laws protecting the handicapped.*

prohibited discrimination on the basis of handicap in any federally assisted program (Section 504 of the Rehabilitation Act of 1973).

An inherent conflict exists between competency testing requirements and the recent federal laws protecting the handicapped. Competency testing programs are based on the concept that all students should meet a uniform standard of achievement, while PL 94-142 and Section 504 offer assurances of an individualized program to meet varying educational needs. There is a potential for conflict between individualized programs and uniform standards of achievement (McClung & Pullin, 1978; Rosewater, 1979).

Exemption of the handicapped from competency testing is, on the other hand, also in question. Such exemption of the handicapped could be discriminatory by prohibiting some students from full participation in an educational environment that is the least restrictive (McClung & Pullin, 1978; Rosewater, 1979).

McClung (1977) has also pointed out some legal and educational policy issues of competency testing for nonhandicapped students. These include (a) potential for racial discrimination in the selection and administration of specific measures, (b) inadequate advance notice and phase-in periods prior to the initial use of the tests, (c) possible lack of validity and reliability of the instruments used, (d) inadequate match between what is taught in the schools and what is tested on the measures, (e) for students who fail the test, remedial instruction that may be inadequate or may reinforce tracking, and

(f) unfair apportionment of responsibility for test failure between students and teachers.

Special educators should carefully analyze the references previously cited in this section—they are key writings for those concerned with measuring functional competencies in both the handicapped and nonhandicapped populations. One fundamental question that special educators must address is how mandated testing programs can be implemented so that opportunity for the handicapped student is consistent with the requirements of PL 94-142 and Section 504. This requires a translation of predominantly legal constraints into educational practices.

## RECOMMENDATIONS

The authors believe there are two approaches to assessment of functional competency of the handicapped that have merit. The first approach applies to those personnel who must immediately begin testing for competency. These professionals should develop a written rationale or philosophy for the measurement of functional competency of the handicapped. Basically this rationale should answer questions on the purpose of testing. For example, is the handicapped student being tested for the purpose of improving his or her educational program, providing an opportunity for participation in the least restrictive environment, determining whether a greater variety of teaching techniques needs to be used, or determining whether a school program is meeting its obligations to educate its students? The

114    answers to these and other questions should provide a basis for determining whether a handicapped student should participate in the testing program. The committee that determines the individualized educational program can use the rationale to delineate the type of involvement most appropriate for a particular student. This process should provide an opportunity for most students and their parents to specify the type and amount of participation in the competency testing program for each handicapped individual.

The authors feel more comfortable in recommending the repeal of all legislation that mandates competency testing for any student (either handicapped or nonhandicapped). A review of the literature has pointed out the following aspects of the current state of the art on functional competency testing:

- The construct itself is not well understood.
- The terms used to describe this construct vary as well as their definitions.
- There are considerable differences throughout the United States regarding the policies and practices in assessment of both handicapped and nonhandicapped students.
- Some individual states' legal and educational practices relative to competency testing and the handicapped may conflict with PL 94-142 and Section 504.

It is inappropriate for decisions to be made regarding a person's competency and the issuance of a diploma until data are available demonstrating that such decisions have social and educational benefits.

Finally, the authors recognize that their recommendation that all laws be repealed will have little effect. Many, probably most, readers will dismiss these observations as the impractical thoughts of academicians and parents. For the most part, legislators will continue to pass laws and educators will continue to implement policies regarding competency testing. Eventually, however, the schools will most likely be sued by irate parents, minority groups, and students themselves. With the state of the art regarding assessment of functional competency being what it is, it is unlikely that the schools will have a defensible case.

## REFERENCES

Bormuth, J. R. Reading literacy: Its definitions and assessment. *Reading Research Quarterly*, 1975, 74, 7-66.

Buchanan, D. W. Two visions of literacy. *English Quarterly*, 1975, 10, 73-75.

Cook, W. *Adult literacy education in the U.S.* Newark, Del.: International Reading Association, 1977.

Dauzat, S. V., & Dauzat, J. A. Literacy: In quest of a definition. *Adult Literacy and Basic Education*, 1977, 1, 1-5.

Davis, R. G. Needed: Functional literacy skills, curricula and tests. *Educational Technology*, 1977, 17, 52-54.

Elgin, S. H. The real literacy crisis. *Change*, 1978, 10, 10-11.

Florida Bureau of Education for Exceptional Students. *A resource manual for the development and evaluation of programs for exceptional students.* Tallahassee, Fla.: Florida Department of Education, 1978.

Grattan, C. *American ideas about adult education.* New York: Teachers College, Columbia University, 1959.

Harman, D. Illiteracy: An overview. *Harvard Education Review*, 1970, *2*, 226-243.

Kerlinger, F. N. *Behavioral research: A conceptual approach*. New York: Holt, Rinehart & Winston, 1979.

Larson, C. A. Problems in assessing functional communication. *Communication Education*, 1978, *27*, 304-309.

Lieb-Brilhart, B. What if Johnny could read and write?. . . Another look at the literacy issue. *Communication Education*, 1977, *26*, 251-253.

Linde, J. C. *Competency testing, special education and the awarding of diplomas*. Washington, D. C.: National Association of State Directors of Special Education, 1979.

McClung, M. S. Competency testing: Potential for discrimination. *Clearinghouse Review*, 1977, 439-448.

McClung, M. S., & Pullin, D. Competency testing and handicapped students. *Clearinghouse Review*, 1978, 922-927.

Miller, G. A. *Linguistic communication: Perspectives for research*. Newark, Del.: National Reading Council, 1973.

Murphy, R. T. Assessment of adult reading competence. In D. M. Neilsen & H. F. Hjelm (Eds.), *Reading and career education*. Newark, Del.: International Reading Association, 1975.

Northcutt, N. W. Functional literacy for adults. In D. M. Neilsen & H. F. Hjelm (Eds.), *Reading and career education*. Newark, Del.: International Reading Association, 1975.

Norton, J. R. Back-to-basics and student minimal competency evaluation: How to spell "school" with three R's and an E. *Contemporary Education*, 1979, *50*, 98-103.

Pipho, C. State activity: Minimal competency testing. Denver: Education Commission of the States, 1979.

Powell, W. R. Levels of literacy. *Journal of Reading*, 1977, *20*, 488-492.

Robinson, H. A. Libraries: Active agents in adult reading improvement. *American Library Association Bulletin*, 1963, *57*, 416-421.

Rosewater, A. *Minimum competency testing programs and handicapped students: Perspectives on policy and practice*. Washington, D.C.: Institute for Educational Leadership, 1979.

Smith, L. L. Literacy: Definitions and implications. *Language Arts*, 1977, *54*, 135-138.

Sticht, T. G. *Reading for working*. Alexandria, Va.: Human Resources Research Organization, 1975.

Wiemann, J. M. Needed research and training in speaking and listening literacy. *Communication Education*, 1978, *27*, 310-315.

# Discontinuity and Instability in Early Development: Implications for Assessment

*Carl J. Dunst, Ph.D.*
*Western Carolina Center*
*Morganton, North Carolina*

*Regina M. Rheingrover, M.A.*
*University of Maryland*
*College Park, Maryland*

THE TERM *development* implies a high degree of continuity and stability in *behavior change* across time. Yet, in general, the preschool years are characterized by instabilities in development and lack of continuity in behavior change. In examining the implications of developmental discontinuities and instabilities for the assessment of infant and preschool-aged children, this article emphasizes the *interpretation* of assessment-related data. The term *assessment* will be used broadly to mean measurement activities whose goals and functions include screening, diagnosis, prognosis, and both the qualitative and quantitative description of an individual's patterns and styles of performance—the purpose of these activities being to design interventions specific to the needs of the individual (Dunst, in preparation).

The article examines several different types of stability-instability and continuity-discontinuity, and focuses on three categories of assessment procedures: psychometric intelli-

*Appreciation is extended to Jean Benson and Phyllis Dale for assistance in the preparation of this article.*

117

118

gence tests, Piagetian-based assessment instruments, and several nontraditional-oriented approaches to the assessment of early cognitive competence. The focus is restricted primarily to cognitive and intellectual assessment during the early preschool years for two reasons. First, instabilities and discontinuities in these areas of development tend to be greatest during these years. Second, there is a need to clarify several common misconceptions regarding interpretation of cognitive and intellectual assessment data.

## DEFINITION OF TERMS

### Development

The term *development* refers to intraindividual change in behavior across time and the extent to which changes in interindividual performance is similar or different (Baltes, Reese, & Nesselroade, 1977). *Intra*individual change means behavior change that is manifested by a single individual across time; *inter*individual change refers to the similarities and differences in manifested changes in two or more individuals. When intraindividual change across time is nearly identical in different individuals, the change is described as a developmental function (Wohlwill, 1973, 1980). A developmental function may be thought of as a map of the course of development of an attribute, trait, or some other behavior characteristic. The *form* or *pattern* of change in vocabulary size, mental age, the structure of intelligence, and height—all plotted across age—represent several types of developmental functions.

### Stability

Emmerich (1964) made a fundamental distinction between stability and continuity in development that will be used here. Stability refers to the preservation of an individual's rank ordering within a group on some behavior measure(s) when the measurements are made across time. To the extent that the individual's position relative to the position of others remains the *same* across measurement occasions, the correspondence is described as stability in performance. For example, if the same group of individuals is administered an IQ test twice, and persons who scored high on the first test occasion also score high on the second and those who scored low on the first test score low on the second, the between-test correspondence in scores is referred to as stability in performance. The statistical index of stability is typically a cross-time correlation coefficient computed from the scores obtained on two measurement occasions.

Kagan (1971) makes a distinction between two types of stability: homotypic and heterotypic. *Homotypic* stability refers to interindividual invariance in the relative positions of persons within a group when the response measures taken are the *same* at two different ages. A high correlation between children's height at 1 year of age and 5 years of age would represent homotypic stability. *Heterotypic* stability refers to interindividual invariance in the relative positions of persons within a group when the response measures taken across time are *different* but theoretically related. For example, if amount of smiling at 10 months of age were taken as an index of developing "sociability," and nonsmiling infants turned out to be the more introverted 5-year-olds, this would indicate that there was heterotypic stability in development.

Several things need to be made clear regarding the measurement of stability in development. First, a stability coefficient (i.e., a correlation) tells us nothing about the *levels* or *amount* of the attribute individuals manifest across measurement occasions. The scores obtained on a second occasion could go down, go up, or remain relatively the same, and yet the individuals comprising a sample could maintain their relative positions within the group across the two measurement occasions.

> *It is important to recognize that stability refers to* inter*individual differences ... in development, and tells little about ...* intra*individual changes in behavior.*

Second, because the magnitude of a stability coefficient is not dependent on the average (i.e., mean) scores obtained by the same group of persons across time, a stability index tells us little about the nature of the changes, if any, manifested by the group. Third, it is important to recognize that stability refers to *inter*individual differences (or similarities) in development, and tells little about the specific nature of *intra*individual changes in behavior. (See Wohlwill, 1980, for a discussion of other aspects of the stability-interindividual differences features of behavior change.)

## Continuity

The concept of continuity–discontinuity pertains to the nature of developmental functions (McCall, 1979a, 1979b). In contrast to stability, continuity refers to several aspects of the nature of *intraindividual* changes in behavior. There are several different types of continuity.

Sequential continuity refers to (a) the form of a developmental function—for quantitative changes in behavior, and (b) the specification of the invariant order of acquisition of hierarchically arranged responses—for qualitative changes in behavior (Wohlwill, 1973, 1980). The form of a developmental function for the quantitative variable weight plotted against age would provide a basis for specifying the sequential nature of weight change. The invariant order of acquisition of behaviors characteristic of each of the six stages of the sensorimotor period (Piaget, 1952) exemplifies the sequential nature of qualitative behavior change.

Functional continuity refers to the nature of causal, antecedent-consequent relationships between successive points on a developmental function (Flavell, 1970; Wohlwill, 1970). Identifying a functional continuity in development is no simple task. For example, weight gain during the preschool years cannot be attributed solely to amount of food intake, but is related as well to such variables as the nutritional quality of food, stature, and the age of the child (Eichorn, 1979; Thompson, 1954). The establishment of a functional relationship between behavioral changes of a psychological nature is even more difficult. Take, for example, the psychological construct *mental age* (MA). Although it is easy enough to plot MA against chronological age to discern the relatively linear relationship between the two quantitative variables, it is something else to be able to verify or even claim a functional relationship between MAs of, say, 2 and 3 years.

McCall (1979a, 1979b) contends that qualitative changes in behavior by their very nature constitute discontinuities in development. However, it is argued here, in line with Lewis and Starr (1979) and Wohlwill (1970), that if a causal, antecedent–consequent relationship could be established between discrete, qualitatively different behavior responses, functional continuity could be claimed.

Structural continuity refers to the extent to which the structure of the "item pool" of some measure of a psychological trait or construct remains identical across time, or the cognitive processes or operations underlying some psychological phenomenon remain similar at different points along a developmental function (Emmerich, 1964; Wohlwill, 1980). For example, insofar as the nature of intellectual abilities at 1 year of age is identical to the nature of intelligence at subsequent ages, there is structural continuity in the development of the psychological phenomenon (Nesselroade, 1970; Wohlwill, 1980). Structural continuity is generally studied through examination of the *patterns of relationships* among theoretically related variables. This is typically done using multivariate techniques such as factor analysis and cluster analysis, which tell us the extent to which groups of items, different measures of a hypothesized psychological construct (e.g., intelligence), or different scales of measurement tend to "go together."

### Developmental stability and continuity

According to McCall (1979b), stability and continuity measures provide potentially independent and distinct *types of information* about behavior change. McCall (1979a) also notes that there is a need to consider both in the analysis of developmental processes. In fact, McCall hypothesizes that instabilities in development may be clues to discontinuity. Wohlwill (1980) makes the point that intraindividual and interindividual behavior change and constancy are to some degree interdependent in a statistical sense. For example, factor analysis, a procedure often used to determine structural continuity in development (see, e.g., Nesselroade, 1970; Reinert, 1970), is based on the interindividual patterns of responses (i.e., correlations) between items on some criterion measure. To the extent that interindividual patterns of responses at different ages are characteristic of intraindividual change, the developmental function is considered a prototypic model (Wohlwill, 1980).

## CONTINUITIES AND STABILITIES IN DEVELOPMENT

### Psychometric assessment instruments

#### Constancy of the IQ

The extent to which IQ scores and their counterparts—the DQ (Gesell & Amatruda, 1947), MDI (Bayley, 1969), and GQ (Griffiths, 1954, 1970)—show homotypic stability across time has been well studied (see Bayley, 1970; Brooks & Weinraub, 1976; Honzik, 1976; and Wohlwill, 1980, for reviews). These studies have sought to determine the predictive validity of the IQ—that is, to what extent do IQ scores of infants and preschool-aged children show within-group invariance in the school-age and adult years?

Honzik (1973) summarized the research to date and stated that there is a "clear relation between the magnitude of the correlation and both the age of the child on the first test and the interval between tests. The younger the child on a first test, and the longer the time interval between tests, the lower" the stability of the IQ (p. 647). In general, tests administered to children under 2 years of age do not predict preschool, school-age, or adult intelligence. It is only toward the late preschool years that the predictive value of the IQ emerges.

The above conclusions are drawn from studies with normally developing and nonimpaired children. Considerably better stability has been found in studies with retarded and handicapped children (see Brooks & Weinraub, 1976; DuBose, 1977; McCall, 1979a). In fact, it appears that the more handicapped or retarded the population, the higher the stability of the IQ.

The well-known findings just recapitulated are often interpreted as meaning that a person's IQ score in the infant or preschool years cannot be used to predict that person's IQ score in the school and adult years. Is this accurate? This question cannot be answered from stability data. As discussed earlier, stability in development reveals little or nothing about intraindividual change in performance. All that can be said about instability in IQ performance is that a person's IQ, relative to the IQs of other individuals in the reference group (typically the standardization sample), changes its rank order position across occasions. That particular person's IQ score may or may not have changed.

Honzik (1973) reported data illustrating the restrictions on the interpretability of stability data. One pair of subjects showing nearly identical IQ scores throughout the preschool years had, at the age of 14, IQs of 84 and 160. In contrast, two subjects whose IQ scores differed by as much as 25 points throughout their preschool years were found to have identical IQs as adults. Similarly, Dubose (1977) found, despite a high correlation ($r = .81$) between the IQ scores of severely handicapped children tested some 30 months apart, that for some subjects scores changed very little, and for others scores on the two tests differed by as much as 25 to 30 points. McCall, Applebaum, and Hogarty (1973) have reported findings very similar to those of DuBose and Honzik.

Thomas (1970) pointed out that the predictive value of preschool IQ tests should not be based on actual test-score correlations, but instead should be based on ability to predict an individual's diagnostic classification (e.g., profound, severe, moderate, or mild) across test occasions. Several studies have attempted this (see Brooks & Weinraub, 1976; Thomas, 1970), but they have been plagued with problems (see Thomas, 1970, for a discussion of the difficulties). Until better studies are conducted, the interpretation of stability data is restricted to statements concerning interindividual differences and cannot shed any light on intraindividual change in behavior (or lack of change).

### Structural continuity

The organizational and structural features of infant and preschool intelligence have been examined in numerous studies (see Bayley, 1970; Dunst, 1978; Horn, 1970; Stott & Ball, 1965, for reviews). It has, for the most part, been found that there are both quantitative and qualitative shifts in the structure of infant and preschool intellectual abilities. The work of McCall and his colleagues (McCall, 1979a,

1979b; McCall, Eichorn, & Hogarty, 1977; McCall, Hogarty, & Hurlburt, 1972) is perhaps the best on the topic.

In one investigation (McCall et al., 1972), the responses of infants on the Gesell scales at 6, 12, 18, and 24 months were subjected to factor analysis to discern the structural features of the "item pools" at the different developmental junctures. The items that "went together" at the four ages differed considerably. The primary content of these item pools at the four ages was manipulation of objects at 6 months; motor imitation and social skills at 12 months; verbal imitation, production, and comprehension at 18 months; and verbal production and grammatical maturity at 24 months.

In a second study (McCall et al., 1977), the same analyses were performed on the responses of infants and preschool-aged children administered several different intelligence tests at 25 ages between 1 and 60 months. The results showed even more marked qualitative shifts in the nature of the items that went together at successively older ages. Both of the McCall et al. investigations demonstrate structural discontinuities in development, although the discontinuities are due partly to the nature of the items comprising the tests used as the criterion measures (see McCall, 1979a).

The obvious implication of these structural discontinuities is that we should not expect to find infant and preschool-aged children manifesting the same types of intellectual competencies at different ages. A not-so-obvious implication is to use the items that "go together" at different ages as a basis for assessing a child's competencies. Children who have acquired the majority of tasks within a core of items can be considered to have mastered the particular competency measured, whereas children passing only selected tasks within a set of items can be considered to be just learning that intellectual competency. This assessment strategy would place less emphasis

122

on individual items, and favor the discernment of an individual's unique *patterns* of responses (Dunst, in preparation). This is an approach that appears not to be widely used in the assessment of infant and preschool-aged children.

### Heterotypic stability

For the most part, attempts to use early preschool year IQ scores to predict subsequent academic achievement and performance in other areas of development (e.g., social development) have proved futile (see e.g., Bayley, 1970; Wohlwill, 1980, for reviews). However, in a number of studies (reviewed by Honzik, 1976; and McCall, 1979a), vocalizations by infants under 12 months of age during test situations have been found to predict subsequent school-age and adult IQs, but only for females.

How are we to interpret these heterotypic stability and instability data? Heterotypic instability tells us that relative to the reference group tested, there is little or no invariance in the rank order positions of individuals on the two measurement occasions. What of the vocalization–IQ heterotypic stability? What this tells us is that infants who vocalize more during test situations subsequently are found to have higher IQs, and vice versa. If the same type of stability manifested itself among a group of retarded children, what conclusion could be drawn? Is it possible that the retarded children who vocalized more had IQs of the same magnitude as the IQs of nonretarded persons who vocalized more? Absolutely not. Stability in performance is a measurement that is independent of actual levels of performance, and consequently we can only conclude that there is heterotypic stability with *reference to* a particular group of individuals. The highest IQs of the retarded and nonretarded persons in different groups reporting the same type of stability could be 50 or more points apart.

### Piagetian-based assessment procedures

#### Sequential continuity

The extent to which normally developing infants and retarded and handicapped children acquire sensorimotor behaviors in the six-stage sequence posited by Piaget (1952) has been well studied. To discern sequential continuity, it is determined whether subjects, in response to a series of items ranked by stage difficulty, succeed to a certain point and fail all subsequent stage items. In studies by Corman and Escalona (1969) and Uzgiris and Hunt (1975) with normally developing infants and in a number of studies with impaired populations (Decarie, 1969; Kahn, 1976; Rogers, 1977; Woodward, 1959), sequential continuity has been established. In several investigations, sequential continuity has not been found for all areas of sensorimotor development (Kopp, Sigman, & Parmelee, 1973; Rogers, 1977; Silverstein, Brownlee, Hubbell, & McLain, 1975). However, these studies attempted to establish sequential continuity for within-stage as well as between-stage placement items. Piaget claimed ordinality for between stages of development only, and not for within-stage items. When Rogers (1977) scaled stage placements instead of both within- and between-stage items, she found that her sample manifested sensorimotor behaviors in a stage progression manner, but they did not when intermediate stage items were included in the analysis.

The establishment of sequential continuity for a particular sensorimotor construct (e.g., object permanence) provides a basis for discerning the progressively more complex levels of the construct. It does not, as has been suggested (e.g., Uzgiris & Hunt, 1975), establish functional continuity between the successive levels of achievement (Brainerd, 1978; Flavell, 1970, 1972; Kagan, 1980). There have been no direct empirical tests designed to establish functional continuity for Piagetian-type sensorimotor progressions, although there

> *Until functional continuity is established, interpretations of sensorimotor progressions must be confined to statements regarding the sequences of steps ... and not claim any causal antecedent-consequent relationship between adjacent items.*

have been several proposals about how to do so (Dunst, in press; Fischer, 1980; Flavell, 1972). Until functional continuity is established, interpretations of sensorimotor progressions must be confined to statements regarding the sequences of steps in the genesis of particular constructs that do not include claims regarding causal, antecedent-consequent relationship between adjacent items in the sequences.

### Structural continuity

Piaget (1973) claimed that cognitive development is characterized by considerable temporal concomitance in the appearance of structurally equivalent types of cognitive behaviors, and also considerable covariation in the acquisition of parallel developing cognitive competencies. A number of studies have investigated the extent to which infants manifest the same stage performance (temporal concomitance) in different domains of sensorimotor intelligence, and the extent to which performance on one scale of development correlates (covaries) with performances on other scales.

Corman and Escalona (1969) and Kopp, Sigman, and Parmelee (1974) found that among infants followed longitudinally, stage of performance in one sensorimotor area of development did not generally correspond to the stage of performance in other areas of development at any of the ages examined. In cross-sectional studies with both normally developing (see Uzgiris, 1976) and mentally

retarded (Dunst, Brassell, & Rheingrover, 1981) children, the same results have been reported. In studies examining the correlations between performances on different domains of sensorimotor intelligence, little covariation in performance has been found (Dunst et al., 1981; King & Seegmiller, 1973; Kopp et al., 1974; Rogers, 1977; Uzgiris, 1973; Wachs and Hubert, 1981).

In instances in which temporal concomitance and covariation in performance are found, there are generally shifts in the structural and organizational nature of the scales that go together at different ages (Dunst et al., 1981; King & Seegmiller, 1973; Uzgiris, 1973; Wachs & Hubert, 1981). The shifts in the organizational features of the scales indicate structural discontinuities in the genesis of sensorimotor intelligence. There is also structural discontinuity for another reason. The shifts that occur at different ages represent the progressively more complex operations that infants are capable of performing (Fischer, 1980; Piaget, 1952; Uzgiris, 1973).

The structural discontinuities in sensorimotor development have several implications for the assessment of early cognitive competencies. First, the fact that infants do not generally manifest the same stage competencies in different sensorimotor domains at a given age indicates a need to assess the specific levels of performance achieved in separate branches of development (e.g., Uzgiris & Hunt, 1975) to ensure an accurate portrayal of a child's cognitive abilities (see Dunst, 1980). Second, a child's "overall" level of sensorimotor performance should not be characterized by a single scale of development. This will generally prove to be inaccurate. For example, object permanence is often used as a principal measure of sensorimotor performance, yet level of development in this domain is generally unrelated to level of performance in other sensorimotor areas (Dunst et al., 1981; Uzgiris, 1976). Third, knowledge of the types of competencies that go together at different

124

ages could help identify the patterns of organization that can be expected, and thus provide a basis for judging whether or not an individual child's "profile of abilities" is typical or atypical (see Dunst, 1980).

### Homotypic stability

There have been a number of attempts to determine the extent to which level of performance in a particular sensorimotor area at one age predicts level of performance in the same domain at subsequent ages (King & Seegmiller, 1973; Uzgiris, 1973). For the most part, homotypic stability has not been found to be characteristic of developmental progress along a particular sensorimotor continuum (e.g., spatial relationships or means-ends abilities).

The failure to find homotypic stability indicates simply that infants who are precocious in their level of performance at one age level are not necessarily the same infants who are most advanced in their level of development at subsequent ages. Consequently, an infant's status at one age cannot be used to predict the age at which the child will attain either the next landmark or higher level attainments along a developmental continuum. Homotypic instability indicates, as Uzgiris (1973) pointed out, that the *rate of progress* in the genesis of a sensorimotor construct such as means-ends abilities or vocal imitation can be expected to be different for different infants.

### Heterotypic stability

There have been a number of attempts to relate sensorimotor performance to subsequent development in other areas (see Uzgiris, 1976). For example, Bates and her colleagues (Bates, Benigni, Bretherton, Camaioni, & Volterra, 1977a, 1977b) have attempted to establish a functional relationship between sensorimotor intelligence and communicative competence. They have shown that attainments in certain domains of sensorimotor intelligence

do correlate significantly with subsequently acquired nonverbal and verbal communicative competencies. These investigators claim that these across-time correlations are evidence of a functional relationship between the two types of development.

Are Bates et al. correct in their claim? Perhaps, but the type of analyses they performed demonstrates only heterotypic stability in development and not functional continuity. Across-time correlations between different but theoretically related response measures establish that there is interindividual invariance in the relative positions of individuals on the two measures; however, they do not confirm a causal, antecedent-consequent relationship for intraindividual change. This is often a point of misinterpretation of data of this sort. Heterotypic stability and functional continuity may be the reverse sides of the same coin, but they are not equivalent aspects of behavior change.

## Nontraditional cognitive measures

### Cognitive mastery

Lewis and Starr (1979) have argued that if it could be demonstrated that a particular behavior(s) served the *same* function or had the *same* meaning at different points along either a continuous or discontinuous developmental function, *response continuity* could be claimed. Studies of cognitive mastery and effectance have tried to establish this type of relationship (see Harter, 1978; McCall & McGhee, 1977; Wachs, 1977, for reviews). For example, smiling has been found to be a particularly reliable index of cognitive mastery among infants and older children (e.g., Harter, 1974; Harter, Schultz, & Blum, 1971; Schultz & Zigler, 1970; Zelazo & Komer, 1971). In response to cognitive tasks ranked according to difficulty, infants and older children smile very little in response to tasks that are solved easily; smile most in response to tasks that are optimally difficult; and, of course, do not smile in response to difficult tasks that are not solved at all.

The smiling that follows the successful solution of optimally challenging tasks is assumed to be an overt indicator of intrinsic gratification. The extent to which smiling actually serves this function throughout the infant and preschool years has, unfortunately, been demonstrated only for certain age ranges and only with selected sets of cognitive tasks (see McCall & McGhee, 1977). What is needed are data to support or refute the contention that behaviors like smiling serve the same function for sequences of cognitive tasks that tap progressively more complex problem-solving behaviors. Data from a study by Dunst (1981) are suggestive regarding the response continuity of the smiling behavior. Among retarded infants studied over a 4-month period of time, subjects were found to smile more frequently to their successful solutions to tasks on the Uzgiris and Hunt (1975) scales than to tasks not solved correctly. Dunst noted that perhaps the onset of smiling behavior to successful problem solving followed by a decrease in positive affect to repeated successes on such tasks could be used as an overt indicator of cognitive effectance, and thus serve as a basis for judging whether an infant has adequately mastered the behaviors being practiced.

## Cognitive expectancy

Zelazo (1979) describes an assessment technique that shows that there is considerable response continuity for visual fixation, vocalizations, and heart rate used as measures of cognitive understanding among 3- to 30-month-old children. The procedure consists of measuring these responses when the expectations of infants and toddlers are disconfirmed. In this paradigm, a subject is shown a standard series of events until a clear expectation is established. Once this occurs, a discrepant event is presented. The infant's responses to

this expected-discrepant series of occurrences are recorded. The findings show that specific clusters of responses to the presentation of a discrepancy can be expected, and that the response clusters reflect the subject's understanding of the "change of events." McCall and McGhee (1977) review other assessment procedures that rely on violations of expectations as a means to measure cognitive levels of understanding.

Kearsley (1979) has used the above procedures to assess cognitive performance among different groups of handicapped children. Perhaps the most interesting result is that some children who show significant developmental delays on standardized tests function at an age-appropriate level on the expectancy series. Kearsley argues that for children for whom standardized tests are inappropriate (e.g., those afflicted with cerebral palsy), the "expectancy test" may be a much more accurate measure of cognitive understanding. To round out these findings, it would be desirable to have some norm-type data showing the specific clusters of responses that can be expected to be manifested in response to progressively more complex discrepancy situations, and the extent to which there is response continuity or discontinuity at different levels of complexity.

• • •

This article has presented extremely oversimplified accounts of complex issues regarding intraindividual and interindividual behavior change. (See especially Kagan, 1980;

---

*There is very little stability in development during the preschool years, and, with the exception of sequential continuity, most studies have not found functional or structural continuity in development.*

126

Lewis & Starr, 1979; McCall, 1979a, 1979b; Wohlwill, 1980, for more in-depth discussions of continuity and stability in development.) Most of the studies reviewed found that there is very little stability in development during the preschool years, and, with the exception of sequential continuity, most studies have not found functional or structural continuity in development. Developmental discontinuities and instabilities, as noted repeatedly, restrict the types of interpretations that can be made with assessment data. It is particularly important to be aware that stability in development is not sufficient evidence for claiming a causal, antecedent-consequent relationship between successive points along a developmental function as has often been done.

The two nontraditional measures for assessment of cognitive performance—the cognitive mastery and cognitive expectancy approaches—appear to have the potential for demonstrating response continuity in development. Although there is a need for additional data to support or refute this contention, these types of cognitive measures may prove useful for assessing cognitive and intellectual processes not measured by either psychometric- or Piagetian-based assessment scales.

## REFERENCES

Baltes, P., Reese, H., & Nesselroade, J. *Life-span developmental psychology: Introduction to research methods.* Monterey, Calif.: Brooks/Cole, 1977.

Bates, E., Benigni, L., Bretherton, I., Camaioni, L., & Volterra, V. *Cognition and communication from 9–13 months: A correlational study* (Institute for the Study of Intellectual Behavior Report No. 12). Boulder: University of Colorado, 1977. (a)

Bates, E., Benigni, L., Bretherton, I., Camaioni, L., & Volterra, V. From gesture to the first word: On cognitive and social prerequisites. In M. Lewis & L. Rosenblum (Eds.), *Interaction, conversation, and the development of language.* New York: Wiley, 1977. (b)

Bayley, N. *Manual for the Bayley Scales of Infant Development.* New York: Psychological Corporation, 1969.

Bayley, N. Development of mental abilities. In P. Mussen (Ed.), *Carmichael's manual of child psychology* (3rd ed). New York: Wiley, 1970.

Brainerd, C. The stage question in cognitive-developmental theory. *Behavioral and Brain Sciences,* 1978, *2,* 173–213.

Brooks, J., & Weinraub, M. A history of infant intelligence testing. In M. Lewis (Ed.), *Origins of intelligence: Infancy and early childhood.* New York: Plenum Press, 1976.

Corman, H., & Escalona, J. Stages of sensorimotor development: A replication study. *Merrill-Palmer Quarterly,* 1969, *14,* 351–361.

Decarie, T.G. A study of the mental and emotional development of the thalidomide child. In B. Foss (Ed.), *Determinants of infant behavior* (Vol. 4). London: Methuen, 1969.

DuBose, R. Predictive value of infant intelligence scales with multiply handicapped children. *American Journal of Mental Deficiency,* 1977, *81,* 388–390.

Dunst, C.J. The structure of infant intelligence: An historical overview. *Intelligence,* 1978, *2,* 321–331.

Dunst, C.J. *A clinical and educational manual for use with the Uzgiris and Hunt scales of infant psychological development.* Baltimore: University Park Press, 1980.

Dunst, C.J. Social concomitants of cognitive mastery in Down's syndrome infants. *Infants Mental Health Journal,* 1981, *2,* 144–154.

Dunst, C.J. Toward a social-ecological perspective of sensorimotor development among the mentally retarded. In R. Sperber, C. McCawley, & P. Brooks (Eds.), *Learning, cognition, and mental retardation.* Baltimore: University Park Press, in press.

Dunst, C.J. Infant and preschool assessment. In C.J. Dunst (Ed.), *Infant and preschool assessment techniques: Reliability, validity, and utility.* Baltimore: University Park Press, in preparation.

Dunst, C.J., Brassell, W.R., & Rheingrover, R.M. Structural and organisational features of sensorimotor intelligence among retarded infants and toddlers. *British Journal of Educational Psychology,* 1981, *51,* 133–143.

Eichorn, D. Physical development: Current foci of research. In J. Osofsky (Ed.), *Handbook of infant development.* New York: Wiley, 1979.

Emmerich, W. Continuity and stability in early social development. *Child Development,* 1964, 35, 311–332.

Fischer, K. A theory of cognitive development: The control and construction of hierarchies of skills. *Psychological Review,* 1980, 87, 477–531.

Flavell, J. Concept development. In P. Mussen (Ed.), *Carmichael's manual of child psychology* (3rd ed). New York: Wiley, 1970.

Flavell, J. An analysis of cognitive developmental sequences. *Genetic Psychology Monographs,* 1972, *86,* 279–350.

Gesell, A., & Amatruda, C. *Developmental diagnosis.* New York: Harper & Row, 1947.

Griffiths, R. *The abilities of babies.* London: University of London Press, 1954.

Griffiths, R. *The abilities of young children.* London: Child Development Research Centre, 1970.

Harter, S. Pleasure derived by children from cognitive challenge and mastery. *Child Development,* 1974, *45,* 661–669.

Harter, S. Effectance motivation reconsidered: Toward a developmental model. *Human Development,* 1978, *21,* 34–64.

Harter, S., Schultz, T., & Blum, B. Smiling in children as a function of their sense of mastery. *Journal of Experimental Child Psychology,* 1971, *12,* 396–404.

Honzik, M. The development of intelligence. In B. Wolman (Ed.), *Handbook of general psychology.* Englewood Cliffs, N.J.: Prentice-Hall, 1973.

Honzik, M. Value and limitations of infant tests: An overview. In M. Lewis (Ed.), *Origins of intelligence: Infancy and early childhood.* New York: Plenum Press, 1976.

Horn, J. Organization of data on life-span development of human abilities. In L. Goulet & P. Baltes (Eds.), *Life-span developmental psychology: Research and theory.* New York: Academic Press, 1970.

Kagan, J. *Change and continuity in infancy.* New York: Wiley, 1971.

Kagan, J. Perspectives on continuity. In O. Brim & J. Kagan (Eds.), *Constancy and change in human development.* Cambridge, Mass.: Harvard University Press, 1980.

Kahn, J. Utility of the Uzgiris and Hunt scales of sensorimotor development with severely and profoundly retarded children. *American Journal of Mental Deficiency,* 1976, *80,* 663–665.

Kearsley, R. Iatrogenic retardation: A syndrome of learned incompetence. In R. Kearsley & I. Sigel (Eds.), *Infants at risk: Assessment of cognitive functioning.* Hillsdale, N.J.: Erlbaum, 1979.

King, W., & Seegmiller, B. Performance of 14- to 22-month-old black, first-born infants on two tests of cognitive development. *Developmental Psychology,* 1973, *8,* 317–326.

Kopp, C., Sigman, M., & Parmelee, A. Ordinality of sensory-motor series. *Child Development,* 1973, *44,* 821–823.

Kopp, C., Sigman, M., & Parmelee, A. Longitudinal study of sensorimotor development. *Developmental Psychology,* 1974, *10,* 687–695.

Lewis, M., & Starr, M. Developmental continuity. In J. Osofsky (Ed.), *Handbook of infant development.* New York: Wiley, 1979.

McCall, R. The development of intellectual functioning in infancy and the prediction of later IQ. In J. Osofsky (Ed.), *Handbook of infant development.* New York: Wiley, 1979. (a).

McCall, R. Qualitative transitions in behavioral development in the first two years of life. In M. Bornstein & W. Kessen (Eds.), *Psychological development from infancy: Image to intention.* Hillsdale, N.J.: Erlbaum, 1979. (b).

McCall, R., Applebaum, M., & Hogarty, P. Developmental changes in mental performance. *Monographs of the Society for Research in Child Development.* 1973, *38*(3, Serial No. 150).

McCall, R., Eichorn, D., & Hogarty, P. Transitions in early mental development. *Monographs of the Society for Research in Child Development,* 1977, *42*(3, Serial No. 171).

McCall, R., Hogarty, P., & Hurlburt, N. Transitions in infant sensorimotor development and the prediction of childhood IQ. *American Psychologist,* 1972, *27,* 728–748.

McCall, R., & McGhee, P. The discrepancy hypothesis of attention and affect in infants. In I. Uzgiris & F. Weizman (Eds.), *The structuring of experience.* New York: Plenum Press, 1977.

Nesselroade, J. Application of multivariate strategies to problems of measuring and structuring long-term change. In L. Goulet & P. Baltes (Eds.), *Life-span developmental psychology: Research and theory.* New York: Academic Press, 1970.

Piaget, J. *The origins of intelligence in children* (M. Cook, trans.). New York: International Universities Press, 1952.

Piaget, J. *The child and reality: Problems of genetic psychology* (A. Rosen, trans.). New York: Grossman, 1973.

Reinert, G. Comparative factor analytic studies of intelligence throughout the human life-span. In L. Goulet & P. Baltes (Eds.), *Life-span developmental psychology: Research and theory.* New York: Academic Press, 1970.

Rogers, S. Characteristics of the cognitive development of profoundly retarded children. *Child Development,* 1977, *48,* 837–843.

Schultz, T., & Zigler, E. Emotional concomitants of visual mastery in infants: The effects of stimulus movement on smiling and vocalizing. *Journal of Experimental Child Psychology,* 1970, *10,* 390–402.

Silverstein, A., Brownlee, L., Hubbell, M., & McLain, R.

128

Comparison of two sets of Piagetian scales with severely and profoundly retarded children. *American Journal of Mental Deficiency*, 1975, *80*, 292–297.

Stott, L., & Ball, R. Infant and preschool mental tests: Review and evaluation. *Monograph of the Society for Research in Child Development*, 1965, *30*(3, Serial No. 101).

Thomas, H. Some problems of studies concerned with evaluating the predictive validity of infant tests. *Journal of Child Psychology and Psychiatry*, 1970, *8*, 197–205.

Thompson, H. Physical growth. In L. Carmichael (Ed.), *Manual of child psychology* (2nd ed). New York: Wiley, 1954.

Uzgiris, I. Patterns of cognitive development in infancy. *Merrill-Palmer Quarterly*, 1973, *19*, 181–204.

Uzgiris, I. Organization of sensorimotor intelligence. In M. Lewis (Ed.), *Origins of intelligence: Infancy and early childhood*. New York: Plenum Press, 1976.

Uzgiris, I., & Hunt, J. McV. *Assessment in infancy: Ordinal scales of psychological development*. Urbana: University of Illinois Press, 1975.

Wachs, T. The optimal stimulation hypothesis and early development. In I. Uzgiris & F. Weizman (Eds.), *The structuring of experience*. New York: Plenum Press, 1977.

Wachs, T., & Hubert, N. Changes in the structure of cognitive-intellectual performance during the second year of life. *Infant Behavior and Development*, 1981, *4*, 151–161.

Wohlwill, J. Methodology and research strategy in the study of developmental change. In L. Goulet & P. Paltes (Eds.), *Life-span developmental psychology: Research and theory*. New York: Academic Press, 1970.

Wohlwill, J. *The study of behavioral development*. New York: Academic Press, 1973.

Wohlwill, J. Cognitive development in childhood. In O. Brim & J. Kagan (Eds.), *Constancy and change in human development*. Cambridge, Mass.: Harvard University Press, 1980.

Woodward, M. The behaviour in idiots interpreted by Piaget's theory of sensorimotor development. *British Journal of Educational Psychology*, 1959, *29*, 60–71.

Zelazo, P. Reactivity to perceptual-cognitive events: Application for infant assessment. In R. Kearsley & I. Sigel (Eds.), *Infants at risk: Assessment of cognitive functioning*. Hillsdale, N.J.: Erlbaum, 1979.

Zelazo, P., & Komer, J. Infant smiling to nonsocial stimuli and the recognition hypothesis. *Child Development*, 1971, *42*, 1327–1339.

# Measurement References in the Assessment of Preschool Handicapped Children

*James L. Hamilton, Ph.D.*
*William W. Swan, Ed.D.*
*U.S. Education Department*
*Washington, D.C.*

A S WITH many other areas of human service, those involved in special education for handicapped preschool children are struggling to make their field less of an art and more of a science. There are many indicators that progress is being made in this effort: the formulation of research and evaluation questions increasingly reflects the complexities of the developing child; increasing numbers of educational programs are based on theoretical positions and empirical findings; research and evaluation activities are becoming commonplace in many programs; and measurement activities are becoming an integral feature of special education. Though these may be considered important milestones, few if any professionals are satisfied with the field's rate of progress.

While many factors impede more rapid progress in improving the identification and education of young handicapped children,

This article was written by the authors in their private capacity. No official support or endorsement by the U.S. Education Department is intended or should be inferred.

130 limitations in measurement are among the most significant. What to measure? when to measure? and how to measure? are issues that demand increasingly greater attention. Because not all variables of interest can be measured continuously, the measurement questions at issue are probably more appropriately stated as what, when, and how to sample, and does the sample provide the needed information? Another central issue is: what is the reference against which a given measure should be compared?

## IDENTIFYING REFERENCES

The reference for a measure is but one of many measurement issues that deserves attention; however, it is critical when measures are selected or constructed, and then used in preschool programs.

It is generally accepted that a child's performance on a test (or test item) has little or no meaning as an event unless it can be compared to some other event, i.e., a reference. In absolute terms, a referencing event can only be selected from some dimension of time or space. Thus a referent may be an event occurring in the past, present, or future, and/or it may be an event occurring within or external to the child. There are many possible referents for a child's performance on a test. If a severely mentally retarded child achieves a score of "62" on a test, the meaning of that 62 can only be derived by comparing it to some other event. The following questions illustrate the kinds of referencing events that can be identified:

1. Has the child taken the same test before? If so, what score was achieved on that occasion?
2. How does the child's performance on the test compare to the child's future performance on the test?
3. How does the child's performance on the test compare to the test performance of other severely mentally retarded children, of moderately or mildly retarded children, of normal children, of adults?
4. How does the child's test performance relate to the functioning of older children or adults who took the same test when they were younger?
5. How does the child's test performance compare to the test constructor's or to someone else's standard or cutoff score indicating proficiency on the test?

There are several points that should be made about this illustration. First, it does not apply only to test scores. Any reliable measure of child performance (frequency counts, ratings, checklist data, or anecdotal records) could be appropriately substituted for test performance in the illustration. Second, although the answer to each of the questions will increase the meaningfulness of the score 62, the answers are not equally informative. For example, a response to the first question of "the child previously achieved a score of 45" would undoubtedly stimulate many more questions designed to add meaning to the facts. Third, the time-space framework for selecting references is not the only way to consider potential referencing events. For example, it is just as appropriate to consider the child's performance across time as the reference in questions 1 and 2, other persons' performance as the reference in questions 3 and 4, and the test itself as the reference in question 5.

Finally, these questions do not exhaust the possible references that can provide meaning to the child's performance. Consider two other questions:

6. How does the child's test performance in one setting compare to the child's test performance in another setting?
7. How does the child's performance on the test compare to that of children who have had significantly different environmental experiences (e.g., children who

earlier took part in a special intervention program)?

Question 6 addresses generalization of child performance to a second setting. In question 7, the child's performance is tied—albeit indirectly and not necessarily with cause-effect implications—to the child's external experience.

## MAJOR REFERENCE TYPES

Of the three general sources of references (the child's performance, others' performance, and the test itself), it is the last two that have been dominant in measurement theory and practice. Respectively, they are most often

---

*Of the three general sources of measurement references (the child's performance, others' performance, and the test itself) the last two have been dominant in measurement theory and practice.*

---

referred to in the context of a specific instrument or class of instruments under the rubrics "norm-referenced" and "criterion-referenced," although the denotation of the latter is not uniform among professionals (see Hambleton, Swaminathan, Algina, & Coulson, 1978, for a recent discussion of criterion-referenced, domain-referenced, and objectives-referenced tests). Norm-referenced measurement, originating largely in early studies of individual differences, has by far the longest tenure. Criterion-referenced measurement has a much shorter history (its beginnings are generally traced to papers by Glaser, 1963, and Popham & Husek, 1969), which may account for some of the yet-to-be-resolved problems of terminology and of procedures to estimate the psychometric properties of these measures.

The other general source, child performance across time or setting, is typically not singled out as a reference category. One possible reason for this omission is that, as seen above, a "child-referenced" measure may not provide enough information to either describe or evaluate the child's performance. Or, it may be argued that a child-referenced measure is best combined with a reference outside the child, such as criterion or normative information. Although these arguments have merit, child-referenced measurement should be retained as an important source of information in deriving meaning about a given child's performance, especially in the context of an instructional setting.

To summarize, norm-referenced measures are designed to determine an individual's standing relative to an internal or external norm group. The emphasis is on measuring individual differences, and on determining whether an individual has more or less knowledge, interest, or ability than other members of a reference group. Criterion-referenced measures compare the individual not to other individuals, but in relation to the level of performance that has been specified as mastery or proficiency on the measure being used. In contrast, child-referenced measures compare the child's performance on one occasion and in one setting with the child's performance on another occasion or in a different setting.

Given the above, the question remains: which reference(s) is (are) likely to satisfy best the measurement purposes that are common to preschool programs for handicapped children?

## MATCHING REFERENCES WITH MEASUREMENT OBJECTIVES

### Screening

In selecting or constructing a measure to identify a child for early intervention, the

132 most common reference is the performance of others on the same measure. The Denver Developmental Screening Test (Frankenburg & Dodds, 1968) is an example of a normative measure of this kind. The relative standing of a child on this measure can be readily determined by comparing the child's score with the scores obtained from many other children. The essential task of a norm-referenced screening test is to determine whether a given child's performance is sufficiently different from the performance of many other children that special intervention (or further testing) is warranted. However, the reference for such a measure is usually not limited simply to the performance of many other children of the same chronological age.

Information is also provided about how accurately the measure identifies children for intervention or further testing, typically by giving information about the later performance of children tested with the measure at an early age. These test-accuracy data usually take the form of predictive validity estimates, percentage of classification errors, or some index of the number of false positives or false negatives associated with particular cutoff scores. (References for a norm-based screening test are suggested in questions 3 and 4 of the illustration.)

Unfortunately, for all but the more extreme and severe cases, the detection of young children who will display significant developmental or learning problems later in life has been a limited success. This is particularly true of infants, as can be seen in several reviews of the accuracy of infant measures in predicting later cognitive functioning (Bayley, 1970; Stott & Ball, 1965; Yang & Bell, 1975).

To improve the detection of children who require early intervention, many professionals are measuring other variables that relate to a given child's later performance (such as home environment, family socioeconomic status, and parent-child interaction patterns). Al-though these measures are useful in improving detection (McCall, Appelbaum, & Hogarty, 1973; Bradley & Caldwell, 1976; Yarrow, Rubenstein, & Pedersen, 1975), it may also be possible to improve child performance measures by further consideration of their referential base. Most screening tests were developed by observing the development of normal children, and describing behaviors that occur "naturally" or that can be prompted at certain age levels. Viewed along a developmental continuum, however, certain classes of behaviors that are salient at one age may not be salient, and therefore may not be measured or sampled, at another age. Furthermore, some behaviors seen at one age, though they certainly precede behaviors at a later age, may not be prerequisites for the later behaviors. Thus a potentially more appropriate reference for a screening test would not be normal development per se, but a set of developmental milestones which represent longitudinally consistent categories of behavior, and which are known to be prerequisite (functionally related) to later appearing behaviors. Finally, by measuring the same classes of behaviors at different ages, the screening procedure could also, and more easily, include the child's own performance on different occasions (or in different settings) as an additional reference.

## Diagnosis

The diagnostic process related to programs for preschool handicapped children usually consists of three phases. In the first phase, measurements are taken to: (1) verify that the screening process correctly identified the child as needing early intervention, and (2) determine the child's general level of performance in a variety of broad-based skill areas (motor development, cognitive ability, and social skills), some of which may be measured in more than one setting. Most of the measures used in this phase of diagnosis will be norm-referenced in either a formal or informal sense. That is, in addition to measures such as a norm-referenced intelligence test (formal), measures may be taken of the child's social skills with some (informal) reference to the social skills of normal or other higher functioning children.

In the second phase, more specific information is sought regarding the child's level of functioning. At this stage norm-referenced measures are for the most part replaced by criterion-referenced tests that specify the child's strengths and weaknesses in more specific areas of performance. For example, while the first phase of diagnosis may have measured the child's general level of communication ability, the second would focus on more specific receptive and expressive language skills.

The third phase of the diagnostic process aims at determining what the child can and cannot do within very specific skill areas. How many letters of the alphabet the child can name might represent the third-phase level of measurement. The frequency of stereotyped behaviors or aggressive behaviors toward peers (as well as environmental events preceding and following these behaviors) might also be measured at this point. The ultimate aim during this phase is to identify specific child performance skills so that instructional objectives can be established and instructional plans made. Given this aim, the reference for measurements here will consist primarily of the tests themselves or the child's own performance.

As noted above, the diagnostic process moves from general to specific measurements of child performance. In doing so, it uses all three classes of measurement references, with norm-referenced measures gradually replaced by criterion- and child-referenced measures. The extent to which the child's performance skills and deficits are accurately diagnosed depends largely on the scope and quality of the measures selected during each phase of the process.

## Instruction

Many of the measurements taken during the final phase of diagnosis not only serve to identify instructional objectives, but also provide baseline information about the child's pre-instructional performance levels in a variety of skill areas. As Smith and Neisworth (1969) have suggested, the educator's next task is to help the child reach higher and higher levels of competency in those areas. Once instruction has begun, the role of measurement is to determine whether the instruction is helping the child become more competent. What, then, is the most useful reference for measures of child progress? This depends in part on whether short-term (daily or weekly, for example) or long-term (yearly, for example) progress is to be measured.

To measure short-term progress, the logical choice would be criterion-referenced measurement. Indeed, criterion-referenced measurement was originally conceived as an alternative to norm-referenced measurement in measuring the achievement of students (see Glaser, 1963). It should be noted, however, that most available criterion-referenced measures are more appropriately called *objectives-referenced* rather than criterion- or domain-referenced if the definitions given by Hambleton et. al (1978) are accepted. Their distinction is that criterion- or domain-referenced tests are made up of items that are a representative set of items from a clearly defined domain of behaviors measuring an objective; in an objectives-referenced test, no domain of behaviors is specified, and items are not considered to be representative of any behavioral domain. To date, because of requirements and the complexities of their construction, relatively few real criterion- or domain-referenced tests have been developed.

134

Many special educators, however, have experience in dividing a general skill into its component parts, and in determining which of those parts a child has mastered. But the result of this procedure is most accurately called an objectives-referenced measurement. Regardless of precise terminology, however, the rationale for selecting a criterion-type rather than norm-referenced measure at this level is that the educator is more interested in determining whether the child has reached a specific objective (or its component parts) than in comparing the child's performance to the performance of others.

To ascertain whether or not the child is making progress as a result of instruction or other factors, the educator must be able to compare the child's performance on two or more occasions. Such a child-referenced measure is important for several reasons. First, it provides information about the child's performance across time or setting (the performance may be better, worse, or the same). Second, it may (depending on whether or not proper controls are used) provide information about the effectiveness of instructional procedures. Though this information is important to obtain, it should be understood that the interpretation of child performance changes is limited to better or worse. A final reason that child-referenced measures are important relates to the fact that not all children served in special education programs will be able to achieve established instructional objectives (or proficiency performance, cutoff scores, or mastery levels). In such instances, determining

> *Determining that the child is becoming increasingly competent relative to himself or herself, as shown on a child-referenced measure, may be more important than criterion-related information.*

that the child is nevertheless becoming increasingly competent, as shown on a child-referenced measure, may be more important than criterion-related information.

## Program evaluation

The general aim of evaluating a preschool program for handicapped children is, by definition, to make a judgment about the program's merit or worth. If the judgment is to focus on the achievement of the children served in the program, two major issues must be addressed before the study is undertaken. First, what is the standard or benchmark against which the program will be compared? For example, should the evaluation study compare the performance of program children with:

1. the program children's performance prior to exposure to the program, as in a simple before-after design or an interrupted time-series design;
2. the performance of a similar group of children who are exposed to a competitor program;
3. the performance of a similar group of children who are exposed to no educational program;
4. the performance of a similar group of children who are exposed to an abbreviated version of the program, or who have partial exposure to an identical program; or
5. the performance of other children as reported in standardized test norms or in research findings reported in the professional literature?

The second major issue is the kind of measure or measures that will be used to index the performance of the program children (and comparison children, if any). In addition to general considerations of validity, reliability, and standardized administration, the measure selected should be sufficiently sensitive to detect change in children's performance and should have reasonable correspondence with program goals and objectives. A further consideration is the kind of reference (norm, criterion, child) associated with the measure. The decision to be made in this regard will depend in part on the study design. For example, a norm-, criterion-, or child-referenced measure can be used in an interrupted time-series design. However, this is probably not the design of choice given the time interval associated with program evaluations, and given the rival hypotheses related to this design. The designs suggested in comparisons (2), (3), and (4) above can successfully use either a norm- or criterion-referenced test. However, special care must be taken to ensure that in designs (2) and (4) children in both programs are exposed to instruction on similar goals and objectives. This is especially important if a criterion-referenced test only is used. Finally, in (5) above, the design itself calls for the use of a norm-referenced measure.

Although there is considerable debate regarding the relative utility of criterion- versus norm-referenced measurement in program evaluation (cf., Sax, 1974 and Millman, 1974), most professional evaluators suggest the use of multiple measures (e.g., Campbell, 1969; Airasian, 1974). This was done in evaluating a program for normal and handicapped preschoolers, and recently reported by Mac-Turk and Neisworth (1978).

Progress in improving the identification and education of preschool handicapped children is in part tied to the quality of measurements used to index child performance. In deciding what, when, and how issues related to measuring child performance, attention should be given to the reference(s) associated with different measures. At a minimum, to a "How good is that?" or "So what?" question regarding a score of 62, one should be able to say, "That performance is better than what the child displayed last week," or "That score represents proficiency on the test," or "That score means that the child performed better than 28 percent of the children who make up the test's norm group."

To conclude, Rosner (1975) has pointed out that the dialogue between proponents of norm-referenced and criterion-referenced measurement about the relative merits of each approach is much like that of carpenters arguing over the relative usefulness of nails and screws. Each is useful and, although their functions may overlap at times, each tends to be specifically appropriate for certain situations. This analogy can hardly be improved upon, although child-referenced measures may be appropriately added to it, and in certain situations a combination of measures may be the most appropriate approach.

## REFERENCES

Airasian, P.W. Designing summative evaluation studies at the local level. In W.J. Popham (Ed.), *Evaluation in education: Current applications.* Berkeley: McCutchan, 1974.

Bayley, N. Development of mental abilities. In P.H. Mussen (Ed.), *Carmichael's manual of child psychology* (3rd ed., Vol. 1). New York: Wiley, 1970.

Bradley, R.H., & Caldwell, B.M. Early home environments and changes in mental test performance in children from 6 to 36 months. *Developmental Psychology,* 1976, *12,* 93–97.

Campbell, D.T. Reforms as experiments. *American Psychologist,* 1969, *24*(4), 409–429.

Frankenburg, W., & Dodds, J. *Denver developmental screening test.* Denver: University of Colorado Medical Center, 1968.

Glaser, R. Instructional technology and the measurement of learning outcomes. *American Psychologist,* 1963, *18,* 519–521.

Hambleton, R.K., Swaminathan, H., Algina, J., & Coulson, D.B. Criterion-referenced testing and measurement: A review of technical issues and developments.

136

*Review of Educational Research,* 1978, *48*(1), 1–47.

MacTurk, R.H., & Neisworth, J.T. Norm referenced and criterion based measures with preschoolers. *Exceptional Children,* 1978, *45*(1), 34–39.

McCall, R.B., Appelbaum, M.I., & Hogarty, P.S. Developmental changes in mental performance. *Monographs of the Society for Research in Child Development,* 1973, *38* (Serial No. 150).

Millman, J. Criterion-referenced measurement. In W.J. Popham (Ed.), *Evaluation in education: Current applications.* Berkeley: McCutchan, 1974.

Popham, W.J., & Husek, T.R. Implications of criterion-referenced measurement. *Journal of Educational Measurement,* 1969, *6,* 1–9.

Rosner, J. Testing for teaching in an adaptive educational environment. In W. Hively & M.C. Reynolds (Eds.), *Domain-referenced testing in special education.*

Reston, Va.: The Council for Exceptional Children, 1975.

Sax, G. The use of standardized tests in evaluation. In W.J. Popham (Ed.), *Evaluation in education: Current applications.* Berkeley: McCutchan, 1974.

Smith, R.M., & Neisworth, J.T. Fundamentals of informal educational assessment. In R.M. Smith (Ed.), *Teacher diagnosis of educational difficulties.* Columbus: Merrill, 1969.

Stott, L.H., & Ball, R.S. Infant and preschool mental tests: Review and evaluation. *Monographs of the Society for Research in Child Development,* 30, 1965.

Yang, R.K., & Bell, R.Q. Assessment of infants. In P. Reynolds (Ed.), *Advances in psychological assessment* (Vol. 3). San Francisco: Jossey-Bass, 1975.

Yarrow, L.J., Rubenstein, J.L., & Pedersen, F.A. *Infant and environment.* New York: Wiley, 1975.

# Developmental Scales and Development Curricula: Forging a Linkage for Early Intervention

Stephen J. Bagnato, Jr., D.Ed.
Milton S. Hershey Medical Center
Pennsylvania State University
Hershey, Pennsylvania

THE EXPANDING interdisciplinary union of school psychologists and early intervention specialists on behalf of young handicapped children underscores the need for devising practical and reliable methods to link developmental assessment and curriculum planning (Bagnato & Neisworth, 1979, in press-a).

Functional developmental assessments for young handicapped children require the use of more adaptive process methods (Dubose, Langley, & Stagg, 1979; Haeussermann, 1958). The essence of this perspective is portrayed by Chinn, Drew, and Logan (1975): "Precision prescriptive teaching demands better performance of the evaluator, which frequently results in the criterion-referenced use of instruments that were originally developed on a norm-referenced basis" (p. 73). Simply, assessment results should serve as "baseline guides" for individualized educational planning.

Despite frequent calls for assessment-curriculum linkages in preschool IEP construction (Kamii & Elliott, 1971; Chase, 1975; Bagnato & Neisworth, 1979; Bagnato, 1981),

138

few clinicians capitalize on the criterion-based utility of traditional developmental scales. The inertia in this area can be traced to the ingrained criticism that traditional scales are poor predictors of later intellectual functioning (Yang & Bell, 1975; Lewis, 1973), although data on this question are in fact somewhat equivocal (Illingworth, 1970; Knobloch & Pasamanick, 1974). In overemphasizing the predictive validity question, critics have obscured the worth of traditional developmental scales as baseline skill analysis measures.

Recent research and clinical practice strongly support the view that norm-referenced developmental scales are reliable, effective monitors of *current* child functioning as well as of child progress and program efficiency (Simeonsson & Weigerink, 1975; MacTurk & Neisworth, 1978; Capute & Biehl, 1973; Bagnato & Neisworth, 1980; Bagnato & Neisworth, in press-b). Moreover, when matched with developmentally sequenced curricula and used as criterion-based measures, the scales generate results that form effective "target-links" to initial curriculum goal planning (Gordon, 1975; Meier, 1976; Bagnato & Neisworth, 1979; Bagnato, 1981). Two factors signal the pressing need for change in this area: (1) the proliferation of highly useful, but technically inadequate infant-preschool scales and (2) the mandate to provide effective diagnostic-intervention services to young handicapped children.

Focusing on this need, the study reported here was designed to demonstrate that diagnostic data from traditional developmental scales could be reliably matched with curriculum goals to facilitate the construction of initial IEPs for young exceptional children. Both the curriculum-based utility of the scales and the most effective mode of communicating their results were assessed. Thus, the efficacy of an assessment-curriculum linkage method was evaluated.

## METHOD

### Subjects

The study group consisted of early childhood teachers (N = 48) in two regional programs for developmentally disabled infants and preschoolers. The teachers were selected according to their familiarity with developmentally sequenced curricula and the length and range of their experience with early intervention ($\bar{x}$ = 3.7 years). Group 1 (N = 24) was experienced in using the *Comp-Curriculum* (HICOMP) developed by Forsberg, Neisworth, and Laub (1977) for individualized educational planning while Group 2 (N = 24) commonly employed the Project MEMPHIS (Quick, Little, & Campbell, 1974) curriculum materials. Teachers were randomly assigned to experimental and control group conditions. They then completed assessment-curriculum linkage, IEP exercises on a sample handicapped child, using developmental data from one of two diagnostic report styles and the particular curriculum they were familiar with.

### Developmental measures

The following developmental instruments were selected for use in the study in order to assess the level of congruence or "match" between tasks within traditional scales and those in commonly employed preschool curricula (see Figure 1).

*The Gesell Developmental Schedules*

---

*The study was designed to demonstrate that diagnostic data from traditional developmental scales could be reliably matched with curriculum goals to help construct IEPs for young exceptional children.*

| Measure | Congruent Functional Domain | | | |
| | Motor | Cognitive | Language | Personal-social |
|---------|-------|-----------|----------|-----------------|
| Gesell | Motor | Adaptive | Language | Personal-social |
| MEMPHIS | Motor (GM/FM) | Perceptuo-cognitive | Language | Personal-social |
| HICOMP | Motor | Problem-solving | Communication | Own-care |

**Figure 1.** Matching developmental domains for GDS, HICOMP, and MEMPHIS measures.

(GDS) (Knobloch & Pasamanick, 1974). The GDS is the precursor of comprehensive developmental scales on which all other measures have been directly modeled. It samples four functional domains (language, personal-social, motor, adaptive) and generates separate age-range indexes for each domain to describe variations in current functioning from 4 weeks to 72 months.

*The Project MEMPHIS Curriculum* (Quick et al., 1974). The MEMPHIS materials were constructed for teacher use with the exceptional preschool child in mind. The objectives in the MEMPHIS Scale (MCDS) cover the age range 3 to 60 months and provide a broad-scope assessment of skills in fine motor, gross motor, language, personal-social and perceptual-cognitive areas.

*HICOMP Comp-Curriculum* (Forsberg et al., 1977). The HICOMP materials constitute a behaviorally based, normalized curriculum which focuses on handicapped infants and preschoolers aged 0 to 5. The curriculum matches developmental skills, teaching strategies and materials, and evaluation methods for 800 behaviors across four functional domains (communication, own-care, motor, and problem solving).

## Simulated exercises and formats

Diagnostic results from the GDS (Ames, Gillespie, Haines, & Ilg, 1980) on a handicapped preschooler were portrayed in two different reporting formats. These two styles—traditional and translated—formed the basis for completing assessment-curriculum linkage exercises in the control and experimental groups respectively. Research by Meier (1976) and MacTurk and Neisworth (1978) supports the use of the GDS both as a diagnostic measure for curriculum programming and as a monitor of child progress.

*Traditional Developmental Diagnostic Report.* In order to construct the assessment-curriculum linkage exercise for control group teachers, a developmental report detailing performance on the Gesell Schedules for a referred child was selected from clinic files. The report's portrayal of the GDS data on this child was judged by an expert panel of three school psychologists and three preschool teachers to be representative of typical diagnostic reports written by school psychologists. This "traditional" developmental report consisted of the following features:

- discussion of reason for referral, brief developmental history, and behavioral observations;
- narrative report of attained developmental quotients (DQ) for language, personal-social, motor, and adaptive areas;
- brief citation of strong and weak skill areas;
- application of a diagnostic label (moderate retardation); and
- general recommendations for placement.

Control group teachers received the traditional developmental report as a vehicle for

140 matching Gesell task results to HICOMP or MEMPHIS curriculum goals.

*Translated Developmental Diagnostic Report.* GDS diagnostic results from the original report and from the Gesell score sheet were reorganized and reinterpreted to form the "translated" developmental report for the experimental group teachers. The translated reporting format presented the following features:

- behavioral observations regarding child interactions and strategies used to enhance attention and on-task performance;
- diagnostic profile of differences in age-level functioning across multiple areas;
- developmental ages (DA) for each functional domain;
- behavioral narrative of specific skills analysis organized by developmental domain—language, personal-social, motor, and adaptive; and
- a description of developmental "ceiling" targets appropriate to functional level to be stressed in programming.

The experimental group received the translated developmental report as their vehicle for matching Gesell task results to HICOMP or MEMPHIS curriculum goals.

*Assessment-Curriculum Linkage Exercise.*

Each teacher in the experimental (translated report) and control (traditional report) groups created *assessment-curriculum linkages* for the child within several developmental areas: language, personal-social, motor, and adapative. These linkages involved the matching of performance tasks from the GDS with similar instructional objectives from both the HICOMP and MEMPHIS curriculum sequences. (See Figure 2.) These "linkages" were constructed using a procedure developed previously by Bagnato and Neisworth (1979) to match traditional scales and commonly used preschool curricula.

The expert review panel (three school psychologists and three preschool teachers) independently judged the accuracy of these teacher-constructed linkages by creating a standardized answer sheet reflecting appropriate GDS-HICOMP and GDS-MEMPHIS matches for both translated and traditional report styles. Two measures were used to evaluate the accuracy of teacher-constructed linkages: (1) the total number of HICOMP/MEMPHIS curriculum objectives matched with Gesell ceiling tasks in the two types of reports and (2) the percentage of agreement with the expert standard. (An index of $r = .91$ described the judges' inter-rater agreement.)

| CHILD: Dionne | C.A.: 34 mo. | D.A: 18–24 mo. | DIAGNOSIS: Congenital anomalies |
|---|---|---|---|
| **Gesell targets** | **Rating ±** | | **MEMPHIS goals** |
| Formboard: places 2–3 shapes | ± | | Places round & square blocks in formboard |
| Drawing: scribbles spontaneously | ± | | Spontaneous scribble is present |
| M. cubes: tower of 3–4 | ± | | Builds a 4-block tower |
| Pegs: sequential placement | – | | Puts large pegs in a pegboard |
| Voc.: 10 words including name | ± | | Repeats single words heard |
| Test obj.: names 2 | ± | | Labels any 3 common objects |
| Picture card: identifies 3–5 | ± | | Identifies 3 objects on pictures |
| Cup-cubes: 10 into cup | ± | | Places cubes in-out of cup |
| Pellet & bottle: dumps responsively | – | | Secures pellet from bottle |
| Paper: folds once imitatively | – | | Folds paper demonstrated |

**Figure 2.** A sample developmental assessment curriculum linkage for the cognitive-adaptive domain.

## Procedure and research design

The protocol for the study involved two basic phases: (1) random assignment of HICOMP and MEMPHIS teachers to experimental (translated developmental report) and control (traditional report) groups and (2) completion by teachers of the diagnostic-prescriptive linkage exercises after reading and analyzing the assigned report of GDS results. There were 24 teachers in the translated-GDS group (12 HICOMP and 12 MEMPHIS) and 24 in the traditional-GDS group (12 HICOMP and 12 MEMPHIS).

A randomized-control-group, post-test-only design was used to evaluate the GDS-HICOMP/MEMPHIS linkages and thus the advantages of the translated versus traditional developmental diagnostic formats on which the linkages were based. Such a design allows the omission of a pretest which would inject a training-biasing effect. Randomization ensures the equivalence of all groups (Campbell & Stanley, 1973, p. 25).

## RESULTS

The study was intended to evaluate the curriculum-based utility of the information provided by traditional developmental scales and to assess the most effective mode of communicating developmental diagnostic results for curriculum goal planning. This permitted the efficacy of a pragmatic method of forging assessment-curriculum linkages to be tested.

## Efficacy of the assessment-curriculum linkage mode

A one-factor analysis of variance (ANOVA) was conducted using the Gesell/HICOMP-MEMPHIS linkage data to evaluate the differential efficacy of the traditional and translated report modes as a basis for creating assessment-curriculum linkages. Results revealed a significant main effect for the diagnostic reporting modes ($F = 246.94$; critical $F = 5.18$; df $= 1,45$; $p < .01$). Posthoc data analysis using Tukey's HSD multiple comparison method showed significant differences between the translated and traditional report modes as means of communicating developmental diagnostic data ($\bar{x} = 41.47$ vs. $\bar{x} - 16.25$; $p < .01$).

Comparative means and standard deviations for the experimental and control groups' linkages, irrespective of curriculum employed, reflected the traditional-translated mode difference. Descriptive raw score analysis (see Table 1) reveals that the experimental group using the translated linkage mode made significantly greater-total numbers of Gesell-curriculum matches than the control group using the traditional report mode. Agreement with the expert standard was also significantly higher in the translated made group. In general, regardless of whether they used the HICOMP or MEMPHIS curriculum, teachers employing the translated linkage mode were significantly more accurate (.87 vs. .54), more productive (664 vs. 273), and more homogeneous (.81 vs. .22) in creating Gesell-curricu-

**Table 1.** Percentage teacher linkage agreement with expert standard across curriculum areas by report mode

| Report mode | Communication | Self-care | Motor | Problem solving | Total |
|---|---|---|---|---|---|
| Translated | .87 | .86 | .92 | .82 | .87 |
| Traditional | .48 | .57 | .62 | .54 | .54 |

142

lum matches than teachers using the traditional report mode.

### Gesell-curriculum task congruence

A two-by-two (curriculum × linkage report mode) ANOVA was performed to determine the impact of using different developmental curricula on the linkages generated. The data in Table 2 show clearly that the type of developmental curriculum employed did not affect the total numbers or accuracy of teacher linkages (HICOMP $\bar{x}$ = 41.69 vs. 16.25; MEMPHIS $\bar{x}$ = 41.25 vs. 14.50; $p <$ .01). Yet, the developmental sequential nature of the curricula is not a critical factor in accommodating assessment linkages. Again teachers using the translated report mode demonstrated higher levels of agreement, accuracy, and productivity in matching Gesell tasks to both HICOMP and MEMPHIS curriculum objectives for the sample child. The agreement levels for both curricula are nearly identical (87% vs. 86%). In other words, HICOMP and MEMPHIS teachers using the translated linkage mode independently agreed on matching objectives for the sample child nearly 90 percent of the time.

Finally, within the experimental group, Pearson Product-Moment correlations were conducted on the teacher linkages between performance ceiling tasks on the Gesell Developmental Schedules (GDS) and objectives in the HICOMP and MEMPHIS curricula. An index of r = .75 provided evidence of the concurrent relationship among assessment-curriculum tasks as well as of the stability and homogeneity of teacher-constructed linkages. This relationship attests to the essential similarity because developmental behaviors on the GDS and objectives within major developmental curricula. Moreover, these results are congruent with the research of MacTurk and Neisworth (1978) and provide strong supporting evidence for using comprehensive developmental scales as criterion-based measures, at least in the *initial* stages of individualized curriculum goal planning. Such a use of the scales aids the preschool teacher in initially pretesting children on important curriculum tasks that objectify dysfunctional developmental processes that need to be stressed in programming.

## CONCLUSIONS AND IMPLICATIONS FOR PRACTICE

The overall results of the research concerning linkages between developmental assessment and curricula support two major conclusions:

1. Traditional norm-referenced developmental scales have the potential to be utilized as reliable criterion-based curriculum measures in at least the initial stages of individualized goal planning.
2. The mode of communicating develop-

**Table 2.** Total Gesell linkages and percentage agreement with the expert standard by report mode and curriculum

| Report mode | Total linkage | | % agreement | |
|---|---|---|---|---|
| | HICOMP | MEMPHIS | HICOMP | MEMPHIS |
| Translated | 334 | 330 | .87 | .86 |
| Traditional | 145 | 128 | .53 | .55 |

*The mode of communicating developmental diagnostic results to teachers significantly influences the reliability, homogeneity, and scope of the data for creating assessment-curriculum linkages.*

mental diagnostic results to teachers significantly influences the reliability, homogeneity, and scope of the data for constructing assessment-curriculum linkages, and thus for creating IEPs.

Moreover, the results of the study and of related research point to the following strategies for making school psychological practice more responsive to early special education:

1. Select scales that match the curriculum employed within the early intervention program, i.e., those that are developmentally sequenced, cover multiple functional domains, and sample congruent tasks and processes.

2. Choose a diagnostic battery composed of a variety of measures reflecting both *qualitative* and *quantitative* child performance data. The use of adaptive process measures enhances this aspect

(Haeussermann, 1958; Dubose, Langley, & Stagg, 1979).

3. Organize developmental diagnostic reports by multiple behavioral domains rather than by the individual measures given to facilitate the synthesis of child data, comprehensive coverage, and a balanced curriculum-area goal planning.

4. Report developmental ages (DA) for *each* functional area rather than a global developmental quotient (DQ) to portray general child functioning. Research indicates that no unitary factor of infant intelligence ("g") exists (Lewis, 1973).

5. Provide a behavioral narrative that discusses in detail the strengths, weaknesses, needed management, strategies, and modes of operation that characterize the child's developmental functioning within each area.

6. Use "advance" or "summary" organizers for highlighting critical child performance data to guide assessment-curriculum linkages, i.e., lists of developmental ceilings, functional levels, skills sequences, and instructional needs.

"Little did Doll and Gesell know that the scales they developed . . . could be better used to plan courses of individualized training and instruction" (Bijou, 1977, p. 10).

## REFERENCES

Ames, L.B., Gillespie, C., Haines, J., & Ilg, F. *The Gesell Institute's child from one to six: Evaluating the behavior of the preschool child.* New York: Harper & Row, 1980.

Bagnato, S.J. Developmental diagnostic reports: Reliable and effective alternatives to guide individualized intervention. *Journal of Special Education*, 1981, *15*(1), 65–76.

Bagnato, S.J., & Neisworth, J.T. Between assessment and intervention: Forging an assessment/curriculum linkage for the handicapped preschooler. *Child Care Quarterly*, 1979, *8*(3), 179–195.

Bagnato, S.J., & Neisworth, J.T. The intervention effi-

ciency index (IEI): An approach to preschool program accountability. *Exceptional Children*, 1980, *46*(4), 264–269.

Bagnato, S.J., & Neisworth, J.T. *Linking developmental assessment and curricula: Prescriptions for early intervention.* Rockville, Md.: Aspen Systems, in press. (a)

Bagnato, S.J., & Neisworth, J.T. Subjective judgment vs. child performance measures: Congruence in developmental diagnosis. *Analysis and Intervention in Developmental Disabilities*, in press. (b)

Bijou, S.W. Practical implications of an interactional model of child development. *Exceptional Children*, 1977, *44*(1), 6–14.

**144**

Campbell, D.T., & Stanley, J.C. *Experimental and quasi-experimental designs for research.* Chicago: Rand McNally, 1973.

Capute, A.J., & Biehl, R.F. Functional developmental evaluation: Prerequisite to habilitation. *Pediatric Clinics of North America,* 1973, *20*(1), 3–26.

Chase, J.B. Developmental assessment of handicapped infants and young children: With special attention to the visually impaired. *The New Outlook for the Blind,* October 1975, 341–348.

Chinn, P.C., Drew, D.J., & Logan, D.R. *Mental retardation: A life cycle approach.* St. Louis: C.V. Mosby, 1975.

Dubose, R.F., Langley, M.B., & Stagg, V. Assessing severely handicapped children. In E.L. Meyen, G.A. Vergason, & R.L. Whelan (Eds.), *Instructional planning for exceptional children.* Denver, Colo.: Love Publishing, 1979.

Forsberg, S.J., Neisworth, J.T., & Laub, K. *Comp-Curriculum.* University Park, Penna.: HICOMP Preschool Project, Pennsylvania State University, 1977.

Gordon, R. *Evaluation of behavioral change: Study of multi-handicapped young children.* New York: New York University Medical Center, 1975.

Haeussermann, E. *Developmental potential of preschool children.* New York: Grune and Stratton, 1958.

Illingworth, R.D. *The development of the infant and young child: Normal and abnormal.* London: E. & S. Livingstone, 1970.

Kamii, C., & Elliott, D.L. Evaluation of evaluations. *Leadership,* 1971, *28,* 827–831.

Knobloch, H., & Pasamanick, B. *Developmental diagnosis.* New York: Harper & Row, 1974.

Lewis, M. Infant intelligence tests: Their use and misuse. *Human Development,* 1973, *16,* 108–118.

MacTurk, R.H., & Neisworth, J.T. Norm-referenced and criterion based measures with preschoolers. *Exceptional Children,* 1978, *45*(1), 34–39.

Meier, J.H. Developmental inventory—profile and base for curriculum planning. In John Mier (Ed.), *Developmental and Learning Disabilities.* Baltimore: University Park Press, 1976, 190–200.

Quick, A.D., Little, T.L., & Campbell, A.A. *Project Memphis: Enhancing developmental progress in preschool exceptional children.* Belmont, Calif.: Fearon Publishers, 1974.

Simeonsson, R.J., & Wiegerink, R. Accountability: A dilemma in infant intervention. *Exceptional Children,* 1975, *41,* 474–481.

Yang, R.K., & Bell, R.Q. Assessment of infants. In P. McReynolds (Ed.), *Advances in pscyhological assessment* (Vol. III). San Francisco: Jossey-Bass, 1975.

# PART III:
# ASSESSMENT FOR SPECIFIC GROUPS

# Nonbiased Assessment of Minority Group Children

*Thomas Oakland, Ph.D.*
*University of Texas*
*Austin, Texas*

THE NEED TO KNOW and to fully understand pupils is one of the strongest tenets of the educational profession. Educators also believe that knowledge of pupils is increased by acquiring information through various assessment techniques. Formal and informal methods have been developed that enable educators to describe and evaluate children's academic, intellectual, perceptual, linguistic, social, and emotional characteristics. Assessment has become a cornerstone of the profession.

Educators also know assessment techniques have their limitations. For example, tests have been criticized because they may rigidly shape school curricula and restrict educational change, promote a view that human abilities are fixed and unmodifiable, foster undesirable biases and expectations, invade a person's privacy, and imperfectly predict future behaviors (Cronbach, 1975; Holmen & Docter, 1972; Oakland, 1974).

147

148    Tests have always been criticized. However, during the last decade, critics have become more vocal, adamant, and numerous—particularly among blacks, Hispanics, and other racial and ethnic minorities (Samuda, 1975). Critics have demonstrated how tests denigrate minority persons' dignity and pride, restrict educational and vocational opportunities, serve to dehumanize and institutionalize decision-making practices, and maintain prejudicial attitudes (Oakland, 1973).

This article examines issues regarding the assessment of minority group children from three perspectives. The first section reviews potential problems that impede attempts to develop suitable psychoeducational programs for minority group children. The second section looks specifically at points before, during, and after assessment that may bias assessment. The third section presents suggestions for providing nonbiased programs.

## A BROAD VIEW OF POTENTIAL PROBLEMS

Discussions of nonbiased assessment tend to focus on tests and testing. One often concludes, after considering limited information, that tests are bad.

This categorical position is incorrect. It also helps to perpetuate a set of attitudes that impede the development of appropriate diagnostic-intervention techniques for minority group children. To be effective, educators who use these techniques must consider a number of potential problems that arise in working with children generally and with minority group children in particular.

### Children

Children who are uncooperative and poorly motivated, who devalue education, are unable to take tests, and exhibit obstreperous behaviors impede educators' ability to acquire a complete and accurate assessment of what they can and cannot do.

### Parents

Parents may know a Monday night television schedule more thoroughly than their children's daily schedule. Others are caught up in the "me" generation and lack a proper sense of dedication to their children. Some are unable to make objective, intelligent decisions regarding their children's welfare. They may be uncooperative, apprehensive, and afraid of the school. They may not have time—or know how—to help. Various values of the home may be inconsistent with those of the school. For example, parents may encourage children to remain at home to do chores or to get a part-time job (which often escalates to a full-time job). Families may move frequently. Some urban schools experience a 100% student turnover rate yearly.

### Examiners

Some examiners are poorly trained. They lack knowledge of minority groups, rigidly approach each case in the same repetitive way, and seek shortcuts to complicated situations.

## Assessment Techniques

All assessment techniques may not be equally suited to children from different racial, ethnic, and cultural groups and for those families of lower socioeconomic status. Only by knowing a test's reliability and validity data, standardization sample, and other appropriate characteristics can educators know under what conditions a test can be used most confidently. Standardized tests are but one way to assess children. Other techniques include informal observations; interviews; class records and reports; criterion-referenced tests; behavioral assessment; reports from peers, teachers, parents, and other significant adults; anecdotal information; sociograms; questionnaires; and informal personality measures. Nonbiased assessment is achieved by choosing the most suitable techniques that help us acquire the information we want.

## Educators

Teachers who want to rid their rooms of a particular child, refuse to try different educational and behavioral strategies, distort information, are uncooperative, and think that the children's environment is so deleterious that nothing they do will be beneficial also stand in the way of developing suitable programs.

*Principals* impede good programs when they provide insufficient support for special services; are uncomfortable working with children with special handicaps, those in minority groups, or those from families of low socioeconomic status; adopt dictatorial leadership styles rather than facilitative problem-solving styles;

and draw rigid boundaries between the school and the neighborhood, thus inhibiting teachers and parents from forming important and mutually supportive relationships regarding their children.

## School Districts

School district policies often promote development of a bureaucratic network insensitive to the individual needs and characteristics of children, their families, and teachers. During the last 20 years the federal government has actively shaped school policies and programs through legislation and judicial decisions. In implementing school policies to comply with the law, educators may lose sight of their primary goal: to provide high-quality professional services to children and their families. School districts that identify many children for special education programs so that they ensure themselves their full share of state and federal funds are but one common example of this trend.

Many urban school districts are financially troubled, constantly facing the threat of strikes and other disruptions in their programs, and having a high turnover rate and low morale among professional staff and children. These problems exacerbate attempts to develop programs

---

*In implementing school policies to comply with the law, educators may lose sight of their primary goal: to provide high-quality professional services to children and their families.*

---

150

suitable for children who come from diverse racial, ethnic, cultural, and social class groups.

Isolated rural districts also have their limitations and problems. They, too, tend to lack financial resources and personnel and are tradition-bound; changes often occur slowly.

### PL 94-142

The effect of PL 94-142 has been significant and far reaching on education generally and on nonbiased assessment specifically (see, in this volume, Martin). One effect has been to encourage school psychologists to assess more children directly and to not provide consultation services to teachers, principals, and parents. This has resulted in dramatically increasing the number of children being referred for appraisal. Through their consulting activities, school psychologists and other assessment specialists often are able to work directly with teachers and parents to arrive at viable solutions to children's educational and psychological problems without doing a complete appraisal, thus permitting greater numbers of children to be seen.

Some legal requirements seem beyond the capabilities of school districts. Consider that the schools in New York and Chicago are responsible for assessing and teaching those children whose native language may be 1 of 200 languages and dialects. This obligation is not being—and probably cannot be—met. Clearly problems in assessing minority group children have no one source. They may be due to children; parents; examiners; assessment

techniques; teachers; principals; district policies, practices, and financial abilities; and legal issues.

### POSSIBLE BIAS POINTS

Educators and psychologists have direct control over only some of the conditions that directly influence nonbiased assessment, mainly situations occurring at school. Some of these conditions occur *prior* to assessment; others occur *during* assessment; still others occur *following* assessment.

### Bias Points Prior to Assessment

#### REFERRAL AND SCREENING

The diagnostic-intervention process begins when a teacher refers a child for special services. Administrative procedures for processing referrals differ among districts. In some, children's names are put on a waiting list to be screened and evaluated. In other districts, names are referred to a within-school committee responsible for screening the referral after collecting existing data and obtaining additional information, including an appraisal of whether resources exist within the school to meet the children's needs.

The nature of the behaviors that actually stimulate the referral may constitute a bias point. Teachers may refer as academic problems those children who are not the lowest academically in class but whose behaviors they find disturbing. Other teachers have lower expectations for children who live in mobile homes, come from lower-class homes, attend unconventional churches, dress poorly, come from one-parent families, speak a foreign language, recently arrived in town, or have other distinguishable characteristics. A child's skin color or last name may stimulate other deep-seated prejudices. Prejudices may result in identifying qualities that are not present, encouraging the development of latent qualities, and overlooking other characteristics. For example, speech problems among children from bilingual backgrounds or those who speak nonstandard dialects often are overlooked. Health problems teachers readily detect among middle-class children may be unattended in lower-class children.

In New York City, over 90% of children referred for special services are found eligible for those services. Some districts may have even higher ratios of referred children to eligible children. An imbalance in the number of children from minority groups placed in special education begins at this point. Thus an examination of referral and screening procedures may indicate this to be a significant source of bias.

### TEST NORMS

One assumption underlying assessment is that the child being tested could have been included in the test's standardization sample (i.e., the children whose scores constitute the test norms). The norms for many tests are large, heterogeneous, and well selected to adequately reflect the full range of children's characteristics. Others have a restricted and narrow standardization sample. No test is inherently biased. Bias enters when someone *uses* a test with an inappropriate standardization sample. Thus knowing a test's standardization samples is prerequisite for a nonbiased assessment program.

### TEST RELIABILITY

Reliability refers to the stability of a person's performance. For test scores to be accurate, they must be stable. Although the reliability of test scores for majority- and minority-group children tend to be similar, school districts should conduct their own studies to decide the degree of confidence they can have in their test data. One also should keep in mind that objectively acquired data from formal measures (e.g., from standardized achievement and intelligence tests) tend to be more reliable than data from informal and less objective techniques (e.g., class grades, behavior observation, and teacher reports). Designing nonbiased programs requires the selection and use of reliable data-gathering techniques.

### TEST VALIDITY

Valid measures accurately assess behaviors they are designed to measure. When measures are valid, accurate decisions are made and the results used with confidence; when they do not, inaccurate decisions flourish. Thus the degree of confidence educators can have in using measures is contingent on knowing this information. No test is accurate for all purposes. Tests are selected for specific reasons and to provide accurate information to specific questions.

152 While the prevailing data suggest that intelligence test validity is similar for majority and minority children (Jensen, 1980), other studies suggest this is not always the case. For example, one study (Oakland, 1978) reports the ability of the Metropolitan Readiness Test to predict Metropolitan Achievement Test scores 2 years later to be .77% for whites, .30% for Mexican-Americans, and .15% for blacks. This should not be interpreted as an indictment of all tests. Local, regional, and statewide studies are needed to ascertain the validity of tests used with minority group children. Only by knowing the validity of the data can a program be certified as nonbiased.

## Bias Points During Assessment

Characteristics that can lead to bias during the assessment include child characteristics, examiner characteristics, and the adequacy of diagnostic-intervention techniques.

### CHILD CHARACTERISTICS

*Language.* Children's ability to understand and communicate in English is very important. School success partly depends on the ability to understand, speak, read, and write English. Knowing children's listening and speaking proficiency in English is important in judging whether their language skills are sufficiently developed to enable them to take other tests adequately.

Conventional measures requiring a high level of English proficiency cannot be used with children whose English language skills are poorly developed. Paucity

---

*Conventional measures requiring a high level of English proficiency cannot be used with children whose English language skills are poorly developed.*

---

of language might be due to general language deficiencies among English-speaking children or to language differences due to either the child's exposure to nonstandard dialects or to the child's exclusive knowledge of a language other than English. Tests used in schools generally are not intended to directly assess language skills but use language to assess intelligence, achievement, personality, and other characteristics. In working with children with language differences, educators need to alter their conventional assessment techniques to obtain a valid picture of intellectual, personality, and social characteristics.

*Test wiseness.* In giving tests, educators assume that children possess certain abilities prerequisite to taking tests. For example, they assume that children can understand the directions (which might include concepts such as right, left, up, down, same, and different), that children will consider all possible responses before choosing an answer, that children can work on one item at a time and not be distracted by other items, and that children are involved and attentive during the full test. These and other abilities (Oakland, 1972) constitute basic test-taking skills. Children must have these prerequisite skills for tests to be valid (see, in this volume, Reid & Hresko).

*Motivation and anxiety.* Adequate test performance requires that children be properly motivated (Oakland & Matuszek, 1977). Too often, children randomly select answers on a multiple-choice test or refuse to cooperate in other ways. Other children may be extremely anxious and unable to attend to the test. A nonbiased assessment program must consider the attitudinal characteristics of children to ensure that they are properly motivated. Results from aptitude and achievement tests are valid only when children are fully motivated to try to do their very best work.

*Cultural differences.* Minority children often come from restricted environments or from cultural settings that provide opportunities for growth and development differing significantly from those of most children (Cole & Bruner, 1971; Newland, 1973). These differences may be seen in child-rearing practices, expectations and aspirations, language experiences, informal and formal learning experiences, and other factors that constitute acculturation patterns. The acculturation patterns of minority group children and those from lower socioeconomic homes may be significantly different from acculturation patterns of children included in a test's standardization sample. Confidence in a test decreases when a child's acculturation patterns with respect to the characteristics being assessed are judged to be significantly different from those of the standardization sample.

Not all children from minority or lower socioeconomic status groups differ significantly from children included in the standardization sample. The decision on whether a child's acculturation patterns are similar to those of other children must be made for each child *individually* and can be made competently only with thorough knowledge of each child's background and knowledge of the test's standardization sample.

*Expectations.* Individuals' behavior tends to move toward the expectations others hold of them. When children are expected to be well behaved and these expectations are communicated to them, the prevalence of good behavior increases. Children tend to adopt and accept the expectations their peers, family, and teachers communicate to them. Knowing a child's expectations enables educators to more accurately appraise the child's future and to alter their interpretations of the assessment data. A child who expects to fail on tests is likely to underperform on tests. Thus low expectations tend to exacerbate other problems and decrease the validity of test data.

EXAMINER CHARACTERISTICS

The assessment specialist plays a central role in designing and implementing a nonbiased assessment program. Three particular areas serve as guides.

*Bias attitudes.* Teachers' attitudes toward children affect their behavior toward children. Teachers who feel attachment and concern toward students behave differently from those who feel rejection or indifference toward students. Moreover, teachers' attitudes are directly affected by children's characteristics. Educators generally tend to favor bright, achieving, linguistically competent, academically motivated, compliant, conforming stu-

154  dents. But many children being referred for assessment exhibit different characteristics. Furthermore, some persons have strong and fixed opinions regarding persons of identifiable racial, ethnic, and social class groups. These prejudices act as roadblocks that prevent persons from getting to know and understand the characteristics of each individual. Assessment specialists are not immune to these prejudices. They, too, may have their biases. Thus it is important to assess the extent to which bias may discolor and alter both the information acquired and the interpretations made of this information while working with persons of different racial or ethnic groups.

*Who is the client?* The Ethical Standards of Psychologists (American Psychological Association, 1972) emphasize the belief in the dignity and worth of the individual, a commitment to freedom of inquiry and communications, and a concern for the best interest of clients, colleagues, and society in general. Psychologists are strongly encouraged to respect the integrity and protect the welfare of persons with whom they work. When a conflict arises among professional workers, psychologists should be more concerned with the welfare of their clients (e.g., a child) than with the interest of their professional group.

However, this principle is not always adhered to. Some examiners are most concerned about job security, friendships, and serving the school system that employs them. Persons in this frame of mind will not fully investigate all school-related factors that may attenuate a child's performance. To find a deficit within the child and to fault the child's home and neighborhood often is easier than to identify important teacher and other school-related variables that are retarding the child's development. A nonbiased assessment of programs assumes that the examiner has an open mind and investigates both school- and home-related factors that may be hampering a child's development.

*Competency.* Examiners tend to be highly trained, competent, and dedicated. However, some know assessment superficially and mechanically. They are poorly prepared in child-clinical techniques and behavioral assessment and have not kept up with other advancements made in the field of appraisal. Many minority group parents and those with low incomes have come to depend on the public schools to provide good quality education and psychological services. These parents do not have the financial means to purchase these services privately. Thus the standards governing the provision of educational and psychological services in public schools must remain as high as those for the private sector. Nonbiased assessment is based on providing the highest quality of services to children and their families through public schools. Services short of this goal cannot be justified or tolerated.

### ADEQUACY OF DIAGNOSTIC-INTERVENTION TECHNIQUES

Recently all assessment specialists in a large eastern school district were told to identify children for the resource room by administering 4 of 12 subtests from the Wechsler Intelligence Scale for Children, one figure drawing, and a visual-motor test. Fortunately, the assessment specialists recognized the gross inadequacies of this plan and refused to comply with the directive. Specialists should not be called on to make important decisions based on meager information derived from short-cut strategies. They need multiple kinds of information. They need information about the medical, social, psychological, and educational characteristics of children. Because the human being is a complex organism, problems in one or more of these areas affect development in other areas. Thus one strong focus must include multiple kinds of information on children's characteristics (see memorandum from the Office for Civil Rights, in Oakland, 1973).

Home and school factors that may be contributing to the child's problems also need to be understood. This requires an ecological focus in which educators examine interrelationships among child, home, and school. Rarely is there one single cause for significant school problems. Usually many factors either cause or support dysfunctional school behavior. To be complete, nonbiased assessment must consider a variety of school and home factors in addition to children's characteristics.

### Bias Points After Assessment

Assessment is a process—not a goal. It provides ways to collect and interpret information relevant to making decisions. The goal within education is to make wise and informed decisions that will benefit the child educationally, psychologically, and socially. Thus the effectiveness of our nonbiased assessment program hinges on what happens to the child following assessment. Three principal barriers must be removed to have a proper program following assessment.

### NO INTERVENTION

The fundamental principle underlying a nonbiased assessment program is that, if necessary, some attempt will be made to facilitate children's development. Yet in all too many situations, specialized interventions do not occur. While new labels may be placed on the child, resulting in a different class assignment, important and more effective curricular and behavioral strategies may not follow.

The diagnostic-intervention model put forth by Cromwell, Blashfield, and Strauss (1975) merges assessment information with interventions and thus helps to establish a standard for our practices. Four components of this model are described briefly.

The first component is concerned with acquiring historical information to assist educators in understanding a child and his or her environment. Information of a historical nature helps educators identify and understand important antecedent events in a child's life.

The second component seeks information that describes current characteristics of the child and his or her environment. Thus the first two components constitute a diagnostic side of the diagnostic-intervention strategy.

The third component focuses on interventions. Interventions include any process over which educators have control

156 and are developed from information gathered from the first two components.

A fourth component estimates the successfulness of the interventions. Given these previous and current characteristics, educators should be able to forecast the likelihood of a particular intervention's helpfulness to the child.

Thus a complete diagnostic-intervention program would acquire historical and current information on children and their environment. It would compare these two sources of information to draw associations between their previous and current characteristics. It would use this information to specify viable interventions and then would conduct follow-up studies to examine their effectiveness.

### NO REEXAMINATION

The fourth component of this model provides for evaluating the effectiveness of interventions. This will require periodic review and reexamination of children to determine the extent to which progress is being made. With the goal of providing beneficial interventions, educators need to continuously update information and readjust interventions. Failure to reexamine children contributes a significant degree of bias.

### DISPROPORTIONATE ASSIGNMENT TO INFERIOR EDUCATIONAL PROGRAMS

A third bias point is reached when large numbers of minority children are routinely placed in lower ability groups, educable mentally retarded classes, and other administrative structures judged to be ineffective and inferior to regular education programs (Laosa & Oakland, 1974).

---

*A third bias point is reached when large numbers of minority children are routinely placed in lower ability groups, educable mentally retarded classes, and other structures judged to be inferior.*

---

For example, blacks constituted 9% of California's population and 26% of the educable mentally retarded (EMR) population. Given the strong and pervasive notion that such classes are ineffective educational dead-ends, minority groups believe their disproportionate assignment to these classes provide prima facie evidence for discriminatory practices.

*One Approach to Nonbiased Assessment: PL 94-142*

Involvement of the federal government in education has mushroomed during the last 25 years, particularly after the *Brown v. Board of Education* decision. The government increased its involvement to protect the constitutional and statutory rights of minorities following the unwillingness or inability of states and local districts to alter allegedly discriminatory educational policies and practices.

The federal district courts considered allegations that educational programs for minorities are inferior, that schools discriminate against non-English-speaking students, that tests and assessment practices are biased, and that parents' rights are abrogated. By enacting PL 94-142 the government established uniform guidelines for schools to help overcome these and other problems.

While the scope of issues addressed by PL 94-142 is much broader than assessment and minority group children, the law has shaped nonbiased assessment practices more than any other source (Bateman & Herr, in press; Ysseldyke & Shinn, in press; and in this volume, Martin). As a federal law, if affects school districts in all 50 states and territories. All state education agencies have rewritten their policies and procedures to conform to this law. Principal features pertaining specifically to nonbiased assessment programs include the following rights.

RIGHT TO DUE PROCESS

Procedure safeguards guarantee the rights of parents to a meaningful role within the diagnostic-intervention process. The due process provisions include the right to examine all relevant records; to obtain an independent evaluation of the child; to receive written notices in their native language before the school district proposes to initiate a change or refuses to initiate the change in identifying, evaluating, or placing a child; the right to present complaints with respect to any matter relating to identifying, evaluating, or placing their child; the right to a hearing conducted by an impartial hearing officer employed by the state education agency; the right to appeal decisions to the state education agency; the right to be advised by legal counsel, to present evidence, to cross-examine witnesses, and to compel the attendance of witnesses; the right to a verbatim record of such hearings; the right to written findings of facts and decisions; and the right to bring civil action in any state or district court of the United States.

RIGHT TO EDUCATION WITH NONHANDICAPPED CHILDREN

Handicapped children should be educated to the maximum extent possible with nonhandicapped children. Special classes, separate schools, and other administrative arrangements which move handicapped children from regular education should occur only when the nature and severity of the handicapped are not appropriately met through regular classes or the use of supplementary aids and services.

RIGHT TO TESTS THAT ARE NOT CULTURALLY DISCRIMINATORY

Tests will be selected and administered so as to not be racially or culturally discriminatory. Tests and other evaluation materials must be validated for the specific purpose for which they are used. Tests must be administered by trained personnel in accordance with the standardized instructions, in the child's native language, and for the specific purpose for which the tests were developed. When testing children with impaired sensory, manual, or speaking skills, tests must be selected and administered so as to accurately reflect the children's characteristics rather than their impairments. Finally, the evaluation must be directed to assess specific areas of educational need, not merely general constructs such as intelligence.

RIGHT TO A MULTIDIMENSIONAL,
TEAM-BASED ASSESSMENT

Multiple kinds and sources of information should be acquired during the assessment (Gerry, 1973). The child is assessed in all areas relating to the suspected disability, including, whenever appropriate, health, vision, hearing, social and emotional status, general intelligence, academic performance, communicative status, and motor abilities. Information is also needed on the child's social and cultural background and adaptive behavior. In addition, information should be obtained from teachers, including their recommendations for the child.

Placement decisions must be made by groups of persons who are knowledgeable about the child, the evaluation data, and placement options. The evaluation made by a multidisciplinary team is a cornerstone to nonbiased assessment. An appropriate education program considers all data; no single procedure is used as the sole criterion for determining an appropriate educational program.

Periodic reevaluation of children receiving special education and related services must occur. Thus decisions must be regularly reviewed, with options open for each child to be maintained in special education or brought back into regular education.

## Other Attempts to Achieve Nonbiased Assessment

Educators and psychologists have attempted to devise more appropriate psychoeducational assessment procedures for minority groups in various ways.

Most techniques have focused on testing and examiners, some have focused on system changes, and a few have focused on changing children (Davis, 1974).

### CHANGING TESTS

The development of culture-free tests during the 1940s and 1950s represented an attempt to find assessment techniques that could be used internationally and would not reflect cultural and socioeconomic differences. The strong influence a particular culture has on shaping behaviors is now widely realized. Cultures can differ dramatically in the behaviors they encourage people to develop. Thus the development of culture-free tests of important and meaningful characteristics in the behavioral sciences is not possible.

Culture-fair testing then became a goal (Eells, 1951; Jensen, 1970). A test is judged to be culture-fair if four conditions exist: (a) the mean scores and standard deviations for all racial, ethnic, and social-class groups within one country are the same, (b) persons from various racial, ethnic, and social class groups are included in the standardization sample, (c) the items minimize reading and language abilities, and (d) the test is untimed. Few tests meet these four conditions. For example, the mean scores on supposedly culture-fair tests tend to be lower for children from the lower social classes. Moreover, these tests often have low validity.

Culture-specific tests (Williams, 1971) also were seen as an answer. Tests were developed for a specific racial or ethnic group having a common identifiable cultural and geographic area. However, the scope of assessment is so large within the United States that this solution is impractical. There are not enough resources to develop culture-specific tests. Moreover, their reliability and validity are also questionable.

Criterion-referenced measures (Drew, 1973) also were described as an answer. By assessing the specific educational goals educators attempted to make testing more relevant to educational interventions. While criterion-referenced measures are helpful, they have a narrow scope and do not elicit reasons why children may be doing poorly in school.

The System of Multicultural Pluralistic Assessment (Mercer & Lewis, 1978) is one of the newer approaches to nonbiased assessment. It presents a more complete battery consisting of independent measures of children's medical, psychological, and social characteristics but does not consider information on children's educational achievement.

Translating tests from English into black dialects or foreign languages attempts to facilitate communication and make the tests more relevant linguistically. It is difficult to translate tests and yet maintain the integrity of the abilities being assessed. Moreover, there are no national linguistic standards for nonstandard dialects. An English-language test translated into Spanish for children in the Texas valley is inappropriate linguistically when used with Mexican-American children in California, Puerto Rican children in New York, and Cuban children in Miami.

*An English-language test translated into Spanish for children in the Texas valley is inappropriate linguistically when used with Puerto Rican children in New York and Cuban children in Miami.*

The development of racial and ethnic norms also was suggested as a means of implementing nonbiased assessment techniques. Tests could provide separate norms for blacks, Mexican-Americans, Indians, and children from other racial or ethnic groups. While most test standardization samples now include minority groups, their numbers are often too small to use as a basis for establishing separate norms. Moreover, presenting separate racial norms invites invidious comparisons.

Pluralistic norms and estimated learning potential (Mercer & Lewis, 1978), the upward adjustment of test scores earned by lower socioeconomic children so as to normalize mean score differences, have provoked much interest recently. However, pluralistic norms and the estimated learning potential presently lack conceptual clarity and empirical support (see *School Psychology Digest*, 1979, 8, 1 & 2).

Identification of item bias also has been tried (Green, no date; Jensen, 1975; Oakland & Feigenbaum, 1979, 1980). The statistical data currently are published on a few tests, and the results are not well known. Moreover, this line of investigation fails to deal with other professional, political, and social problems associated with the assessment of minority group children.

160 CHANGING EXAMINERS

Pairing examiners and children of the same race and language abilities has been used as a means to effect nonbiased assessment. Some people have assumed that performance of black children will be higher with black examiners and Mexican-American children with Mexican-American examiners. However, the evidence does not support this idea (Sattler, 1973). Interpersonal skills, rather than the racial characteristics of the examiner, appear to be more crucial in obtaining maximum performance from children.

Other examiner characteristics, such as the quality and recency of their training and their knowledge of minority group children and adults, have been discussed as an important component of nonbiased assessment. In-service training and continuing education continue to be used as a means of sensitizing and informing examiners to various issues pertinent to nonbiased assessment.

CHANGING SYSTEMS

Various changes have been attempted or proposed that effect broad and sweeping changes in the ways educators assess minority group children. For example, a moratorium on testing was advocated by the National Education Association (Bosma, 1973) and other groups, presumably to secure more equitable assessment techniques. However, a moratorium is a radical response that does not correct the problem. In fact, the contrary is being proposed: a basic tenet of nonbiased as-

sessment is to require more testing, not less.

Offering cultural awareness seminars for the school staff also was used to facilitate work with minority group children and their families. The early seminars often were poorly planned. They raised expectations of significant changes in attitudes in a very short time. Yet the need for educators and psychologists to understand and be active in the minority communities remains a pressing need.

Screening and referral policies more recently have been examined as a source of bias (Ysseldyke, 1979). While there is a strong tendency to blame tests for putting children into ineffective programs, placement actually starts when teachers observe undesirable differences and subsequently refer children for special services. Information on bias associated with screening and referral is just beginning to be obtained and evaluated.

Many school systems have set informal quotas on the number of children from each racial or ethnic group included in their EMR programs and lower abilities groups. This is a political decision. It does not consider the real needs of children.

As was previously discussed, one way to effect changes toward nonbiased assessment has been by challenging school practices in the state and federal court systems (Bateman & Herr, in press; Laosa & Oakland, 1974; Ysseldyke & Shinn, in press). Typically a local school district or state education agency is made to defend its policies and practices by plaintiffs who initiate class action suits on behalf of a group of minority children. The resolution of allegations may occur by the plaintiffs and defendants negotiating with one another, by the court issuing a judgment of policies and procedures on nonbiased assessment, or by a court-appointed group of qualified experts who arrive at a decision.

State and federal legislation has provided strong influence regarding what constitutes basic nonbiased assessment programs. Of course, legislation carries with it the weight of the executive branch of government, which can force a school system to comply with the law. Clearly the most rapid progress toward defining appropriate nonbiased assessment practices has occurred through legislative and judicial actions.

CHANGING CHILDREN

Educators have attempted to improve assessment for minority group children by trying to improve their test-taking abilities and to encourage them to be more reflective and less impulsive in taking tests. This would allow them to more effectively express what they can and cannot do.

CONCLUSION

Significant advances have been made toward developing more appropriate assessment services with minority group children. Educators have a better understanding of the broad as well as specific problems, and they can anticipate and thus make provisions for potentially bias-producing points before, during, and after assessment. Guidelines have been provided on which to base nonbiased programs.

However, educators are not ready to turn their attention elsewhere. Problems still exist. Educators need to discover better ways to help uncover and identify various talents and abilities that otherwise remain hidden and undeveloped. Better methods are needed of finding academic, cognitive, social, and emotional strengths which too often remain shrouded by bigotry, biases, poverty, or culture.

However, educators' responsibilities do not end by discovering talent. It is necessary to help foster the development of various abilities and talents. Once discovered, this information must be used to improve the development and status of all persons—to use test results to benefit children rather than to restrict their development or rigidify their status. Finally, educators are expected to help individuals make appropriate decisions. Children, parents, teachers, administrators, school board members, lawyers, judges, and others need reliable and valid information that is objectively obtained and offered.

Instead of using tests to limit educational and vocational opportunities, educators need to continue to seek ways to discover and foster talents. Instead of using tests to denigrate the dignity and pride of minority groups, educators must seek ways to destroy prejudicial attitudes and practices. Information should be used to set minds free and to humanize interpersonal relationships. Assessment techniques were developed to be of service to all citizens. Educators need to work to establish this principle in practice.

## 162  REFERENCES

American Psychological Association. *Ethical standards of psychologists.* Washington, D.C.: APA, 1972.

Bateman, B., & Herr, C. Law and special education. In J. M. Kauffman & D. P. Hallahan (Eds.), *Handbook of special education.* Englewood Cliffs, N.J.: Prentice-Hall, in press.

Bosma, B. The NEA testing moratorium. *Journal of School Psychology,* 1973, *11,* 304-306.

Cole, M., & Bruner, J. S. Cultural differences and inferences about psychological processes. *American Psychologist,* 1971, *26,* 867-876.

Cromwell, R. L., Blashfield, R. K., & Strauss, J. S. Criteria for classification systems. In N. Hobbs (Ed.), *Issues in the classification of children* (Vol. 1). San Francisco: Jossey-Bass, 1975.

Cronbach, L. J. Five decades of public controversy over mental testing. *American Psychologist,* 1975, *30,* 1-14.

Davis, F. *Standards for educational and psychological tests.* Washington, D.C.: American Psychological Association, 1974.

Drew, C. Criterion-referenced and norm-referenced assessment of minority group children. *Journal of School Psychology,* 1973, *11,* 323-329.

Eells, K. *Intelligence and cultural differences.* Chicago: University of Chicago Press, 1951.

Gerry, M. H. Cultural myopia: The need for a corrective lens. *Journal of School Psychology,* 1973, *11,* 307-315.

Green, D. *Racial and ethnic bias in test construction.* Monterey, Calif.: California Test Bureau/McGraw-Hill, no date.

Holmen, M. G., & Docter, R. *Educational and psychological testing.* New York: Russell Sage Foundation, 1972.

Jensen, A. J. Another look at culture-fair testing. In J. Hellmuth (Ed.), *Disadvantaged child,* Vol. 3, New York: Brunner/Mazel, 1970.

Jensen, A. J. *Test bias and construct validity.* Paper presented at the Annual Convention of the American Psychological Association, Chicago, September 1975.

Jensen, A. J. *Bias in mental testing.* New York: Free Press, 1980.

Laosa, L. M., & Oakland, T. D. Social control in mental health: Psychological assessment and the schools. Paper presented at the 51st Annual Meeting of the American Orthopsychiatric Association, San Francisco, April 1974.

Mercer, J. R., & Lewis, J. F. *System of multi-cultural pluralistic assessment* (SOMPA). New York: Psychological Corporation, 1978.

Newland, T. E. Assumptions underlying psychological testing. *Journal of School Psychology,* 1973, *11,* 315-322.

Oakland, T.D. Effects of test-wiseness materials on standardized test performance of preschool disadvantaged children. *Journal of School Psychology,* 1972, *10,* 355-360.

Oakland, T. D. Assessing minority group children: Challenges for school psychologists. *Journal of School Psychology,* 1973, *11,* 294-303.

Oakland, T. D. Assessment, education, and minority-group children. *Academic Therapy,* 1974, *10,* 133-140.

Oakland, T. D. Predictive validity of readiness tests for middle and lower socioeconomic status Anglo, black, and Mexican American children. *Journal of Educational Psychology,* 1978, *70,* 574-582.

Oakland, T. D., & Feigenbaum, D. Multiple sources of test bias on the WISC-R and Bender-Gestalt. *Journal of Consulting and Clinical Psychology,* 1979, *47,* 968-974.

Oakland, T. D., & Feigenbaum, D. Assessment of test bias on the Adaptive Behavior Inventory for Children. *Journal of School Psychology,* 1980, *18* (4).

Oakland, T. D., & Matuszek, P. Using tests in nondiscriminatory assessment. In T. D. Oakland (Ed.), *Psychological and educational assessment of minority group children.* New York: Brunner/Mazel, 1977.

Samuda, R. S. *Psychological testing of American minorities: Issues and consequences.* New York: Dodd, Mead & Co., 1975.

Sattler, J. Racial experimenter effects. In K. S. Miller & R. M. Dreger (Eds.), *Comparative studies of blacks and whites in the United States.* New York: Seminar Press, 1973.

Williams, R. Danger: Testing and dehumanizing black children. *The School Psychologist,* 1971, *25,* 11-13.

Ysseldyke, J. Issues in psychoeducational assessment. In D. Reschly and G. Phye (Eds.), *School psychology: Perspectives and issues.* New York: Academic Press, 1979.

Ysseldyke, J., and Shinn, M. Psychoeducational diagnosis. In J. M. Kauffman and D. P. Hallahan (Eds.), *Handbook of special education.* Englewood Cliffs, N. J.: Prentice-Hall, in press.

# Special Problems of Deaf Adolescents and Young Adults

*Kenneth R. Nash, Ed.D.*
*University of Rochester*

*William E. Castle, Ph.D.*
*National Technical Institute*
*for the Deaf*
*Rochester, New York*

INFORMATION ON the effects of deafness on adolescents and young adults is rather limited, but it is clear that the developmental impact of childhood hearing loss can be profound and long lasting. In this article we briefly discuss some of the special academic, psychosocial, and career problems of adolescents and young adults resulting from early severe auditory deprivation.

For the purpose of this article, a deaf person is defined as one whose hearing disability precludes successful processing of linguistic information through audition, with or without the use of a hearing aid (Conference of Executives of American Schools for the Deaf, 1974). Among the school-age deaf children currently in special schools, programs, or classes in this country, more than 86% were born deaf or became deaf before age 3, the critical period for language development. Less than .05% had normal hearing but be-

164 came deaf before they could develop English linguistic competence.

It is widely recognized that reduced linguistic competence markedly influences academic, personal, social, and career development. Therefore the age at which a person becomes deaf is highly significant. Numerous other variables influence the way deafness affects the individual, such as the cause of the hearing loss, intellectual capacity, age at the time of identification, age at the time of educational and psychological intervention, types of interventions, family background and degree of acceptance, religious convictions, socioeconomic status, and the rate and sequence of biological change. Given the range and scope of these variables, it is clear that although deafness affects maturation of all persons in a somewhat similar fashion, its influence on a particular individual's academic, psychosocial, and career development will vary greatly as a function of the interaction of these factors.

## ACADEMIC DEVELOPMENT

There are deaf businessmen, social workers, engineers, lawyers, accountants, and architects who are self-actualized individuals, functioning at their capacity. Such occupations are realistic goals for some deaf adolescents and young adults; but for the majority, such aspirations are not realistic. A major barrier to the achievement of such goals is that, compared to their hearing peers, deaf persons progress academically at substantially reduced rates. Jensema (1975), for example, assessed the academic achievement of 6,873 hearing impaired children in special classes as measured by the special edition of the 1973 *Stanford Achievement Test for Hearing Impaired Students*. He found that from ages 8 to 18, average hearing impaired students increased their vocabulary only as much as average normal hearing students do between the beginning of kindergarten and the latter part of second grade. The deaf students' performance on the reading comprehension, math concepts, and math computation subtests showed similar discrepancies. Jensema also found strong relationships between achievement levels and the age of onset of deafness, cause of hearing loss, extent of hearing loss, and other handicapping conditions.

Trybus and Karchmer (1977) investigated the educational performance level of over 6,000 hearing impaired students in special school programs and classes for the deaf. The researchers found that half read at less than mid-fourth-grade level; that is, below or barely at a newspaper literacy level. Of the high-achieving group, only 10% of the hearing impaired 18-year-olds nationally can read at or above an eighth-grade level. These results clearly suggest that the average deaf child faces special academic problems.

The achievement levels of the new students accepted into the National Technical Institute for the Deaf (NTID) in 1979 highlight the magnitude of the problem: the overall mean grade equivalent of the entering class was 8.8, with a standard deviation of 1.35, on the Stanford Achievement Test, Advanced Battery. This level of performance is markedly higher than that of the average deaf 19-year-old, but it is clearly not at a level competitive with the deaf students' hearing counterparts.

Though more systematic research is necessary to find ways to assess and remediate the effects of early auditory deprivation on language acquisition, some progress is being made. For example, there is ample evidence that if trained to use residual hearing, many deaf people can use hearing aids to gain information valuable for understanding and using speech (Sanders, 1971). Until recently, however, many hearing impaired adolescents and young adults concerned with peer acceptance have faced an awkward choice: to declare their handicap to the world to assure amplification or to sacrifice the hearing aid in an attempt to avoid stigma. Given the need to conform, young people frequently have rejected aids or selected them for reasons of cosmetics rather than communication (Karchmer & Kirwin, 1977). Recent technical advances may make such decisions less frequent, however; behind-the-ear aids can now provide gains in excess of 60 dB with a frequency response range extending to 500 Hz. For those who can benefit, in-the-ear aids are also available with gains up to 50 dB.

Many educators have maintained that once a deaf student reaches age 17 or 18, little improvement in reading, writing, or even speech skills can be expected. For example, in the areas of English proficiency, several investigators have found that the average deaf student progresses approximately .2 grade points per year in the area of reading comprehension (Cooper & Rosenstein, 1966; DiFrancesca, 1972). Several recent efforts, however, have shown that when provided with suitable instruction, deaf adolescents and young adults can make far greater progress than previously anticipated (Hammermeister, 1971; Orlando, 1975). Reporting on the English proficiency and progress made by 265 NTID freshmen, Crandall (1980) found that after four quarters of instruction "those students enrolled in the standard curriculum demonstrated a mean improvement of 1.47 grade points in the area of reading vocabulary and 1.24 grade points in the area of reading comprehension." As this student population entered NTID with grade equivalent scores of 7.38 and 8.46 in vocabulary and comprehension, respectively, Crandall concluded that the students are improving their English skills at a faster rate than their past educational history would indicate.

Such advances may eventually lead to a better academic future for deaf people, but by themselves such approaches are insufficient. To overcome the special academic problems will require systematic research programs that lead to additional major breakthroughs and a cadre of skilled content specialists prepared to work with the deaf in advanced academic areas as well as the basics.

*Recent efforts have shown that when provided with suitable instruction, deaf adolescents and young adults can make far greater progress than previously anticipated.*

## 166 PSYCHOSOCIAL DEVELOPMENT

The transition from adolescence to adulthood is a difficult period for hearing adolescents and their families, and it can be a time of particular stress for hearing impaired adolescents and their parents (Schlesinger & Meadow, 1971). Although most deaf adults lead independent and productive lives, research data suggest that early childhood deafness can significantly affect psychosocial development. For example, deaf adolescents and young adults have often been characterized as emotionally immature. Levine (1956) referred to this constellation of behavior in terms of egocentricity, easy irritability, impulsiveness, and suggestibility. Altshuler (1974) described the deaf as showing egocentricity, dependency, impulsivity, and a lack of empathy. Several investigators have found that the prevalence of emotional or behavioral problems is significantly higher among deaf children than among hearing children in otherwise comparable circumstances (Meadow & Trybus, 1979; Schlesinger & Meadow, 1972).

Deaf adolescents and young adults tend to have relatively poor self-concepts compared to their hearing counterparts (Schroedel & Schiff, 1972; Sussman, 1973). Garrison and Tesch (1978), however, cautioned that such interpretations may be the result of inappropriate tests rather than the students' true self-perceptions. Preliminary studies of NTID students suggest that over half of the entering freshmen have major gaps in their knowledge of the personal and social information needed to function in college and to work in community environments. In addition, many deaf students are several years behind their hearing classmates in social and personal maturation. A survey of the personal-social needs of NTID students indicates that the greatest personal-social problems confronting NTID students are lack of responsibility and poor decision-making skills (Covill-Servo & Garrison, 1978).

Studying the social perception of nonverbal cues, Schiff (1973) found that deaf students had less success in extracting information and made more errors in social perception than their hearing counterparts. Evans (1976) found that deaf children in residential schools had limited opportunities for personal and social growth. It is important to remember that these findings do not apply to all persons with profound prelingual auditory deprivation and that extreme caution must be exercised in the interpretation of test results (Garrison, Tesch, & DeCaro, 1978). However, it is clear that deafness can pose special psychosocial problems for deaf adolescents and young adults.

Emerton, Hurwitz, and Bishop (1979) suggest that the gap in social maturity between deaf and hearing peers is the result of limited knowledge and life experiences, rather than a manifestation of a generalized alteration of the balance of psychological processes, as proposed by Myklebust (1964). Levine (1971), recognizing the psychological retardation of many deaf people, concluded that they suffer from "educational and psychological malnutrition otherwise known as cultural deprivation." Levine believes that such cultural deprivation is a result of failure by teachers, parents, and peers to provide the information and experiences deaf children need for development. Stinson (1972) found that parents of deaf children were often overprotective, denying them experiences allowed to their hearing siblings. Mindel and Vernon (1971), Freeman, Malkin, and Hastings (1975), and Schlesinger and Meadow (1972) support the hypothesis that deafness itself does not cause personal and social problems among deaf people. Rather deafness creates conditions that lead to experiential deprivation that in turn causes the special personal and social problems of deaf adolescents and young adults.

NTID is trying several approaches to developing competence among young adults. The first assumes that personal-social competence can be developed as a result of experiences in a variety of settings. Based on this approach a broad range of activities and opportunities are made available to students, including participation in classes and social activities with hearing peers, integrated dormitory arrangements with special program activities, extensive work simulations, and cooperative work experience on the job. The second approach assumes that some personal and social skills can be formally taught. Based on this hypothesis, special courses are being designed to focus on specific skill areas (Bishop, Emerton, & White, 1977).

Though such approaches may be useful at the postsecondary level, much work must be done at earlier ages. One key to successful psychosocial development is effective parent counseling. Over 95% of deaf children have parents who had abso-lutely no contact with deafness before the birth of their child (Schein & Delk, 1974). Therefore they have no experience on which to base a relationship with their deaf child. If parents are to help their children through the difficult period of adolescence and young adulthood, the parents themselves must be helped to deal with their feelings of frustration, anger, and resentment before they affect their children. Unfortunately, professionals do not always explain the problems of deafness in clear, realistic terms; in addition, some parents are unable to accept what they hear and see. As a result, when the deaf child reaches adolescence, both parents and child may face unique difficulties. Educators, counselors, and others must be prepared to help the child and parents resolve the problems of deciding in which "culture" their child will be most happy and fulfilled—deaf, hearing, or both—and find ways to make their joint decision enhance the quality of family relationships.

## Career Development

Historically, deaf persons have been underemployed but not unemployed (Moores, 1969; Schein & Delk, 1974). However, the impact of rapid technological change combined with unique academic and psychosocial problems could easily result in new and more severe career problems for deaf adolescents and young adults in the future. It has been predicted that by the year 2000, half the people in the country will be working in fields that do not even exist today. These circumstances present the deaf adoles-

168

*The impact of rapid technological change combined with unique academic and psychosocial problems could easily result in new and more severe career problems for deaf adolescents and young adults in the future.*

cent and young adult with several requirements: selection of a career, preparation for that career, and continued education to maintain it.

Too often, deaf adolescents and young adults are unaware of the career options available to them and therefore cannot make thoughtful career choices. In addition, they often lack the personal, social, communication, and technical competencies required for job advancement (Updegraff, Bishop, Steffan, & Dodd, 1978). Given the radically changing status of the job market, such competencies are increasingly necessary for success.

Until recently, deaf students had few opportunities to receive postsecondary training. For example, until 1964 the only postsecondary program for the deaf in the country was Gallaudet in Washington, D.C., a liberal arts college exclusively for the deaf. In 1965, Congress established NTID to provide technical education to deaf students. NTID is one of the ten colleges of the Rochester Institute of Technology. The 900 deaf students live in the same dorms, participate in the same campus activities, and take courses with their 7,000 hearing peers. Since the mid-1960s, there has been an explosion in postsecondary programs. In 1978 over 55 postsecondary programs met the guidelines suggested by the Conference of Executives of American Schools for the Deaf (Stuckless, 1973).These programs, situated primarily in junior colleges, enroll over 4,000 students (Rawlings, Trybus, & Biser, 1978). As Section 504 of the amendments to the Vocational Rehabilitation Act of 1973 is implemented, additional colleges and universities will make programs available to deaf students. This massive increase in program options enhances the opportunities for deaf individuals to enter fields previously closed to them.

Opportunities for initial placement for the deaf population may continue to be high, but continuing education programs are also needed. Without such programs the deaf population will soon find itself with obsolescent skills. Currently, at least one of ten adults in the general population participates in adult and continuing education annually. No specific figures on the deaf population are available, but the level of participation is extremely small. Continuing education as well as initial postsecondary training will be required to assure the career success of deaf adolescents and young adults.

## OPENING THE FUTURE FOR HEARING IMPAIRED INDIVIDUALS

Many deaf adolescents and young adults encounter special problems in academic, psychosocial, and career development as the result of experiential deprivation caused by early auditory loss: academic achievement may be retarded, personal and social skills may not be fully developed, and career options may be less clear and more difficult to maintain. These difficulties notwithstanding, many deaf adolescents and young adults lead meaningful and rewarding lives. Opportunities for academic, psychosocial, and career growth could be further enhanced, however, by several factors, including continued programmatic research, preparation of better trained professionals, and appropriate and timely counseling of parents and students.

## REFERENCES

Altshuler, K. The social end psychological development of the deaf child: Problems, their treatment and prevention. *American Annals of the Deaf*, 1974, *119*, 365-376.

Bishop, M., Emerton, G., & White, K. *Socialization: Can you really do anything about it?* Unpublished paper. Rochester, N. Y.: National Technical Institute for the Deaf, 1977.

Conference of Executives of American Schools for the Deaf. *Report of the committee to redefine deaf and hard of hearing.* Washington, D. C.: The Conference, 1974.

Cooper, R., & Rosenstein, J. Language acquisition of deaf children. *The Volta Review*, 1966, *68*, 58-67.

Covill-Servo, J., & Garrison, W. *Personal social needs assessment.* Unpublished paper. Rochester, N. Y.: National Technical Institute for the Deaf, 1978.

Crandall, K. English proficiency and progress made by the NTID student. *American Annals of the Deaf*, 1980, *125*, 417-426.

DiFrancesca, S. *Academic achievement test results of a national testing program for hearing impaired students, United States, Spring, 1971.* Washington, D. C.: Gallaudet College, Office of Demographic Studies, 1972.

Emerton, G., Hurwitz, T., & Bishop, M. Development of social maturity in deaf adolescents and adults. In L. Bradford & W. Hardy (Eds.). *Hearing and hearing impairments.* New York: Grune & Stratton, 1979.

Evans, A. Experiential deprivation: An unresolved factor in the impoverished socialization of deaf school children in residence. *American Annals of the Deaf*, 1975, *120*, 545-554.

Freeman, R., Malkin, S., & Hastings, J. Psychosocial problems of deaf children and their families: A comparative study. *American Annals of the Deaf*, 1975, *120*, 391-405.

Garrison, W., & Tesch, S. Self-concept and deafness: A review of research literature. *The Volta Review*, 1978, *80*, 457-466.

Garrison, W., Tesch, S., & DeCaro, P. An assessment of self-concept levels among postsecondary deaf adolescents. *American Annals of the Deaf*, 1978, *123*, 968-975.

Hammermeister, F. Reading achievement in deaf adults. *American Annals of the Deaf*, 1971, *116*, 25-28.

Jensema, C. *The relationship between academic achievement and the demographic characteristics of hearing impaired children and youth.* Washington, D.C.: Gallaudet College, Office of Demographic Studies, 1975.

Karchmer, M., & Kirwin, L. *The use of hearing aids by hearing impaired students in the United States.* Washington, D. C.: Gallaudet College, Office of Demographic Studies, 1977.

Levine, E. *Youth in a soundless world.* New York: New York University Press, 1956.

Levine, E. Psycho-cultural determinants in personality development. *The Volta Review*, 1971, *73*, 258-267.

Meadow, K., & Trybus, R. Behavioral and emotional problems of deaf children: An overview. In L. Bradford & W. Hardy (Eds.), *Hearing and hearing impairment.* New York: Grune & Stratton, 1979.

Mindel, E., & Vernon, M. *They grow in silence.* Silver Spring, Md.: National Association of the Deaf, 1971.

Moores, D. The vocational status of young deaf adults in New England. *Journal of Rehabilitation of the Deaf*, 1969, *2*, 5.

Myklebust, H. *The psychology of deafness.* New York: Grune & Stratton, 1964.

Orlando, N. Evidence of success in speech and voice training. *Journal of the Academy of Rehabilitative Audiology*, 1975, *8*, 51-63.

Rawlings, B., Trybus, R., & Biser, J. *A career guide to college/career programs for deaf students.* Washington, D.C. and Rochester, N. Y.: Gallaudet College and the National Technical Institute for the Deaf, 1978.

Ries, P., Bateman, D., & Schildroth, A. *Ethnic background in relation to other characteristics of hearing impaired students in the United States.* Washington,

170

D.C.: Gallaudet College, Office of Demographic Studies, 1975.

Saunders, D. *Aural rehabilitation.* Englewood Cliffs, N.J.: Prentice-Hall, 1971.

Schein, J., & Delk, M. *The deaf population of the United States.* Silver Spring, Md.: National Association of the Deaf, 1974.

Schiff, W. Social perception in deaf and hearing adolescents. *Exceptional Children,* 1973, *39,* 289-296.

Schlesinger, H., & Meadow, K. *Deafness and mental health: A developmental approach.* San Francisco: Langley-Porter Neuropsychiatric Institute, 1971.

Schlesinger, H., & Meadow, K. *Sound and sign: Childhood deafness and mental health.* Berkeley: University of California Press, 1972.

Schroedel, J., & Schiff, W. Attitudes toward deafness among several deaf and hearing populations. *Rehabilitation Psychology,* 1972, *19,* 59-70.

Stinson, M. *A comparison of the acquisition of the achievement motive in hearing and hearing impaired children.* Unpublished doctoral dissertation. Ann Arbor, Mich.: University of Michigan, 1972.

Stuckless, R. E. *Principles basic to the establishment and operation of postsecondary programs for deaf students.* Washington, D.C.: Conference of Executives of American Schools for the Deaf, 1973.

Sussman, A. *An investigation into the relationship between self-concepts of deaf adults and their perceived attitudes toward deafness.* Unpublished doctoral dissertation. New York: New York University, 1973.

Trybus, R. & Karchmer, M. School achievement scores for hearing-impaired children: National data on achievement status and growth patterns. *American Annals of the Deaf,* 1977, *122,* 62-69.

Updegraff, D., Bishop, M., Steffan, R., & Dodd, J. (Eds.). *Career development for the hearing impaired.* Rochester, N. Y.: National Project on Career Education, National Technical Institute for the Deaf, 1978.

# Neuropsychological Implications of Diagnosis and Treatment of Mathematical Learning Disabilities

*Ladislav Košč, Ph.D.*
*Research Institute of Child Psychology and*
    *Pathopsychology*
*Bratislava, Czechoslovakia*

THE NATURE and quality of disabilities and performance deficits in mathematics are among the least understood and most complex issues in the field of learning disabilities. Among the many variables that influence mathematical ability are (1) psychological factors, such as cognitive style and intellectual attributes; (2) educational effects of appropriate and inappropriate instructional practices and curriculum patterns; (3) personality factors that influence learning styles and performance capabilities; and (4) the individual neuropsychological pattern or developmental status.

The psychological approach integrates two broad theories of mathematical abilities: (1) the structure of intellect and factor-analytic concepts (Guilford, 1956; Spearman, 1927; Thurstone, 1938) and (2) information processing, strategy utilization, and other aspects of a cognitive psychology perspective (Lloyd, Saltzman, & Kauffman, 1981; Reid & Hresko, 1981). The educational approach views mathematics as a set of knowledge and skills that are acquired through learning and experience (Kosc, in press). Specialists in mathematics,

172 however, tend to approach the problem of failure from the point of instruction and curriculum, whereas special educators tend to explain performance in terms of learner differences (Cawley, 1978). The personality approach, part of neuropsychologists' concerns for some 40 years, focuses on personality differences as the source of variation in mathematical performance. In some instances, these personality factors may be affected by neurological impairments (Lezak, 1976; Schultze, 1965).

The neuropsychological approach stresses the relationship between neurological factors and behavior in dealing with mathematical notions, concepts, relationships, and problem solving. One major neuropsychological approach focuses on the pathological states, features, processes, and functions of persons who have suffered some form of neurological trauma. The second approach examines neuropsychological status from a developmental perspective and focuses on factors such as perception and hemispheric lateralization.

To date, neuropsychology has contributed minimally to understanding mathematics and to mathematics instruction. It is a young discipline that has focused its efforts on problems other than those related to mathematical disabilities. One thing, however, is clear: from the neuropsychological point of view, mathematical disabilities constitute one complex component of the symbolic or symbolic–communicative functions that form the background of communications through different symbol systems. (Among these symbol systems, the most frequently used is the system of spoken and written language.) These symbols consist of spoken and written words and phrases; mathematical symbols, such as numerals, signs, and notations; musical symbols, such as tones, melodies, or written notes; and kinesthetic symbols, such as gestures, mime, and pantomime.

## A HISTORICAL PERSPECTIVE ON BRAIN-BEHAVIOR RELATIONS

Because of the primary use of numerals for decoding and encoding mathematical concepts and relationships, it is fully understandable that the history of interest in mathematical ability disorders started with research in the field of aphasia as a postlesional disorder of spoken language communication. Broca carried on this research in a neurological, clinical setting, with his subjects being primarily soldiers who had received gunshot wounds during World War I.

A second approach influenced mainly by Penfield was directed toward mapping the cortical areas by stimulating different areas of the brain cortex during surgery. The response characteristics of each stimulation were determined from the verbal responses of the patients, who were conscious during the procedure. A third approach experimented with animals, recording with minute electrodes the altered firing rate of individual nerves in the cortex and destroying specific areas of the brain to observe the subsequent changes in behavior.

### Localization studies

These neurological and neurosurgical efforts gave rise to a basic set of relations between cortical areas and functions: It was determined that the cortical lobe in the rear of the cortex mediates vision, the rear central cortex mediates skin and muscle senses, part of the temporal lobes mediates hearing, the front central cortex mediates motor control, and Wernicke's area and Broca's area mediate the comprehension and synthesis, respectively, of speech. Relatively large areas of the cortex are neither activated by sensory stimuli nor involved in directing motor activity. These regions, including those called association areas, were found to be involved in the detailed processing of sensory inputs, in the planning of motor actions, and perhaps in purely mental functions (Lassen, Ingvar, & Skinhoj, 1978).

Comparable efforts were made to locate the centers of mathematical thinking. The early findings were products of studies in the field of aphasia in which the loss of mathematics functions were referred to as *acalculia* (Gerstmann, 1924; Henschen, 1920). The majority of researchers dealing with acalculia have localized its center in the parietal lobes (Hécaen, Angelergues, & Houiller, 1961; Krampf, 1937; Poetzl, 1928). Some authors have claimed that the center for mathematical activities must be in either the left occipital lobe (Kleist, 1934; Lewandowsky & Stadlmann, 1908) or in the frontal lobes (Pick, 1913, cited in Head, 1926). Recently, Luria extensively discussed disturbances in arithmetical operations and the syndrome of acalculia (Luria, 1980; see section entitled, "Disturbances with lesions of the occipital and occipitoparietal regions").

When acalculia is considered as the complete loss of mathematical abilities and other kinds of disorders as partial losses, it is possible to distinguish among several different location centers in the cerebral cortex. The interested reader is directed to Levy (1979) for a summary of the relevant findings. Luria (1980) discussed the relationships between mathematical disabilities and neurological dysfunction. His reexamination of the concepts of function and localization suggests that earlier commitments to localization theories

*Luria's reexamination of the concepts of function and localization suggests that earlier commitments to localization theories were overestimated.*

were overestimated. Recent findings are in opposition to the narrow localization interpretation of the relationships between brain functioning and behavior. Complex mental functions such as conceptualization and problem solving cannot be considered as the result of localized areas in the cerebral cortex. More likely, these functions are the result or the activity of the entire brain, though even this position tends to be extreme.

### Relating studies to children

Much historical evidence was acquired on adult populations and related by analogy to child populations whose primary concerns were with perceptual, perceptual-motor, and attentional problems (Strauss & Kephart, 1955; Strauss & Lehtinen, 1947). Age, however, seems to be an important consideration. Barroso (1976) noted the importance of chronological age as an indicator of functional recovery from neurological trauma. The emerging picture suggests that prior to age 10, either some but not all functions have been lateralized or lateralization has not taken place. Noticeably lacking is comprehensive evidence of the similarities and differences among normal and pathological populations across age levels and levels of severity.

Wedell (1975) pointed out that Strauss and Lehtinen (1947) placed an increasing amount of weight on findings of specific cognitive deficits as evidence of brain damage in children, ultimately reaching a point where they regarded these deficits as evidence in their own right of brain injury. They were thus led to a circular argument in which the symptoms associated with brain injury were in themselves used as evidence of it.

In this connection, Strauss and his coworkers introduced the term minimal brain damage, or minimal brain injury, which was later replaced by the term minimal brain dysfunction (MBD). The term gained wide-

173

spread use in identifying and labeling children with developmental disabilities of different kinds, structural and functional. These disabilities were used as indicators of brain injury, although no direct evidence was provided. Specific dysfunctions were inferred from behavioral and other developmental discrepancies, especially in the cognitive sphere.

The influence of Strauss and his coworkers led to a widespread application of the concept of MBD in educational areas, especially learning disorders or learning disabilities (Helmuth, 1965, 1966, 1968; Kass & Myklebust, 1969; Senf, 1973; Wedell, 1975).

Orton (1937) concentrated on children with reading and writing disorders, which he attributed to a language deficit caused by a failure in the establishment of cerebral dominance. Orton's concepts were later criticized by Zangwill (1960), who took the position that the relationship between hand preference, cerebral dominance, and cerebral localization and spoken and written language were much more complicated than Orton thought. Delacato (1963) associated MBD with an inappropriate development of lateral preference and developed a treatment program that concentrated on the establishment of symmetrical patterns of motor skill development (e.g., alternating movements of the arms and legs in crawling). Comparable motor training activities aimed at modifying neurological functioning have also been advocated by others (Ayres, 1968; Cruickshank, 1961; Frostig & Horne, 1964; Getman, 1961).

All these theories and related training programs have been severely criticized by the American Academy of Cerebral Palsy (Wedell, 1975) and by other associations (Senf, 1973) because of their oversimplification of the character of brain functioning and its correlates to behavior. These relationships are very complicated and difficult to understand especially when one deals with very slight and neurologically unidentifiable symptomatology—particularly in children. According to Wedell (1975, p. 63), one problem in relating much of this work to children is that "ultimately all behavior has a neurophysiological base and that deficits in behavioral and intellectual functioning must in some way be a reflection of underlying organic dysfunction. However, the present state of our knowledge hardly justifies our regarding such an association at other than a hypothetical level."

## CONTEMPORARY THEORIES OF BRAIN-BEHAVIOR RELATIONS

Contemporary theories of brain-behavior relations regard the higher mental processes of speaking, reading, writing, calculating, and thinking as complex functional systems of the brain. Such systems represent a unified organization of working zones, each of which performs its role as part of a complex system in which different and distinct areas of the brain work together (Luria, 1980). This position, which rejects the narrow localization theory and replaces it with a theory of brain activity as a variably structured complex system, has been recently supported in new experimental approaches to the study of brain mechanisms. In particular, strong support comes from Lassen et al.'s (1978) observations of the changes in the amount of blood flowing in different areas of the human cerebral cortex, which reflect changes in the activity of these areas. These changes were graphically recorded with the aid of a radioactive isotope on computer-generated images.

Luria (1973) suggested three basic functional units of the brain: (1) the unit for regulating tone or alertness; (2) the unit for obtaining, processing, and storing information; and (3) the unit for programming, regulating, and verifying mental activity. Each of these units has a hierarchical structure consisting of at least three cortical zones—the prima-

*Brain units are regarded as an interacting whole working in concert to perform mental processes such as the manipulation of mathematical symbols.*

ry, secondary, and tertiary. The relationships among these three zones constantly change during ontogenesis. Brain units are regarded as an interacting whole working in concert to perform mental processes such as the manipulation of mathematical symbols, especially in computation.

Brown (1976) lists four levels of cognitive organization during ontogenesis: (1) the sensorimotor level, (2) the limbic–presentational level, (3) the cortical–representational level, and (4) the symbolic level. The interrelationships among these, arbitrary though they may be, are established as phases in a continuously unfolding pattern.

### The role of cerebral hemispheres

It is very important to take into consideration the role that the cerebral hemispheres play in processing. The new findings in this direction show that "in about 98% of right-handed persons and in about 66% of left-handed persons, the left hemisphere is specialized for analytic, logical thinking in both verbal and numerical operations" (Wittrock, quoted by Battista, 1980, p. 54). Language and the analyses of stimuli are processed in the left hemisphere. For these same groups of people, the right hemisphere predominates for spatial tasks, artistic endeavors, crafts, body image, and recognition of faces; it seems specialized for holistic thinking. The right hemisphere processes information more diffusely than does the left, integrating many simultaneous inputs at one time (Battista, 1980). However, complex thinking, especially of a problem-solving nature, is surely based on

a smooth integration of two hemispheric modes of thought (Wheatley, Frankland, Mitchell, & Kraft, 1978, p. 31).

Klein (1981) examined mathematics, reading, and hemispheric specialization in learning disabled and non–learning disabled children in the third grade. The results of this study indicated: (1) there were no differences between learning disabled and non–learning disabled children in mathematics achievement as measured by the Wide Range Achievement Test (WRAT); (2) non–learning disabled children performed significantly higher in reading as measured by the WRAT; (3) there was a significant left-hand advantage (right hemisphere advantage) for dichaptically presented spatial stimuli in the non–learning disabled sample; but (4) there was no significant advantage for either hand (hemisphere) in the learning disabled sample. Correlational analyses indicated that the degree of right hemispheric specialization is positively correlated with reading achievement in non–learning disabled children. Specialization seemed to distinguish learning disabled from non–learning disabled children at this age level.

Lezak (1976) described the differential effects of brain injury on performance. She pointed out the role of left hemispheric lateralization in verbal functions and the general disorders of communication associated with left hemispheric insult. Some conditions affect calculation per se, whereas others affect the ability to manipulate numbers in spatial relationships. Lezak described the case of a person who gave correct answers to relatively complex multiplication tasks but when given written tasks involving addition, could not integrate the sum of the left-hand column with that of the right-hand column. This disability, spatial dyscalculia, can mislead the diagnostician and teacher.

It is important therefore that one distinguishes between (1) those who can calculate

176

i.e., understand the processes) but in whom other factors result in incorrect responses, (2) those who can calculate but who calculate incorrectly, (3) those who cannot calculate, and (4) those who do not know when to calculate or which calculation to use.

### The effects of lesions

According to Luria (1973, p. 335) "an arithmetical problem always consists of a goal, the statement of the problem in the form of a question to which no ready answer is available, and the conditions from which a scheme for the solution can be prepared by analysis. Thus a strategy leading to the required solution can be decided." This strategy, expressed in words as a hypothesis, initiates a search for the individual operations that will be used to obtain the necessary results. The process of solution ends with a comparison between the method used and the result obtained on the one hand and the questions and the conditions of the problem on the other hand.

Luria described several kinds of mathematical problems from the simplest to the most complex. He noted several types of changes in processes when conditions connected with the work of particular brain systems were removed. He concluded that neuropsychological analysis of arithmetical problem solving demonstrates profound differences in patterns of disorders.

Thus the impairment of thinking involved with the solution of a problem in arithmetic may be caused by a dysfunction in different parts of the functional system involved with the complex mental process. Depending on which factor is impaired, the inability to solve problems manifests itself in different ways (Callahan and Glennon, 1975). Patients suffering lesions located in the left temporal regions of the brain, which disturbs audio-verbal memory, are unable to retain the conditions of the problem and to involve the necessary components in its solution. On the other hand,

lesions impairing the left parietal–occipital region are manifested as an inability to find the appropriate solution to the problem.

Patients with lesions in this area may never lose sight of the goal, may be aware of the discrete elements of the problem, and may be active in attempts to find a solution. However, their system of logical connections necessary to solve the problem is disrupted and, consequently, they are unable to solve the problem. Finally, patients who suffer lesions in the frontal lobes are not able to perceive the problem as a problem and accordingly they fail to attempt the problem. (For more detailed information on this topic, see Luria, 1980; Christensen, 1974.)

## MATHEMATICAL PROBLEMS IN CHILDREN

The deficits in the symbolic–communicative functions of learning disabled children are manifest in the following systems:

1. the system of spoken and written language; speaking, reading, and writing words and sentences; neurologically referred to as *phasia;*
2. the system of mathematical functions; neurologically referred to as *calculia;*
3. the system of musical functions; neurologically referred to as *musia;*
4. the system of kinesthetic functions shown in the form of nonverbal communications by means of gestures, mime, and pantomime; systems of kinesthetic function are not commonly included in the system of symbolic–communicative functions by neurologists, but this placement is justifiable and necessary (see e.g., Kosc, 1980).

The mastery of spoken language is the foundation for the acquisition and manipulation of the graphic system and other symbolic–communicative systems (e.g., mathematics). These systems become increasingly more

*The mastery of spoken language is the foundation for the acquisition and manipulation of the graphic system and other symbolic-communicative systems.*

automated and internalized, thus making it possible to transcode (Weigl, 1974, 1975) from one symbolic system to another or from one form of representation to another. One symbolic system is generally accompanied by some form of activity related to other symbolic systems. For instance, speaking always has its musical aspects (e.g., prosody, intonation, rhythm).

It is important in researchers' experimental approaches to diagnosis and correction to take into account the localization of the blockage. Hypotheses must be derived from the forms and content of the child's production. Therefore the application of a neuropsychological function analysis (Kosc, 1980; Luria, 1973; Seron, 1975) is valuable.

## Terminology

Many terms have no specific denotations and are used differentially. Uncertainty about terminology is confusing and minimizes the effectiveness of communication among professional workers. Prior to directing attention to the problems of diagnosis, it is appropriate to define selected terminology:

- *knowledge*—results of learning; facts;
- *aptitudes, skills*—results of training; actions;
- *abilities*—psychological prerequisites to acquiring knowledge and skills;
- *faculties, competencies, capacities, capabilities, potentialities*—organic, neural, or neurological prerequisites to the development of abilities and thus also of knowledge and skills;
- *functions*—organic prerequisites to the

processing of abilities and aptitudes and to applying knowledge and skills (Kosc, 1974, 1980).

The terms *damage* or *injury* are reserved for indicating organic defects; *disorder* and *disturbance* indicate serious and slight deviation from the normal status, respectively. From the standpoint of neuropsychology, disorders or disturbances of functions are to be terminologically distinguished in the following way:

- *normofunction*—level functioning suitable to the individual and/or statistical norm;
- *hyperfunction*—highly above-average level of functioning (e.g., hypermnesia, hyperkinesis);
- *asthenofunction*—socially conditioned (by deprivation of any kind), under-average global levels of functioning of a particular function (legasthenia, graphasthenia, calculasthenia, etc.);
- *hypofunction*—organically caused, moderately lower-than-average global levels of function in the context of a broader functional system (hypomnesia, hypocalculia, etc.);
- *oligofunction*—organically caused, serious disorder or defect of functioning in a broader functional system (oligophrenia, oligocalculia in the frame of the mental defect, etc.);
- *dysfunction*—organically caused, moderate or more serious functional system disturbance, such that some subfunctions (factors) are at lower levels than others; this leads to marked disintegration of functioning in the system involved (dyslexia, dysgraphia, dyscalculia, dysmusia, etc.);
- *afunction*—loss or decline of functioning in a global functional system (aphasia, alexia, agraphia, acalculia, amusia, etc.);
- *parafunction*—qualitative disturbance (disturbance of the content of function-

ing), as can be observed in psychological disturbances (paramnesia, paracalculia, etc.).

### Developmental dyscalculia

When diagnosing children's problems in mathematics performance, only one of four types of functional disorders—asthenocalculia, hypocalculia, oligocalculia, or dyscalculia—is usually found. The first step is to determine the category into which the child falls. The neuropsychodiagnostic approach should be applied when it can be hypothesized that developmental dyscalculia is present.

According to Kosc (1974, p. 47),

developmental dyscalculia is a structural disorder of mathematical abilities which has its origin in a genetic or congenital disorder of those parts (functional systems) of the brain that are the direct anatomico-physiological substrate of the maturation of the mathematical abilities adequate to age, without a simultaneous disorder of general mental functions.

Developmental dyscalculia has been classified (Kosc, 1974) as follows:

- *practognostic*—characterized by a significantly low level of manipulation with real or pictorial objects (fingers, balls, cubes, staffs, etc.);
- *verbal*—manifested by a disturbed ability to verbally designate mathematical terms and relations (naming numbers of things, digits, numerals, operational symbols, and mathematical operations);
- *lexical*—also called *numerical dyslexia;* manifested by a disability in reading mathematical symbols (digits, numbers, operational signs, and written mathematical operations);
- *graphical*—also called *numerical dysgraphia;* characterized by disturbed manipulation of mathematical symbol systems in writing (analogous to *lexical dyscalculia*);
- *operational*—manifested by a distur-

bance in carrying out mathematical operations or in applying appropriate operational algorithms;
- *ideognostical*—manifested primarily by a disability in understanding mathematical ideas and relations and thus in doing mental calculation.

### Assessment

According to Christensen (1974), the notion of number always rests, to a greater or lesser extent, on some system of coordinates, which may be linear in character or arranged in a tabular system. During addition (or the symmetrical but opposite operation of subtraction) one always operates within a definite internal spatial field. Initially, the operation is performed stage by stage, breaking up the numbers and subsequently adding the remainder while maintaining the correct spatial orientation of the operation. Not until later stages of learning do these operations take on a shortened, direct character. Ultimately, the experienced person performs them automatically. One characteristic of mathematical operations, including multiplication and division, is that they can acquire a verbal character and rest on established verbal stereotypes.

Thus individual assessment addresses the following components:

- comprehension of number structure—understanding, writing, and recognizing figures; numerical differences;
- arithmetical operations—simple automatized calculations, complex arithmetical operations, arithmetical signs, serial arithmetical operations, and series of consecutive arithmetical operations.

(More detailed information on these assessments can be found in Christensen, 1974.)

Assessment should represent as comprehensive a characterization of the client as possible. Kinsbourne (1971) probed extensively into the functioning of the individual, once a reliable deficit had been observed. Items were presented in different ways through the use of alternative modes. This procedure provides insight into the nature of the psychological deficit and the neurological status of the individual.

Taking into consideration that mathematical abilities constitute one complex component of the symbolic–communicative functions, the following are recommended:

1. Determine if the disturbances in mathematical abilities are isolated or combined with disturbances in other symbolic–communicative functions and whether they are primary or secondary in character (Kosc, 1974).
2. Determine the structure of the mathematical abilities and what other factors (e.g., verbal, numerical, reasoning, memory) interrelate to form patterns of strengths and weaknesses (Witryol & Boly, 1962); this form of analysis will help to differentiate between verbal, spatial, reasoning, and other types of dyscalculia.
3. Determine the stage of development of the mathematical abilities structure (i.e., from the practognostical to the ideognostical stages; see Kosc, 1974, for details).
4. Specify the location of the blockage in the functional arc in all symbolic–communicative functions, especially in the mathematical ones (see Kosc, in press).
5. Specify the mechanisms the child uses in working different types of transcodings from one system of symbols to another or from one form of its representation to another (see Kosc, 1980).
6. In all the above-mentioned forms of diagnostic analyses, it is necessary to examine both the achievement and the process of mathematical manipulation used by the individual (Luria, 1966; 1973; Small, 1973). Examining the strategies the child uses in solving problems is particularly important when analyzing

*It is necessary to examine both the achievement and the process of mathematical manipulation used by the individual.*

incorrect responses. It is also important to identify any compensatory strategies that the child uses (see Kosc, 1980). This process may be done through verbalization, writing, or drawing all the steps involved in the problem (Kosc, in press; Perron–Borelli & Perron, 1970; Rubinstějn, 1962).

7. Examine the effects of special assistance already given to the child, particularly in the crucial phases of problem solving. Only after the child has tried unsuccessfully to utilize all appropriate forms of help is it possible to hypothesize that the particular blockage is an endogenous one.
8. Establish hypotheses as to which structures of the functional system of the brain are responsible for the specific type of dyscalculia or other disorder that is impairing performance (Luria, 1973; Christensen, 1974).
9. Study the personality of the individual to determine general and mathematical perspectives in learning (Lee, 1955; Wrigley, 1958).
10. Develop appropriate starting points and a sequence for treatment. Stimulate knowledge, skills, and abilities and use a student's strengths to compensate for blocked functions and subfunctions.

### Treatment

Dyscalculic children, estimated to be about 6% of the population with normal intelligence, present a special treatment problem. Kosc (1977), and Kumorovitzová and Kosc (1980) make the following suggestions:

180

1. The first and basic starting point for the appropriate correction of disturbances of mathematical functions in dyscalculic children is a detailed diagnosis.

2. Researchers generally assume that because of disturbed brain functions, dyscalculic children are not capable of adequate development and that the correction must thus be oriented toward the search for and the acquisition and use of compensatory functions; that is, practitioners must use those structures of mathematical abilities and other symbolic–communicative functions that are relatively well preserved, developed, or functioning.

3. The major principle of correction is cumulative learning. The basis for the treatment of dyscalculic children lies in a systematic orientation toward the convenient use of well-preserved, developed, and functioning partial abilities for the compensation of those that are obviously retarded.

4. Instruction must be individualized. Every dyscalculic child differs not only with regard to the actual state of knowledge and skills and the concrete level and structure of mathematical abilities (and of symbolic–communicative functions in general), but also with regard to the processes of functioning and ways of acquiring mechanisms of compensation at various levels and in various phases of the correction procedure. It is consequently inadequate to apply preestablished programs for the correction of dyscalculic children, especially when such programs are directed only toward the stimulation of their sensory or motor functioning. It is important to have many different illustrative devices available for the corrective work and to vary the ways of manipulating them. It is appropriate to leave the child some freedom of choice in using materials.

5. The successful treatment of the dyscalculic child is not mechanistic but creative, not only from the point of view of the therapist, but also from the perspective of the child. In creative exploration lies the guarantee for the presence and maintenance of the child's motivation for learning in general and for learning mathematics in particular. Although the children may progress toward knowledge and skills very slowly, exploration provides automatic feedback to convince them of their progress.

6. With the truly dyscalculic child, the goal of treatment is not and cannot be a full normalization of the child's knowledge and skills. Instead, the goal is gradual adaptation to the demands of school and life, with expectations determined by the level of seriousness of the disorder. The goal of treatment of the dyscalculic child, in short, is to achieve the child's maximal mathematical functioning.

The accomplishment of these relative goals requires considerable knowledge and experience with treating dyscalculic children and children with other symbolic–communicative dysfunctions. The teacher must take a creative approach to the specific characteristics of each individual child, including appropriate concern for the child's transitory states of mind. Alleviation of the problems of dyscalculic children is a difficult, complicated, but urgent task.

## NEEDED RESEARCH

For the future development of knowledge of and practices regarding dyscalculic children, it seems necessary:

1. to search systematically for more detailed information about the relationships between the brain and behavior (especially when dealing with mathematics learning) in normal as well as seriously disturbed development;

2. to develop a more sophisticated and effective methodology to diagnose abnormal states, personality features, and processes related to the mathematical (not only arithmetical) symbol system, and especially to solving gradually more and more complicated problems;

3. to search for more effective teaching methods, both for normal children and for the abnormally developing ones;

methods of individual and group instruction must respect individual approaches to learning and manipulating symbol systems, especially the mathematical system.

This is only a beginning. From interdisciplinary team efforts will come the development, understanding, and implementation of effective diagnostic and treatment programs for children with dyscalculia.

## REFERENCES

Ayres, A.J. Sensory integrative processes and neuropsychological learning disabilities. In J. Helmuth (Ed.), *Learning disorders* (Vol. 3). Seattle: Special Child Publications, 1968.

Barroso, F. Hemispheric asymmetry of function in children. In R.W. Rieber (Ed.), *The neuropsychology of language.* New York: Plenum Press, 1976.

Battista, M. Interrelationships between problem solving ability, right-left hemisphere processing facility and mathematics learning. *Focus on Learning Problems in Mathematics,* 1980, *2,* 53–60.

Brown, J. Consciousness and pathology of language. In R.W. Rieber (Ed.), *The neuropsychology of language.* New York: Plenum Press, 1976.

Callahan, L.G. & Glennon, V.J. Elementary school mathematics: A guide to current research, 4th ed. Washington, D.C.: Association for Supervision and Curriculum Development, 1975.

Cawley, J.F. An instructional design in secondary school mathematics for learning disabled students. In L. Mann, L. Goodman, & L. Wiederholt (Eds.), *Learning disabled adolescent,* Boston: Houghton Mifflin Co., 1978.

Christensen, A.L. *Luria's neuropsychological investigation.* Copenhagen: Munksgaard, 1974.

Cruickshank, W.A. *A teaching method for brain-injured and hyperactive children.* Syracuse, N.Y.: Syracuse University Press, 1961.

Delacato, C.H. The diagnosis and treatment of speech and reading problems. Springfield, Ill.: Charles C. Thomas, 1963.

Frostig, M. & Horne, D. *The Frostig program for the development of visual perception.* Chicago: Follet Educational Corp., 1964.

Gerstmann, J. Fingeragnosie: Eine unbeschriebene Störung der Orientierung am eigenen Körper. *Wiener Klinische Wochenschrift,* 1924, 37, 1010–1012.

Getman, G.N. Visual success in reading success. *Journal of the California Optometric Association,* 1961, *29,* 1–4.

Guilford, J.P. The structure of intellect. *Psychological Bulletin,* 1956, 53, 267–293.

Head, H. *Aphasia and kindred disorders of speech.* New York: Macmillan, 1926.

Hécaen, H., Angelergues, R., & Houiller, S. Les variétés cliniques des acalculies au course des lésions retrorolandiques: Approche statistique du problème. *Revue Neurologique,* 1961, *105,* 85–103.

Helmuth, J. (Ed.). *Learning disorders.* Seattle: Special Child Publications (Vol. I, 1965; Vol. II, 1966; Vol. III, 1968).

Henschen, S.E. Klinische und anatomische Beiträge zur Pathologie des Gehirns (Vol. V). Über Aphasie, Amusie und Akalkulie, Stockholm, 1920.

Kass, C.E., & Myklebust, H.R. Learning disability: An educational definition. *Journal of Learning Disabilities,* 1969, *2,* 38–40.

Kinsbourne, M. Cognitive deficit: Experimental analysis. In J. McGaugh (Ed.), *Psychobiology.* New York: Academic Press, 1971.

Klein, S. Comparison of reading, mathematics and hemispheric specialization among learning disabled and nondisabled children (tentative title). Dissertation in progress, University of Conn., 1981.

Kleist, K. *Gehirnpathologie.* Leipzig: J.A. Barth, 1934.

Košč, L. Developmental dyscalculia. *Journal of Learning Disabilities,* 1974, 7, 164–177.

Košč, L. Experiences with the correction of dysfunctions of children's mathematical ability. In *International Seminar on Teaching Children with Difficulties in Mathematics.* Budapest: Országos Pedagógiai Intézet, 1977.

Košč, L. Psychologické aspekty problematiky symbolických funkcií z hľadiska teórie informácie. In L. Košč et al. (Eds.), *Vybrané state z vývinovej psychológie a*

182

*patopsychológie.* Bratislava: Slovenské pedagogické nakladateľstvo, 1980, 139–165.

Košč, L. Mathematical abilities and disabilities as the complex components of some broader psychological systems. *Focus on Learning Problems in Mathematics,* in press, 3.

Krampf, E. Über Akalkulie. *Archives Suisses de Neurologie et Psychologie,* 1937, 39, 330–334.

Kumorovitzová, M., & Košč, L. Skúsenosti s korektívnym tréningom pri dysfunkciách v oblasti matematických schopností detí. In L. Kosc et al. (Eds.), *Vybrané state z vývinovej psychológie a patopsychológie.* Bratislava: Slovenské pedagogické nakladateľstvo, 1980, 166–183.

Lassen, N.A., Ingvar, D.H., & Skinhoj, E. Brain function and blood flow. *Scientific American,* 1978, 239, 62–71 (offprint pp. 1–11).

Lee, D.M. A study of specific ability and achievement in mathematics. *British Journal of Educational Psychology,* 1955, 25, 178–189.

Levy, M.K. Dyscalculia: Critical analysis and future directions. *Focus on Learning Problems in Mathematics,* 1979, 1, 31–41.

Lewandowsky, M., & Stadlmann, E. Über einen bemerkenswerten Fall von Hirnblutung und über Rechenstörungen bei Herderkrankungen des Gehirns. *Zeitschrift fur Psychologie und Neurologie,* 1908, 11, 249–265.

Lezak, M.D. *Neuropsychological assessment.* New York: Oxford University Press, 1976.

Lloyd, J., Saltzman, N., & Kauffman, J. Predictable generalization in academic learning as a result of preskills and strategy training. *Learning Disability Quarterly* 1981, 4, 203–216.

Luria, A.R. *Higher cortical functions in man.* New York: Basic Books, 1966.

Luria, A.R. *The working brain: An introduction to neuropsychology.* New York: Penguin Books, 1973.

Luria, A.R. *Higher cortical functions in man* 2nd ed. New York: Basic Books, 1980.

Orton, S. *Reading, writing, and speech problems in children.* New York: Norton, 1937.

Perron-Borelli, M., & Perron, R. L'examen psychologique de l'enfant. Paris: Press Université de France, 1970.

Poetzl, O. Die Aphasielehre von Standpunkte der klinischen Psychiatrie, I. Bd.: Die optisch-agnostische Störungen. Leipzig: F. Deuticke, 1928, 351–358.

Reid, D.K., & Hresko, W. *A cognitive approach to learning disabilities.* New York: McGraw-Hill, 1981.

Rubinštejn, S.J. *Metodiki experimentalnoj patopsichologiji.* Moscow: Medicina, 1962.

Schultze, H.A.F. *Die klinische Analyse der kombinierten Störungen* (Aphasie, Agnosie, Apraxie). Leipzig: Barth, 1965.

Senf, G.M. Learning disabilities. *Journal of Pediatric Clinics of North America,* 1973, 20, 607–640.

Seron, X. Neuropsychologie et rééducation fonctionelle. *Revue Suisse de psychologie Pure et Appliquée,* 1975, 34, 327–345.

Small, L. *Neuropsychodiagnosis in psychotherapy.* New York: Brunner/Mazel, 1973.

Spearman, C. *The abilities of man.* London: Macmillan, 1927.

Strauss, A., & Kephart, N.C. *Psychopathology and education of the brain-injured child* (Vol. II). New York: Grune & Stratton, 1955.

Strauss, A.A., & Lehtinen, L.E. *Psychopathology and education of the brain-injured child* (Vol. I). New York: Grune & Stratton, 1947.

Thurstone, L.L. *Primary mental abilities.* Chicago: Science Research Associates, 1938.

Wedell, K. Specific learning disabilities. In K. Wedell (Ed.), *Orientation in special education.* New York: Wiley, 1975.

Weigl, E. Neuropsychological experiments on transcoding between spoken and written language structures. *Brain and Language,* 1974, 1, 227–240.

Weigl, E. Neuropsychological approach to the problem of transcoding. *Linguistics,* 1975, 7, 105–135.

Wheatley, G., Frankland, R., Mitchell, R., & Kraft, R. Hemispheric specialization and cognitive development: Implications for mathematics education. *Journal of Research in Mathematics Education,* 1978, 9, 20–32.

Witryol, A.G., & Boly, F.L. Positive diagnosis in personality counseling of college students. In J.F. McGowan & L.D. Schmidt (Eds.), *Counseling: Readings in theory and practice.* New York: Holt, Rinehart & Winston, 1962.

Wrigley, J. The factorial nature of ability in elementary mathematics. *British Journal of Educational Psychology,* 1958, 28. 61–78.

Zangwill, O.L. *Cerebral dominance and its relation to psychological function.* London: Oliver & Boyd, 1960.

# Assessment of Severely and Profoundly Handicapped Individuals

*Susan Johnsen Dollar*
*Educational Consultant*
*Austin, Texas*

*Carol Brooks, M.S.Ed.*
*University of Kentucky*
*Lexington, Kentucky*

ONE OF THE SMALLEST defined subgroups in special education is that of severely and profoundly handicapped (SPH) individuals. Depending on the type of handicapping condition considered, prevalence estimates have ranged between 0.1% and 0.9% of the general population (Kauffman & Payne, 1975; Mercer, 1975). For many years SPH children often received little more than custodial care owing to their low incidence and a prevailing attitude among some professionals of their ineducability (Haring & Pious, 1976). With the concerns of the 1960s toward individual constitutional rights, the 1970s litigation decisions toward a zero-reject educational model, and the passage of subsequent legislation, public and professional views began to change. PL 94-142 set service priorities for children with the "most severe handicaps within each disability area" receiving an "inadequate education." This legislative mandate raised im-

184 portant questions related to the area of assessment:

- What criteria should be used in identifying children with the most severe handicaps?
- What criteria should be used in assessing the adequacy of SPH programs?
- How might educational assessment of SPH children differ from other special educational populations?

This article addresses each of these assessment issues.

## ASSESSMENT FOR IDENTIFICATION

To ensure that children with the most severe handicaps received appropriate services, criteria for identification needed to be developed. The Bureau of Education for the Handicapped (1974) described this population by publishing the following definition:

Severely handicapped children are those who because of the intensity of their physical, mental, or emotional problems, need educational, social, psychological, and medical services beyond those which are traditionally offered by regular and special education programs, in order to maximize participation in society and self-fulfillment. Such severely handicapped children may possess severe language or perceptual-cognitive deprivations and evidence a number of abnormal behaviors including failure to attend to even the most pronounced stimuli, self-mutilation, manifestations of durable and intense temper tantrums, and the absence of even the most rudimentary forms of verbal control. They may also have extremely fragile physiological conditions.

This definition delineates three essential characteristics in identifying SPH children: (a) they must have a "severe" or "intense" handicap; (b) they need an educational program requiring greater resources than are normally provided by traditional programs; and (c) they need programs that focus on skills necessary for greater independent functioning and "self-fulfillment." Because the handicap may occur in the physical, mental, or emotional areas, the SPH population may include children with such diverse labels as autistic, cerebral palsied, deaf-blind, mentally retarded, multiply handicapped, schizophrenic, and learning disabled.

### Determining Severity

Numerous attempts have been made by universities, state departments, and local school systems to define the SPH population. While current definitions vary in the use of general or behavioral terms, all include a reference to the degree of the handicapping condition (e.g., "extremely brittle," "intense," "serious," "severe," "profound"). The nature of norm-referenced classification systems required special educators to address the problem of differentiating the severely handicapped from other special education groups. The significant question became: How severe is severe?

The most frequently used criterion for severity is performance four standard deviations or more below the mean (Bricker, Dubose, Alberte, Berkler, Filler, Gast, Holder, Jens, Kauffman, Sears, & Snell,

1978). Problems with this criterion relate to the norm group used and the standardization process itself. First, SPH children are not included or are not adequately represented in most norming samples. Lack of inclusion is often due to the small number of SPH children available. For this reason, most test manuals fail to describe norms or include many items below the third or fourth standard deviation, where most SPH children perform. Second, the severely and profoundly handicapped population is extremely heterogeneous. Even if a representative sample for each subgroup were included, the small number would not be appropriate for standardization purposes. Third, standardized tests require controlled conditions for any valid comparison. Again, the diversity among SPH children and the severity of their handicaps often require a modification of the test instrument itself (i.e., many SPH children lack the necessary communication skills required by most tests).

Aware of the lack of "precision" of most norm-referenced tests, Bricker and Iacino (1977) have used consensus between observers in determining severity. They have found "considerable agreement" in "what constitutes a significant deficiency or impairment" (p. 168).

---

*SPH children are not included or are not adequately represented in most norming samples. . . often due to the small number of SPH children available.*

---

Other professionals have focused on the rate at which new behaviors are acquired as a better indicator of a "severe" deficiency (McKenzie, Hill, Sousie, York, & Baker, 1977). In this model a minimum set of objectives for each developmental year is specified. A minimum rate line is then determined by the number of objectives a child would need to achieve each year to make normal progress. If a child "falls below the minimum rate line for achievement of the birth-to-two-year span of minimum objectives, s/he is eligible for SPH programs" (p. 101).

These latter approaches to identification (i.e., observer consensus and minimum rate) may be more valid and reliable for SPH children than norm-referenced tests. However, early identification is often facilitated by the SPH child's marked physical abnormalities or unresponsiveness to environmental stimuli. It may be more important to develop and use identification procedures that are easy to administer by available personnel to ensure the implementation of "wide-scale screening" and early intervention (Haring, 1976).

## Determining "Greater" Resources

The SPH child often presents a multiplicity of handicaps, requiring services beyond the "traditional" school program. Physicians, physical and occupational therapists, audiologists, psychologists, speech clinicians, social workers, and highly trained teachers are often needed to assess the child's current level of functioning and plan his or her educational program.

186      In addition, the SPH child needs these specialized services for longer periods of time than other children. Bricker and Iacino (1977) have described this type of needed intervention as "longitudinal" as opposed to "episodic." A less "severe" child may require only temporary medical assistance in controlling seizures or short-term physical therapy sessions in developing motor control while the SPH child will need continued assistance. Using this criterion, children who need an episodic intervention would not be eligible for services provided by an SPH program.

### Determining Areas for Programming

Given that SPH children have deficits equal to or greater than four standard deviations below the mean, they will need an educational program that focuses on skills leading to greater independent functioning (Brown, Nietupski, & Hamre-Nietupski, 1976). Sailor and Haring (1977) have described these skills as "basic" as opposed to "academic." Using this criterion, children who need academic instruction would not be referred to an SPH program.

In summary, children must meet three criteria to be eligible for SPH programs:

1. They must have a "severe" handicap. Severity may be determined by norm-referenced tests (a score four standard deviations or more below the mean), agreement between observers (Bricker & Iacino, 1977), or learning rate curves (McKenzie et al., 1977).

2. They need greater resources than normally provided within traditional programs. In addition, these resources are needed on a long-term basis (i.e., longitudinal intervention) (Bricker & Iacino, 1977).

3. They need basic skill development that will lead to greater independent functioning in society or to "self-fulfillment." Because the identification of SPH children is often facilitated by their marked abnormalities or unresponsiveness to environmental stimuli, screening procedures should be efficient and readily accessible to available professionals so that all SPH children receive services at as early an age as possible.

### ASSESSMENT FOR EDUCATIONAL PROGRAMMING

Besides identifying children eligible for service, the other major purpose of assessment is to provide the teacher with the information necessary for planning and evaluating each child's educational program. Assessment instruments used in educational programming should (a) be able to measure the child's current level of functioning so the teacher will know where to begin, (b) have items that are sequenced in a logical hierarchy so the teacher will know what to teach next, (c) describe the testing conditions in which the child performed at an optimal level so the teacher can create the optimum learning environment, and (d) identify criteria used for acceptable performance so the teacher will know when the student is ready to proceed to the next skill. Tests possessing these characteristics have been identified as the "cornerstone for systematic instruction," uniting "testing with teaching" (Dubose, 1978, p. 9).

The need for special educators to examine whether tests used with other special education populations are appropriate in planning and evaluating SPH programs was mentioned earlier. To evaluate these instruments and also provide programming information for the SPH child, professionals have focused on developing criteria for each of the following areas: item content, item sequence, assessment conditions, and mastery criteria.

## Item Content

Two criteria are generally used in determining content areas for SPH assessment and programming: basic behaviors and ultimate functioning. Basic behaviors are those that relate to areas producing greater independence (e.g., self-help, communication). The "criterion of ultimate functioning" means that the task must be one a child might encounter in the "natural" environment (Brown et al., 1976). Consequently item content should be ascertained by observing skills necessary for living and adapting within the immediate community. Any test that measures only academic behaviors would be inappropriate for the SPH population.

Sailor and Haring (1977) have identified the following functional domains from a developmental viewpoint: self-help, sensory-motor, communication, and social skills. Others have developed domains from a remedial or age-appropriate standpoint (Brown, Branston, Nietupski, Pumpian, Certo, & Gruenewald, 1979; Guess, Horner, Utley, Holvoet, Maxon, Tucker, & Warren, 1978). Their curricula include domestic living, vocational training, leisure and recreation time, and community functioning. In addition, competing behaviors (e.g., self-abuse or stereotypic behaviors) often must be eliminated first before the SPH child is ready to learn how to attend or respond to the task situation. Most tests developed and standardized with SPH populations assess these domain areas. Exceptions are tests that focus on a limited age span (i.e., infant scales) or a specific disability (e.g., visual efficiency).

### TEST VARIATIONS

Variations between tests tend to occur in (a) the number of behaviors or skills listed under each domain and (b) the organization of these domains. For example, the TARC System (Topeka Association for Retarded Citizens) (Sailor & Mix, 1975) contains 108 behavioral descriptions organized into four domains, which are further divided into 12 subdomains; the American Association on Mental Deficiency Adaptive Behavior Scale (ABS) (Nihira, Foster, Shellhaas, & Leland, 1974) contains approximately 315 behavioral descriptions, organized into two parts divided into 24 domains and 18 subdomains. The number of items is partly determined by whether the test is intended to be used for only screening or for a more comprehensive assessment (i.e., the more comprehensive the instrument, the more test items). In this manner, Sailor and Haring (1977) have described the TARC as a position I system (i.e., screening instrument) and the ABS as a position III system (i.e., comprehensive).

187

188    However, even within the same level systems there are differences. For example, the Behavioral Characteristics Progression (BCP) (Office of the Santa Cruz County Superintendent of Schools, 1973) and the ABS are both identified as level III systems. Yet the BCP contains 59 strands, whereas the ABS contains 24 domains. These differences are often due to the conceptualization of different domains or strands. Factor analytic studies of part I of the ABS have identified three domains from the original 11 subdomains (Nihira, 1978). The three new major domains included personal self-sufficiency, community self-sufficiency, and personal-social responsibility.

## TEACHER'S STANDPOINT

Because teachers often use tests in determining what to teach within the classroom situation, it may be important to view content organization from a teaching standpoint. Williams and Gotts (1977) have described the importance of teaching skills that are functionally related to one another to facilitate generalization. As opposed to teaching separate tasks for each situational area, a common skill is identified, taught, and generalized across task situations. For example, "taking pants off" is a skill that could be taught and generalized to both undressing and toileting situations. A test could be organized around basic operations (e.g., taking off, putting on, grasping) rather than situations (e.g., dressing, toileting). In selecting future item groupings, perhaps designers of tests for SPH children should consider these functional relationships between skill clusters.

## Item Sequence

Sailor and Haring (1977) have described the sequencing of test items as "done largely on the basis of some attention to normal developmental milestones and pure speculation" (p. 7). The "optimal" sequence has yet to be validated by research. For this reason, current item sequences vary between tests used with SPH populations. The order of items is generally determined in one or more of the following ways: (a) average age norms, (b) SPH norms, (c) degree of independence achieved, and (d) task analysis.

Developmentally determined sequences may not be appropriate in testing or teaching SPH children. For example, a severely cerebral-palsied child will not be able to learn all of the "normal" skills for walking, but may be able to learn how to move with adaptive equipment. Consequently some severely handicapped children never achieve all of the developmental milestones in an area in which they have a severe disability.

Even if an SPH child were physically able to perform certain developmental pinpoints, two other questions would need to be addressed. Is the pinpoint functionally relevant? Are developmental pinpoints able to discern changes or differences in performance? For example, a normal child between 13 and 15 months of age should be able to build a tower with two cubes (Bayley, 1968; Gesell, 1940; Sheridan, 1968; Slosson, 1964). However, owing to the lack of this task's relationship to independent living, it may not be a relevant one to teach or test. In addition, developmental pinpoints may discern changes for normal children but not for

SPH children. An SPH child may achieve only a few items in a given year. Enough items have to be present so that growth can be measured and greater reliability obtained.

## SEQUENCING ACCORDING TO DIFFICULTY

In addressing these problem areas, some test designers have arranged items in increasing order of difficulty for a specific SPH population (e.g., Camelot Behavioral Checklist, Foster, 1974). Difficulty is determined by the percentage of the SPH sample needing training on a particular item. The problem with this approach relates again to the heterogeneity of the SPH population. Given the low incidence and multiplicity of handicaps, homogeneous comparison groups are difficult to obtain.

## SEQUENCING ACCORDING TO INDEPENDENCE

Some tests have sequenced items according to the degree of independence achieved or the number of prompts needed for successful performance. This criterion for sequencing is often used in the self-help area. While this approach does relate to independent functioning, it may not consider variation in physical ability. These differences are sometimes mentioned in the test manual. In these cases the teacher or tester must adapt or omit the sequence on the basis of individual differences.

## SEQUENCING ACCORDING TO TASK ANALYSIS

Most educators of SPH children are now examining sequences based on their functional impact. "Everyday" tasks are analyzed from two standpoints: the prerequisite skills needed to perform the task and alternative ways of completing the same task. Task analysis is used to determine specific concepts and operations needed to perform a behavior. Using this approach, mastery of each subgoal leads the learner to mastery of the terminal goal. The terminal behavior is described and analyzed backward or forward, with subgoals incorporating each of the basic concepts and operations. Variations based upon physical differences are included in the sequence from an assessment of entry behaviors. Because of the complexity of most basic tasks, lattices have been developed to visually describe the interrelationships among various subcomponents (Smith & Snell, 1978).

Some tests have attempted to sequence items according to this task analytic approach but, because of time constraints, are often unable to provide the number and variation in responses required for a complex terminal behavior due to time constraints. Consequently most assessment devices provide only general guidelines or checklists for the teacher's use in planning more comprehensive programming for individual SPH children.

Test item sequences should meet at least two criteria: (a) the item sequence should relate to a functionally relevant behavior, and (b) the number of items included in the sequence should be sufficient for measuring change. Sailor and Haring (1977) have stated: "Education of the severely/multiply handicapped child is still awaiting the development of well-defined skill sequences across curricula domains. At this point much is up to the teacher's creative use of task analysis" (p. 8).

190    *Assessment Conditions*

Criteria for evaluating assessment conditions usually focus on three questions:

1. Does the condition elicit the "best" response?
2. Is the condition relevant to ultimate functioning?
3. Are condition characteristics systematically varied to ensure generalization?

Haring (1976) has pointed out that the child's best responses are more predictive of future performance. To elicit the "best" response, the Balthazar Scales of Adaptive Behavior (Balthazar, 1971) have listed different procedures for eliciting a specific behavior. If the child does not demonstrate the behavior when an opportunity arises, the observer provides materials or verbal reinforcers upon task completion. If these consequences do not strengthen the desired response, then the observer may provide additional cues or demonstrations before performing the task.

VARIATIONS IN TEST CONDITIONS

Like the Balthazar scale, many tests describe moving from "natural" to more "structured" situations in observing the child's responses. Conditions may be described in terms of location (class or home), persons involved in the assessment (parent, teachers, other professionals), material characteristics (visual, auditory, kinesthetic), the degree of child involvement (none to high), and consequences used (specific reinforcers). Responses are then varied under different testing conditions to determine the "best" condition for the "best" response. Test materials point out the need to evaluate "typical" or "spontaneously occurring" behavior (BCP, Office of the Santa Cruz County Superintendent of Schools, 1973; Callier-Azusa Scale, Stillman, 1978).

However, some tests list specific task conditions. For example, in drawing a "straight line between two points" on the Callier-Azusa Scale (Stillman, 1978), the child is given two ¼-inch dots, which "are drawn 4 inches apart" (p. 20). Other items on this scale list a variety of objects to be used (e.g., "places or pastes circle, square, tree, house on outline shape of same size," p. 21). Similarly, the Pennsylvania Training Model (Somerton & Turner, 1975) lists certain conditions in the assessment guide for *gross* screening and only general or no conditions for specific behaviors within the competency checklists.

Given the lack of specifically described conditions and the wide variations in conditions, it is difficult to compare the test performance of different SPH children or even compare performances of a given child on the same test. Such variations in testing conditions, though necessary, inhibit standardization. In contrast, if the testing conditions and "best" responses are recorded during assessment, teachers may receive more information in planning appropriate programs than they would receive from a standard score.

"NATURAL" VERSUS "ARTIFICIAL" SITUATIONS

Besides examining condition characteristics that elicit the best responses, test designers have included more situations that are "natural" as opposed to "artificial." For example, Haring (1976) describes human voices and light as more "natural" than pinpricks or intense stimuli in eliciting infant responses. Because successful performance in an artificial condition does not mean that the learner can demonstrate the same behavior in a more natural situation, test manuals emphasize the importance of evaluating children's behavior over time in naturally occurring situations (e.g., mealtimes, bedtimes, free play, community activities).

Problems arise in the amount of time needed for assessment and the absence of certain "natural" situations. Most professionals now agree that an educational assessment of an SPH child generally requires 2 to 4 weeks of observation (Sailor & Haring, 1977). In addition, "naturally" occurring events at home or in other community settings are not always available to the observer. In these cases information is collected through interviews to determine if the behavior occurs (Balthazar, 1971). The current emphasis on collecting data objectively has influenced other designers to limit the use of their tests to certain settings. For example, Stillman (1978) states that "one must be cautious in interpreting findings when the scale is used outside the classroom" (p. 3). Because instruments do not evaluate learner behaviors in all "natural" situations, the trained observer or special education teacher will need to identify relevant situations in which the behavior should "naturally" occur and collaborate with other care givers in providing a comprehensive assessment.

ZERO-DEGREE INFERENCE STRATEGY

Relevant conditions are a necessary prerequisite to response generalization.

SPH children are often unable to abstract essential characteristics from an irrelevant task to varied environments. For this reason Brown and colleagues (1976) have described the importance of a "zero-degree inference strategy" in assessing performance. Every time the situation changes the SPH child must be reassessed to determine whether or not the response is generalized to the new situation. To ensure this generalization they have described the need to systematically vary the following condition characteristics: (a) person, (b) natural setting, (c) instructional material, and (d) language cue. When the child is able to respond to three different persons in three natural settings using three different instructional materials and three different language cues, the observer can verify that the behavior has been "learned."

Most SPH assessment instruments describe their behavioral checklists as a guide for more extensive observations. The BCP (Office of the Santa Cruz County Superintendent of Schools, 1973) suggests that observations be made "during recess, naps, toileting, bus loading, and meal times as well as during instructional periods" (p. iii). The professional team must assume primary responsibility for varying essential condition characteristics to validate response generalization.

## Mastery Criteria

Mastery criteria depend on certain critical behavioral characteristics. First, the behavior must be observable. It would be difficult to determine whether or not a

192

student has obtained a successful performance level unless the performance itself could be observed. Second, the observed behavior should also be measurable or repeatable (i.e., it has beginning and ending points). This characteristic allows the evaluator a means to determine progress and subsequent mastery. A specific condition is often added to further delineate the behavior. For example, Cartwright and Cartwright (1974, p. 53) have described "sharing" in the following manner:

> If the child is playing with a toy and another child approaches and asks to use the toy, the child gives the toy to the other child without any negative verbal statements.

In both instances the behavior can be observed and measured. This objectivity increases the likelihood of agreement between observers as to whether the behavior was actually performed.

Many SPH assessment instruments use short statements in describing behaviors and are often open to interpretation. For example, the item "plays with other children" does not identify observable behaviors for "play." Consequently "play" might be scored differently by different observers. To avoid this problem, some manuals list behavioral objectives or indicate the need to include more than one observer in scoring each item to increase reliability. For example, the Brigance Diagnostic Inventory of Early Development (Brigance, 1978) includes drawings or pictures for some of the behaviorally stated objectives listed in the manual, particularly in the motor areas.

Third, the observed behavior should be sensitive to changes in performance. As mentioned previously, SPH children progress at a much slower rate than other children. "Washing hands" might take an SPH child many months to master. Therefore components of this terminal behavior need to be specified and measured so that progress can be observed. Comprehensive tests attempt to use a greater number of subcomponents for each terminal behavior. The BCP (1973) has 93 points under the heading of "undressing" and "dressing"; the Pennsylvania Training Model (PTM) (Somerton & Turner, 1975) has 75 points under the same heading. In both cases the article of clothing, the degree of independence required, and a task analysis of the operations are considered in developing items.

If the assessment instrument lists behaviors that are refined, observable, and measurable, then performance criteria may be more easily established. The development of criteria depends on (a) the direction of the desired behavioral change, (b) the stage of learning, and (c) ultimate functioning.

## PHYSICAL AND TEMPORAL BEHAVIORAL CHANGE

White and Liberty (1976) have described two basic types of behavioral change: physical and temporal. Physical changes may involve the use of different muscles or muscle sequences (topographical change), the intensity of the behavior (force), or the direction of the behavior (locus). Temporal changes include the amount of time a behavior lasts (duration), the number of times a behavior occurs within a unit of time (frequency or rate), or the amount of time between a behavior and some event (latency). The method for collecting data and the specification of criteria will vary depending upon the type of desired behavior change. For example, topographical, locus, and duration changes would need to be described for establishing "attention" criteria. The student would need to be able to lower or raise his or her head to a certain degree (topographical), look at the task or teacher (locus), and focus for a certain period of time (duration). On the other hand, changes in "sharing" might involve turning toward a peer (topographical and locus), speaking softly (force), and giving a toy to the peer (topographical and locus) within 10 seconds (latency).

## LEARNING STAGES

Besides including the type of desired change, criteria also need to reflect the stage of learning. Some researchers indicate that there are at least three different learning stages: acquisition, proficiency, and maintenance (Smith & Lovitt, 1976; White & Liberty, 1976). During the acquisition phase the student demonstrates that he or she can accurately perform the desired behavior. Because the SPH child's performance is often inconsistent, acquisition criteria usually include observations over a period of time or trials before mastery is assumed. In addition, Soltman and Rieke (1977) found that one SPH child's mean number of correct responses increased when consecutive trials were changed to intermittent ones. Consequently the nature of the trials may also need to be described in setting an acquisition criterion.

After the acquisition criterion is reached, the student learns to perform the behavior at a faster rate (i.e., proficiency). In this learning stage the student must be provided opportunities for repeated performance in order to attain the proficiency criterion. As described previously, conditions also need to be varied to determine whether the behavior can be demonstrated across situations. To ensure that no inferences are made about performance, these variations should occur in both the acquisition and proficiency stages. Unfortunately "mastery" is often assumed after the acquisition criterion is met within a single setting. In these cases, the probability of maintenance across time is less likely.

Assume a teacher is teaching "housekeeping" skills. The learner is taught initially how to hold and use a broom. Criteria are set for these "holding" and "sweeping" motions. Once the learner can accurately perform these behaviors, criteria are then established for proficiency. At what rate should the learner be able to "grasp," "hold the broom," and "sweep"? Proficiency is attained not only within the classroom but also within the setting in which the behavior is eventually to be performed and maintained (e.g., home, restaurant, motel).

With this example, "ultimate functioning" must obviously be considered in developing performance criteria. Criteria should be similar to those encountered in adult life. Proficiency standards will vary for individual SPH children depending on what is necessary for "successful" living within their immediate environment.

## HIT-AND-MISS CRITERION SETTING

Heterogeneity makes establishment of standard criteria for the SPH population difficult. Most often a criterion is determined by observing persons who are already successfully performing the desired behavior. The severity of the disability often makes normal sample comparisons invalid (i.e., proficiency for a "normal" adult may not be necessary for successful living). In addition, homogeneous SPH samples are difficult to obtain. Criterion setting therefore is more "hit and miss" than scientific and depends on individual characteristics.

## MEASURING COMPETENCY

Perhaps these problems and a lack of research have influenced the inadequate criteria specification apparent in current SPH assessment instruments. Some tests are simply behavioral checklists, using a binary scoring system. The observed behavior is scored as either present or absent. In some cases, the observer is asked to "guess" whether the learner could perform the behavior in different situations or to provide a structured learning situation (Foster, 1974). Other tests use a scale or continuum for scoring each item. The rater is asked to determine whether the behavior occurs "frequently," "occasionally," or "usually" (Nihira et al., 1974; Sailor & Mix, 1975). Phrases such as "many problems," "great difficulty," "is difficult to reach," and "actively seeks" necessitate judgment by the rater.

Other instruments have attempted to base their competency criteria on a more precise measure of behavioral frequency.

For example, on the BCP, criterion is reached if the behavior is performed at a "75% incidence level." The same is true of the PTM. "No competency" is represented by "0% correct response," "moderate competency" by "25% correct response," "adequate competency" by "75% correct response," and "complete competency" by "100% correct response." Percentages are also computed on the Balthazar scales based on the number of times the behavior is evidenced in "familiar" situations across 10 observations. In addition, the Balthazar and the PTM attempt to examine learning rate or proficiency. The Balthazar asks the rater to record the number of seconds for various "eating" behaviors. The PTM's assessment guide asks the observer to record "the total number of days the task was presented, the number of trials to successfully reach criterion, the total time spent on the task, and the total number of correct responses" (p. 3). However, observational conditions are often not precisely identified. The PTM does attempt to identify whether trials were presented consecutively or over a period of time while the Balthazar does not. Owing to the SPH child's often inconsistent performance, it would be difficult to determine mastery of different learning stages without collecting rate data (i.e., number of behaviors per unit of time) over time and across situations.

## FUTURE DIRECTIONS

Assessment of the SPH population is currently more an art than a science. While most tests have provided teachers with a set of basic behaviors, few have developed standard conditions or mastery criteria. For this reason, evaluating or comparing the "appropriateness" of educational programs is difficult. The major problem in developing standardized instruments relates to the heterogeneity and low incidence of the SPH population. Homogeneous subgroups are not easy to obtain. Consequently the Consortium on Adaptive Performance Evaluation (CAPE) developed an assessment and evaluation system for those functioning below the two-year level based on data collected from multiple sites dealing with SPH populations across the nation (Adaptive Performance Inventory). Using this data base, CAPE generated a list of target skills, classified as critical functions or behaviors. It described sequences and interdependencies between these skills, adapting for individual differences. It specified more thoroughly the stimulus and response characteristics of testing conditions. And it established mastery criteria. In addition, a computerized support system is used in the collection of longitudinal data and in the subsequent analysis and revision of the assessment strategy. The final instrument should address some of the current inadequacies present in the assessment of the SPH population. Several future directions for test development have been raised in this article.

---

*Assessment of the SPH population is currently more an art than a science. . . Few tests have developed standard conditions or mastery criteria.*

---

## Item Content

Content should focus on basic behaviors and their functional impact. SPH children may eventually function in different settings ranging from an institution to community-based homes with concomitant differences in daily living activities (e.g., no work to semicompetitive employment). Content should reflect the common adaptive behaviors required across multiple situations. In this way, skills learned or assessed are not situationally bound.

## Item Sequence

Sequences should be task analyzed from this multiple-setting standpoint and adapted for individual differences. Enough items should be included to facilitate the measurement of progress. Therefore multiple sequences may exist for the same terminal behavior.

## Assessment Conditions

Given the zero-degree inference strategy, behaviors should be assessed across several settings to ensure generalization. Conditions will also need to vary for specific severe disabilities. Test designers will need to examine essential stimulus dimensions in determining a relevant set of situations for assessment.

## Mastery Criteria

All test items should present behaviors that are observable and measurable. The type of desired change should be evident, completely described, and varied for specific disabilities. Criteria must be established for each stage of learning. An accurate performance in a single situation will not guarantee proficiency or maintenance. To determine various criteria levels, rate data will need to be collected across various settings.

It may be difficult to develop a single standardized instrument that is both comprehensive and sensitive to the extreme variation within the SPH population. However, the complexity of the task should not preclude efforts in this direction. Not many years ago the SPH population was viewed as uneducable and untestable. Views have changed. SPH children *do* learn. Given current technology, the opportunity for the development of more precise instruments in measuring change and planning appropriate educational programs is available. In the future, refined assessment strategies may enhance the probability of each SPH child's success.

## REFERENCES

Balthazar, E. *Balthazar scales of adaptive behavior.* Champaign, Ill.: Research Press, 1971.

Bayley, N. *Bayley infant scales of development.* New York: Psychological Corp., 1968.

Bricker, D., Dubose, R., Alberte, P., Berkler, M., Filler, J., Gast, D., Holder, L., Jens, K., Kauffman, J., Sears, J., & Snell, M. Issues in certification for teachers of the severely handicapped. Unpublished manuscript, 1978.

Bricker, D., & Iacino, R. Early intervention with severely/profoundly handicapped children. In E. Sontag, J. Smith, & N. Certo (Eds.). *Educational programming for the severely and profoundly handicapped.* Reston, Va.: Council for Exceptional Children, 1977, 166-176.

Bricker, W. Service of research. In M. Snell (Ed.), *Systematic instruction of the moderately and severely handicapped.* Columbus, Ohio: Charles E. Merrill, 1978, 3-18.

Brigance, A. *Brigance diagnostic inventory of early development.* Woburn, Mass.: Curriculum Associates, 1978.

Brown, L., Branston, M. B., Nietupski, S., Pumpian, I., Certo, N., & Gruenewald, L. A strategy for developing chronological-age-appropriate and functional curricular content for severely handicapped adolescents and young adults. *Journal of Special Education,* 1979, *13,* 81-90.

Brown, L., Nietupski, J., & Hamre-Nietupski, S. Criterion of ultimate functioning. In M. A. Thomas (Ed.), *Hey don't forget about me!* Reston, Va.: Council for Exceptional Children, 1976, 2-15.

Bureau of Education for the Handicapped, United States Office of Education, Section 121.2, 1974.

Cartwright, C. A., & Cartwright, G. P. *Developing observational skills.* New York: McGraw-Hill, 1974.

Dubose, R. Identification. In M. Snell (Ed.), *Systematic instruction of the moderately and severely handicapped.* Columbus, Ohio: Charles E. Merrill, 1978, 3-18.

Foster, R.W. *Camelot behavioral checklist manual.* Parsons, Kans.: Camelot Behavioral Systems, 1974.

Gesell, A. *The first five years of life: A guide to the study of the preschool child.* New York: Harper, 1940.

Guess, D., Horner, R. D., Utley, B., Holvoet, J., Maxon, D., Tucker, D., & Warren, S. A functional curriculum sequencing model for teaching severely handicapped. *AAESPH Review,* 1978, *2,* 203-215.

Haring, N. Infant identification. In M. A. Thomas (Ed.), *Hey, don't forget about me!* Reston, Va.: Council for Exceptional Children, 1976, 16-35.

Haring, N., & Pious, C. Future directions in work with severely and profoundly handicapped persons: An overview. In N. Haring & L. Brown (Eds.), *Teaching the severely handicapped.* New York: Grune & Stratton, 1976, 3-16.

Kauffman, J. M., & Payne, J. S. (Eds.). *Mental retardation: Introduction and personal perspectives.* Columbus, Ohio: Charles E. Merrill, 1975.

McKenzie, H., Hill, M., Sousie, S., York, R., & Baker, K. Special education training to facilitate rural, community-based programs for the severely handicapped. In E. Sontag, J. Smith, & N. Certo (Eds.),

*Educational programming for the severely and pro-foundly handicapped.* Reston, Va.: Council for Exceptional Children, 1977, 96-110.

Mercer, J. R. Psychological assessment and the rights of children. In N. Hobbs (Ed.), *Issues in the classification of children* (Vol. 1). San Francisco: Jossey-Bass, 1975.

Nihira, K. Factorial descriptions of the AAMD adaptive behavior scale. In W. A. Coulter & H. W. Morrow (Eds.), *Adaptive behavior: Concepts and measurements.* New York: Grune & Stratton, 1978, 45-57.

Nihira, K., Foster, R., Shellhaas, M., & Leland, H. *American association on mental deficiency adaptive behavior scale.* Washington, D.C.: American Association on Mental Deficiency, 1974.

Office of the Santa Cruz County Superintendent of Schools. *Behavior Characteristics Progression.* Palo Alto, Calif.: VORT Corp., 1973.

Public Law 94-142. *The education for all handicapped children act of 1975.* Washington, D.C.: The National Association of State Directors of Special Education, Inc., 1976.

Sailor, W., & Haring, N. Some current directions in education of the severely/multiply handicapped. *AAESPH Review,* 1977, 2, 3-24.

Sailor, W., & Mix, B. *TARC: Assessment inventory for severely handicapped children.* Lawrence, Kans.: H & H Enterprises, 1975.

Sheridan, M. *The developmental progress of infants and young children.* London: Her Majesty's Stationery Office, 1968.

Slosson, R. *Slosson intelligence test.* New York: Slosson Education, 1964.

Smith, D. D., & Lovitt, T.C. The differential effect of reinforcement contingencies on arithmetic performance. *Journal of Learning Disabilities,* 1976, 1, 32-40.

Smith, P., & Snell, M. In M. Snell (Ed.), *Systematic instruction of the moderately and severely handicapped.* Columbus, Ohio: Charles E. Merrill, 1978, 20-73.

Soltman, S., & Rieke, J. A. Communication management for the non-responsive child: A team approach. In E. Sontag, J. Smith, & N. Certo (Eds.), *Educational programming for the severely and profoundly handicapped.* Reston, Va.: Council for Exceptional Children, 1977, 348-359.

Somerton, M. E., & Turner, K. *Pennsylvania training model individual assessment guide.* Pennsylvania Department of Special Education, 1975.

Stillman, R. *The Callier-Azusa Scale.* Dallas, Tex.: Callier Center for Communication Disorders, University of Texas at Dallas, 1978.

White, O. R., & Liberty, K. A. Behavioral assessment and precise educational measurement. In N. G. Haring & R. L. Schiefelbusch (Eds.), *Teaching special children.* New York: McGraw-Hill, 1976.

Williams, W., & Gotts, E. A. Selected considerations on developing curriculum for severely handicapped students. In E. Sontag, J. Smith, & N. Certo (Eds.), *Educational programming for the severely and profoundly handicapped.* Reston, Va.: Council for Exceptional Children, 1977, 221-236.

# Assessment of Severely Impaired Young Children: Problems and Recommendations

*Rebecca Fewell DuBose, Ph.D.*
*University of Washington*
*Seattle, Washington*

THE PHYSICIAN Arnold Gesell and the epistemologist Jean Piaget meticulously observed and recorded behavior of children in their infancy and early years and left a legacy that many child care agents consider classic. However, neither Gesell nor Piaget studied children who were impaired or were thought to be developing more slowly than their agemates. Very few persons have undertaken careful and systematic observations of behavioral changes in children known to be impaired from birth. Such knowledge as exists about development and learning in young impaired children has come from anecdotal reports, studies of particular groups of children responding to set stimuli, or from very limited performances on traditional and some nontraditional infant measures.

The shortage of documented developmental information on impaired children is one reason examiners are poorly prepared to assess such children. Additionally, many examiners were trained before early interven-

*Portions of this article were originally presented at the HCEEP-DEC Conference, Washington, D.C., December 4, 1980.*

200

tion was a major effort, or before severely handicapped persons participated in the educational system. Practicum experiences were usually limited to the administration of the Wechsler Intelligence Scale for Children, Binet, or similar discipline-related measures to children enrolled in public schools. Inadequate training, knowledge limitations, the lack of adequate assessment measures, and the idiosyncratic characteristics of the target population combine to accentuate the difficulties of assessing impaired children. Regardless of the difficulties, however, assessment is a political reality if children are to receive services.

## DETERMINING PERFORMANCE EXPECTATIONS

Before beginning to assess a child, examiners must have some notion about the behaviors they expect to observe. If told the child to be tested is 3 years old, they immediately begin to think of behaviors 2- to 4-year-olds usually demonstrate—such as speaking in sentences of four to six words, building thee-block pyramids, matching similar pictures, buttoning, and ascending steps by alternating feet but descending steps by marking time—and of tests appropriate to these behaviors. Such expectations are either known or readily available to any examiner thanks to test authors such as Binet and Simon (1905), Frankenburg and Dodds (1967), Gesell (1940), and, more recently, authors such as Cohen and Gross (1979), who have compiled complete sequences of child behavior.

What is not conveyed by these traditional resources is how development and performances will be different when children are deaf, physically impaired, emotionally disturbed, or otherwise disabled. A basic understanding of such behavioral differences is needed so that examiners can formulate expectations and plan assessment strategies that are less likely than standard procedures to penalize the impaired child, and can make decisions about the child's learning and coping skills.

Deafness obviously affects language skill acquisition more severely than it does other skill areas. Language is the major means individuals have of communicating with others; thus, social skill acquisition is delayed and is qualitatively different in deaf children. In most cases motor skill achievement will not be affected by hearing impairments. Cognitive skills are not necessarily affected by deafness, but the many tests that give verbal instructions and require oral responses penalize the deaf child. Schlesinger and Meadow (1972) provide the chronology of both motor and language skills, including signs and fingerspelling, of four deaf children. Their findings will help examiners understand how development and learning are affected when hearing is not present. Awareness that the presence of mental retardation, blindness, or some other problem has a multiplicative rather than an additive effect on the deaf child will enable examiners to proceed cautiously in drawing conclusions with regard to causation of learning difficulties.

Blindness is even more devastating to development in skill domains. Blindness affects children's gross and fine motor skills (Adelson & Fraiberg, 1974); their awareness of spatial relationships, object permanence, and other sensorimotor schemes; self-care and social skills; and, to a lesser degree, verbal and cognitive skills. By not being able to see the nonverbal acts that others use with language, blind children are hampered in "reading" the meaning of what people say. Fraiberg (1977) has expressed the impact of blindness most poignantly: "The hand unites the infant with a world 'out there,' in which the purposeful reach gives intentionality to action and a sense of voluntariness in the formative period . . . .

These hands must come to serve the blind child as primary perceptual organs—something not 'intended,' either, in human biology" (p. 338).

DuBose (1976) described the impact of blindness on sensorimotor development, and Warren (1977) addressed language, cognitive, and social differences between blind and normal children. Fraiberg (1974) captures these early differences in describing her visits to the homes of young blind babies. "There is a large vocabulary of expressive behavior that one does not see in a blind baby at all. The absence of differentiated signs on the baby's face is mirrored in the face of the observer" (p. 217). An obvious example of the expressive behavior Fraiberg refers to is a 5-month-old's lifting of arms when a familiar adult approaches, signaling "pick me up." Fraiberg found the most capable blind babies she studied did not do this until the end of the first year of life when the mother's voice elicited reaching. Of particular interest is the quality of language in blind children whose early experiences are frequently limited to objects, persons, and places immediately available to them. Repetitive and imitative phrases are characteristics of language differences in blind children, particularly those with emotional problems.

Physical impairments have their greatest impact on motor skills; however, delayed skill acquisition is likely in all other domains. Guibor (1953) reported that 50% of all cerebral palsied children have some form of visual impairment. This can be difficult to detect and can have a serious effect on child performance, particularly when midline, visual closure, and visual-motor skills are required for test performance. Auditory and auditory–perceptual problems are also more likely to occur in cerebral palsied children. Fisch (1955) estimated that 20% of all children with cerebral palsy have hearing problems. The frequent occurrence of speech problems in the physically impaired is well-known, and, according to the research of Luria and Yudowich (1959), these problems affect abstract thinking and symbol formation. Personality and emotional disturbances and social and self-concept problems are also commonly associated with severe physical impairments.

Children with severe behavioral and emotional problems are likely to be poor communicators. Ornitz and Ritvo (1968) reported that the earliest nonverbal signals are different in these children. Thus in autistic babies the purpose of their cries is less easily discerned than with normal babies. When early imitative dyadic games such as peek-a-boo and patty-cake emerge in normal children, these behaviors are seldom noted in their autistic age-mates. When sounds do emerge from autistic babies, they are quantitatively and qualitatively different and the ensuing language is so severely affected that abnormal language is always cited as a major problem in autism. Autistic children's mental retardation and their significant delays in some motor milestones such as holding head erect and walking have been described extensively by Ornitz, Guthrie, and Farley (1977). Examiners will also want to remember that in autistic children there is a greater-than-chance occurrence of both hearing losses and visual problems.

Of all problems, examiners are most likely to be aware of the impact of mental retardation on all areas of development. Developmental differences in the sensory perception of retarded children have been a focus of recent research. Miranda and Fantz (1973) examined the visual preferences of Down's Syndrome infants as young as 2 and 4 months of age, and found these infants to be using vision significantly less effectively than normally developing infants. These differences may be due to delayed assimilation of information from the environment. Examiners who are aware of these developmental lags

202

will be better able to explain performance and plan more appropriate intervention strategies.

## SELECTING APPROPRIATE FORMAL TESTS

Before selecting tests to include in an assessment battery, examiners must first determine why the child is being assessed. Morrow and Coulter (1977) describe two separate functions of assessment: identification-placement and intervention-programming. If the purpose of assessment is to identify children who need special services and to decide where services should be delivered, then examiners will most likely need to select standardized or criterion-

---

*Before selecting tests to include in an assessment battery, examiners must first determine* why *the child is being assessed.*

---

referenced tests that are acceptable by the local education agency for determining eligibility for services and placement. For intervention and programming purposes, examiners will want to select tests that examine the concepts and behaviors to be targeted during intervention. These tests are likely to be criterion- or curriculum-referenced.

Unfortunately, many examiners jump into the test-selection task without first determining the kinds of decisions the test data will be used to make. Far too often, test selection is based on local or statewide requirements, examiner preference, test availability, or program policy. Severely handicapped children are likely to be penalized under such conditions, since their impairments may interfere with their performance on traditional assessment measures designed for and standardized on nonhandicapped populations. Sparrow and Cicchetti (1978), Simeonsson, Huntington, and Parse (1980), and Dollar and

Brooks (1980) describe the limitations of formal assessment measures for severely impaired populations. It is incumbent upon examiners to know what tests require of students and what the test information provides for its users, and then to select the tests least likely to penalize each child given his or her particular impairments.

In identifying the test purpose the dichotomous functions suggested by Morrow and Coulter (1977) may serve as a framework. If examiners must use a traditional mental measure in assessing a young severely handicapped child, they should review the test's requirements and seek out studies that show its results when used with populations of handicapped children. When they examined performance differences in 50 high-risk infants, Ramsay and Fitzhardinge (1977) found significantly higher performances on the Griffiths Scales than on the Bayley Scales.

In comparing the traditional infant tests by Griffiths, Cattell, Gesell, Bayley, and Brenet-Lezine, it is important to consider differences in the strategies and sources they use. For example, the Gesell and Griffiths tests rely on parental reports, whereas the Bayley does not. Perhaps this accounts for the Ramsay and Fitzhardinge findings. The point is not whether one test is more accurate than another, but that the information derives from different sources; this must be taken into account in comparing performances across time, tests, or other dimensions.

If testing is intended as a basis for predicting future expectations, caution is required. DuBose (1977) found predictive value in infant intelligence tests when the same tests were given to severely handicapped deaf-blind students 5 years after the initial assessment of those students. Yet the negligible correlation of early and later intelligence in nonhandicapped children is well documented (Honzik, 1976).

Bricker and Bricker (1973) published a monograph containing a series of research reports on the performances of developmentally delayed children on items from the Uzgiris and Hunt Scales (1975) and Albert Einstein Scales of sensorimotor development (Escalona & Corman Scales, 1969). The researchers concluded that these tests could be administered reliably to handicapped children. Others (Kahn, 1976, 1979; Rogers, 1977; Wohlhueter & Sinberg, 1975) found further support for use of these scales with handicapped populations. On the other hand, the use of Uzgiris and Hunt, Escalona and Corman and other traditional developmental scales with severely handicapped populations has been challenged by Switzky, Rotatori, Miller, and Freagon (1979), Swanson (1979), Dollar and Brooks (1980), and White (1980).

It becomes increasingly clear that choosing effective tests for handicapped children is not simple. The evidence that exists is contradictory; no one has provided a substantial longitudinal study of test performances of severely handicapped children that directs examiners toward measures that can be used reliably and validly for identification and placement purposes.

In the absence of consistent, generalizable data, examiners must continue to make decisions on a highly individual basis. Assessment tests and items must be examined carefully in light of the particular child's impairments and decisions made with regard to test administration. It is likely that results from one test will not suffice. Including performances across tests administered under different conditions in different environments will tend to increase the possibility of obtaining more accurate results.

## TEST ADAPTATION

Any time an examiner takes the liberty of changing the guidelines described for administering a test or test item, or modifies the stimulus object or the response requirements, the validity of the test has been violated. Once this has occurred, the purpose for using the test has changed and the scores yielded are no longer accurate.

There are many ways test items or conditions are violated in well-intended efforts to examine children. The room arrangement, the use of readiness exercises, the positioning of the child, the competencies required of the examiner, or the use of the test with a child who is significantly different from those in the standardization population, are all potential sources of test violations. McGuigan (1980), Simeonsson et al. (1980), and Kiernan and DuBose (1974) have noted a number of these concerns. The major problems to be addressed here are those of adapting test items and testing conditions.

If examiners could select from a large number of tests applicable to children with various handicaps, adaptations would not be necessary and violations would be avoided. Unfortunately, only a very few tests have been developed for young severely impaired children. Thus many examiners turn to adapted procedures to elicit information, even though the information they get may not be accurate.

It is possible to maintain the integrity of an adapted test or test item and to get significantly helpful information from it. Knowing how and when to adapt tests requires a careful analysis of the impact that impairments have on a child and an understanding of what each test item is measuring.

A first consideration is to select the test instrument that will yield the most useful information about a particular handicapped child's development and learning. When a condition must be changed to permit a child to perform, one must identify the concept being examined, how the child's sensory or physical impairment will interfere with related task performance, and how the task can be modified.

For example, Langley (1974) designed a magnetic board and magnetized blocks that could be easily manipulated by severely cere-

204 bral palsied children. Langley took mental maturity test items from various tests and attached the choices to the top of the magnetized blocks. The palsied children used elbows, wands, hands, arms, legs, or eyes to indicate choices, in most cases moving the selected answer block into a designated square in the center of the board. Langley reported significant differences in test results when performances were compared to those on a nonadapted measure. Some children tested out several years more mentally mature on the adaptation than one might have expected.

Kiernan (Kiernan & DuBose, 1974) adapted selected items from infant scales to form an experimental scale, the Peabody Intellectual Performance Scale, for use with deaf-blind children. He increased the stimulus value of the items by adding brightness in color for those who had some usable vision, adding texture, increasing item size for ease in handling (e.g., puzzle thickness and block size), and changing a few tasks from two-dimensional to three-dimensional choices. For example, with the color-sorting task from the Merrill-Palmer, instead of flat boxes with thin, round cardboard disks placed on top of each other in the box, Kiernan used clear plastic apothecary jars and Milton-Bradley's "counting bears" that the child could more easily pick up; thus errors could be quickly detected by both child and examiner. In all adaptations Kiernan's first concern was the sensorily impaired child. Item integrity was adhered to as closely as possible. The deaf-blind children scored significantly higher on the experimental scale than on the Cattell Scale. Kiernan acknowledged the problems inherent in the adapted scale; nonetheless, he felt the deaf-blind children's performance on the adapted scale more accurately represented their capabilities. DuBose and Langley (1977) have included many similar adaptations in their Developmental Activities Screening Inventory. The Uniform Performance Assessment System and the Adaptive Performance Inven-

> *Adapted tests cause handicapped children to be viewed differently; therefore, these adaptations must be made cautiously and recorded accurately.*

tory were also designed with adaptations included (White, 1980).

In adapting learning tasks to determine mentally retarded children's level of performance, Carrow (1972) outlined a sequence of increasingly difficult behaviors. The testee: (a) affirms or negates clinician's response; (b) sorts according to categories with model; (c) compares and selects or points to a picture, object, form, or letter to correspond to model; (d) sorts as in (b) but without model; (e) matches pictures, objects, and so on; (f) selects one of a series that is different from others; (g) arranges in series; or (h) verbalizes responses to any of the above tasks. By moving backward from the most advanced performance requirements to less demanding levels, the examiner gains valuable information that helps to design instructional strategies and task criteria within the repertoire of each child.

There are many other ways in which adaptations can be made. Adapted tests cause handicapped children to be viewed differently; therefore, these adaptations must be made cautiously and recorded accurately. The conclusions or statements made on the basis of adapted test performance are delicate, sensitive information that must be carefully conveyed.

## INFORMAL TASKS FOR TESTING AND TEACHING

Since there are so few instruments that can be used with severely handicapped children, it is necessary for many professionals concerned with such children, particularly teachers or educational diagnosticians, to devise informal testing and teaching tasks. Individualized, informal assessment must take into consideration the child's handicaps just as more formal testing does. Informal testing requires that an examiner know what concepts are to be tested, how these concepts develop, the many ways in which children demonstrate they understand the concepts, and how to structure activities to reflect levels of concept development. In addition, informal testing must assess functional skills which may include applications of the concepts assessed in more traditional testing. Unfortunately, this analytical approach to testing and teaching is often overlooked in training teachers and diagnosticians.

Several practical sources and exercises have been helpful to trainees learning to plan informal assessments. DuBose and Langley (DuBose, 1981) introduced student trainees to sensorimotor and preoperational stage theory, to formal tests, to informal experimental scales based on Piagetian theory, and to the impact of handicaps on child development. Later the trainees identified concepts and planned ways to test the concepts-impaired children. Trainees analyzed over 100 typical children's toys and determined the kinds of skills that could be observed as a child played with each toy. This information was placed in a grid of the type shown in Figure 1.

Trainees were also provided experiences from which they could develop analytical skills and become keen observers of child behavior in any task in any setting. Assessment became an ongoing transactional process and was not tied to traditional settings, measures, persons, or conditions. (The Appendix is the guidelines form DuBose and Langley's trainees used in recording observations of young severely handicapped children across multiple assessment environments.)

## TRANSLATING ASSESSMENT FINDINGS INTO EDUCATIONAL PROGRAMS

As noted earlier, the purpose of an assessment has a direct bearing on the test instruments selected. If an assessment's purpose is to make a placement decision, then a score may be all that is needed. If the purpose is to determine a child's educational needs and suggest plans to meet those needs, then the test must yield results relevant to programming.

To interpret test results it is important that the examiner know why a particular test was given, what behaviors the test taps, and what test performances indicate. At all times the impact of impairment on performance must be considered. In addition, DuBose, Langley, and Stagg (1977) suggested consideration of performance differences across variables such as the places in which assessment occurred; the materials or tasks used; rapport with different examiners; level of task comprehension; models of response; and rate, level, and efficiency of skill acquisition. Information of this nature, which can usefully be recorded on the Guidelines form, reduces the guesswork and trial and error that have so often characterized instructional programming for severely impaired learners.

In making instructional decisions, it is not necessary to completely discount the data gathered from tests used in identification and placement decisions. Much of this information can supplement intervention and programming findings if it is analyzed carefully and used cautiously. An example is the cluster analysis of the Bayley Scales by Yarrow and Pedersen (1976). This analysis groups items that tap the same concept and helps identify continuities and discontinuities in performance.

Translating assessment data into educational programs is the heart of the matter. If this does not occur, then testing is for nought, and the same decisions could probably be made using other criteria and procedures that are more cost-efficient and less traumatic for all concerned. Assessment of young severely impaired children is an arduous and challenging task, requiring skilled practitioners, input from care providers, and many hours of obser-

| Toy: Slinky | Visual attention | Reaches/grasps | | Requests reactivation | Juggles on palms | Pulls up and down | "Walks" it | Stretch extend | Compresses it | Language | | Creative play |
| --- | --- | --- | --- | --- | --- | --- | --- | --- | --- | --- | --- | --- |
| | | Left | Right | | | | | | | Rec. | Exp. | |
| Response | | | | | | | | | | | | |
| Resists | | | | | | | | | | | | |
| Mouths | | | | | | | | | | | | |
| Appropriate action | | | | | | | | | | | | |
| Bangs/shakes | | | | | | | | | | | | |
| Physical guidance | | | | | | | | | | | | |
| Verbal/tactual prompt | | | | | | | | | | | | |
| Demonstration | | | | | | | | | | | | |
| Spontaneous trial & error visual comparison | | | | | | | | | | | | |

Attention — Reach—arm extension, Grasp—eye—hand — Causality — Bilateral alternation, midline, eye—hand coordination, transference — Means/ends, oppositional hand movement, eye—hand — Wrist rotation, eye—hand means/ends release — Arm extension, oppositional hand movement, coordination — Midline eye—hand

**Figure 1.** Grid for recording child's interactions with toys.

vation and testing. Results are always tenuous, and they should be. Assessment of these children is a dynamic, elusive process that provides us with but a glimpse of what is actually happening at one point in time.

Examiners must be continually aware that these young children are contributing significantly to their environments, eliciting responses, changing events and persons, and, in turn, being changed by all this themselves.

## REFERENCES

Adelson, E., & Fraiberg, S. Gross motor development in infants blind from birth. *Child Development*, 1974, *45*, 114–126.

Binet, A., & Simon, T. Sur la nécessité d'établir un diagnostic scientifique des états inférieurs de l'intelligence. *L'Année Psychologique*, 1905, 11, 163–190.

Bricker, D., & Bricker, W. *Infant, toddler, and preschool research and intervention project: Report-year III* (IMRID Behavioral Science Mongraph No. 23). Nashville, Tenn.: George Peabody College, 1973.

Carrow, E. Assessment of speech and language in children. In J.E. McLean, D.E. Yoder, & R.L. Shiefelbusch (Eds.), *Language intervention with the retarded*. Baltimore: University Park Press, 1972.

Cohen, M., & Gross, P. *The developmental resource* (2 vols.). New York: Grune & Stratton, 1979.

Dollar, S.J., & Brooks, C. Assessment of severely and profoundly handicapped individuals. *Exceptional Education Quarterly*, 1980, *1*(3), 87–101.

DuBose, R.F. Developmental needs in blind infants. *The New Outlook for the Blind*, 1976, *70*(2), 49–52.

DuBose, R.F. Predictive value of infant intelligence scales with multiply handicapped children. *American Journal of Mental Deficiency*, 1977, *81*, 388–390.

DuBose, R.F. *Final performance report. Innovative diagnostic training: Preparation of diagnostic personnel to serve severely handicapped children.* (USOE-BEH Report #G007701304). Nashville, Tenn.: George Peabody College, August 31, 1981.

DuBose, R.F., & Langley, B. *The developmental activities screening inventory.* Hingham, Mass.: Teaching Resources, 1977.

DuBose, R.F., Langley, M., & Stagg, V. Assessing severely handicapped children. *Focus on Exceptional Children*, 1977, *9*(7), 1–13.

Escalona, S.K., & Corman, H.H. *Albert Einstein scales of sensorimotor development.* Unpublished manuscript, Albert Einstein School of Medicine, 1969.

Fisch, L. Deafness in cerebral palsied school children. *Lancet*, 1955, *2*, 370–375.

Fraiberg, S. Blind infants and their mothers: An examination of the sign system. In M. Lewis & L. Rosenblum (Eds.), *The effects of the infant on its caregiver.* New York: Wiley, 1974.

Fraiberg, S. *Insights from the blind.* New York: Basic Books, 1977.

Frankenburg, W., & Dodds, J. The Denver Developmental Screening Test. *Journal of Pediatrics*, 1967, *71*(2), 181–191.

Gesell, A. *The first five years of life: A guide to the study of the preschool child.* New York: Harper & Row, 1940.

Guibor, G. Some eye defects seen in cerebral palsy with some statistics. *American Journal of Physical Medicine*, 1953, *32*, 342–348.

Honzik, M. Value and limitations of infant tests: An overview. In M. Lewis (Ed.), *Origins of intelligence: Infancy and early childhood.* New York: Plenum Press, 1976.

Kahn, J. Utility of the Uzgiris and Hunt scales of sensorimotor development with severely and profoundly retarded children. *American Journal of Mental Deficiency*, 1976, *80*, 663–665.

Kahn, J. Applications of the Piagetian literature to severely and profoundly mentally retarded persons. *Mental Retardation*, 1979, *17*, 273–280.

Kiernan, D.W., & DuBose, R.F. Assessing the cognitive development of preschool deaf-blind children. *Education of the Visually Handicapped*, 1974, *6*(4), 103–105.

Langley, B. *Comparison of performances on the Columbia Mental Maturity Test and an adapted test for physically handicapped children.* Unpublished manuscript, George Peabody College, 1974.

Luria, A., & Yudowich, F. *Speech and the development of mental processes in the child.* London: Staples Press, 1959.

McGuigan, C. Selecting and evaluating educational tests. In C. Hansen (Ed.), *Child assessment: The process and the product.* Seattle, Wash.: Program Development Assistance System, 1980.

Miranda, S.B., & Fantz, R.L. Visual preference of Down's Syndrome and normal infants. *Child Development*, 1973, *44*, 555–561.

Morrow, H., & Coulter, A. A collection of adaptive behavior measures. In A. Coulter & H. Morrow (Eds.), *The concept and measurement of adaptive behavior within the scope of psychological assessment* (Tech.

**208**

Rep. No. 4). Austin, Tex.: Texas Regional Resource Center, 1977.

Ornitz, E., Guthrie, D., & Farley, A. The early development of autistic children. *Journal of Autism and Childhood Schizophrenia*, 1977, *7*(3), 207–229.

Ornitz, E., & Ritvo, E. Perceptual inconstancy in early infantile autism. *Archives of General Psychiatry*, 1968, *18*(1), 76–98.

Ramsay, M., & Fitzhardinge, P.M. A comparative study of two developmental scales: The Bayley and the Griffiths. *Early Human Development*, 1977, *1*(2), 151–157.

Rogers, S. Characteristics of the cognitive development of profoundly retarded children. *Child Development*, 1977, *48*, 837–843.

Schlesinger, H.S., & Meadow, K.P. *Sound and sign.* Berkeley: University of California Press, 1972.

Simeonsson, R.J., Huntington, G., & Parse, S. Assessment of children with severe handicaps: Multiple problems-multivariate goals. *Journal of the Association for the Severely Handicapped*, 1980, *5*(1), 55–72.

Sparrow, S., & Cicchetti, D.V. Behavior rating scale inventory for moderately, severely, and profoundly retarded persons. *American Journal of Mental Deficiency*, 1978, *82*, 365–374.

Swanson, J. Principles of infant assessment. In B. Darby & M. May (Eds.), *Infant assessment: Issues and applications.* Seattle, Wash.: WESTAR, 1979.

Switzky, H., Rotatori, A., Miller, T., & Freagon, S. The developmental model and its implication for assessment and instruction for the severely/profoundly handicapped. *Mental Retardation*, 1979, *17*(4), 167–170.

Uzgiris, I., & Hunt, J.McV. *Assessment in infancy: Ordinal scales of psychological development.* Urbana: University of Illinois Press, 1975.

Warren, D.H. *Blindness and early childhood development.* New York: American Foundation for the Blind, 1977.

White, O.R. Child assessment. In B. Wilcox & R. York (Eds.), *Quality education services for the severely handicapped: The federal investment.* Washington, D.C.: Bureau of Education for the Handicapped, 1980.

Wohlhueter, M., & Sinberg, R. Longitudinal development of object permanence in mentally retarded children: an explanatory study. *American Journal of Mental Deficiency*, 1975, *79*, 513–518.

Yarrow, L., & Pedersen, F.L. The interplay between cognition and motivation in infancy. In M. Lewis (Ed.), *Origins of intelligence: Infancy and early childhood.* New York: Plenum Press, 1976.

# Appendix

# Guidelines for observing behaviors during the assessment process

Child's Name: _____   Observer: _____

I.   Screening, adaptive or informal assessment
   A.   What did the child do?
   B.   Which tasks were the most difficult for the child?
   C.   Which materials evoked optimal responses from the child?
   D.   What was the average length of time the child attended to each task?
       Did any specific tasks hold his/her attention longer?
   E.   How quickly did the child learn new tasks?  Could s/he generalize new skills to other materials?  Could s/he
       remember new skills over time?
   F.   Through what means did the child approach the majority of tasks?
   G.   What questions would you pursue based on the child's performance?
       What type of tasks will answer your questions?
   H.   How did the child respond to the evaluator?  Was rapport established and how was this accomplished?
   I.   What type of behavioral management techniques were successful?
   J.   What appears to be the origin of the child's cognitive/adaptive delay?
   K.   What informal assessment instruments or subtests would you use to further investigate this child's skills?
       Cognitive   _____
       Language   _____
       Motor   _____
       Social/Self-care   _____
   L.   What is the approximate level of this child's level of functioning?

| | | | |
|---|---|---|---|
| 0-6 mos._____ | 18-24 mos._____ | 36-42 mos._____ | 54-60 mos._____ |
| 6-12 mos._____ | 24-30 mos._____ | 42-48 mos._____ | 60-66 mos._____ |
| 12-18 mos._____ | 30-36 mos._____ | 48-54 mos._____ | 66-72 mos._____ |

       Comments:

   M.   What appears to be the most handicapping condition?  Based on the screening information, how would you rate this
       child's auditory, visual, physical, and intellectual systems?
       Rating key:    0=no or very minimal impairment; 1=impairment that interferes with performance but not
                significantly; 2=severe impairment, system is nonfunctional or extremely damaged.
       Auditory _____   Visual _____   Physical _____   Intellectual _____

II.   Fine Motor Skills
   A.   Did the child approach materials with one hand more than another? Which?
   B.   Did the child: reach_____ grasp _____ release voluntarily _____?
   C.   Did the child hold objects in both hands? _____
   D.   Did the child use two hands together? In the same direction? In opposing directions?
   E.   Did the child cross his/her midline? _____
   F.   How did the child hold (grasp) pegs, blocks, beads, rings, cups, scissors, writing implements?
   G.   Could the child rotate wrists to: RH? LH?
       turn the handle on a jack-in-the-box _____   open a door _____   twist off tops and lids _____
       operate an eggbeater _____   wind a mechanical toy _____
   H.   How would you describe his/her eye-hand coordination?
       Accuracy _____   Control _____   Rhythm _____   Speed _____

    I.    Could s/he plan motorically?

        Paper and markers _____    Beads _____    Blocks _____    Cutting _____

        Paper folding _____    Washers and rings _____

    J.    What is the primary origin of this motor delay?

    K.    What other motor instruments or subtests would you further use?

    _____

    L.    What is approximate developmental level?    _____

### III.  Gross Motor

    A.    What is the primary origin of the gross motor delay?

    B.    Does the child have basic movement patterns?

        Head control _____    Trunk control _____    Sitting balance _____    Cutting _____

    C.    Describe the child's highest level of movement: <u>How</u> did the child do it?

    D.    Did the child maintain balance?

        From a sitting position _____    While walking _____

        While standing on one foot _____    While walking beams _____

    E.    Did the child run?    jump?    climb stairs?    HOW?

    F.    Did the child interact with balls?  Did the child track projectory?  <u>RH</u>, <u>LH</u>

        Catch _____    Throw _____    Kick _____

    G.    Did the child follow a series of movements?

    H.    What formal gross motor instrument or subtests would you use to further evaluate these skills?

    I.    What is the child's approximate developmental motor level?

### IV.  Language

    A.    What is the origin of the child's language delay?

    B.    Does the child's hearing appear intact?  What responses support your answer?

    C.    Does the child use hearing functionally, i.e., for language and communication?

    D.    What cues are being used by the child for comprehension?

        Physical guidance _____    Tactual _____    Contextural situation _____

        Gestures and signs _____    Visual and tactual _____

        Tactual and verbal _____    Verbal and visual _____    Verbal only _____

        Other _____

    E.    Was the child responsive to the evaluator's verbal cues or "tuned out"?

    F.    Does the child vocalize?

        cries and laughs _____    vocal play _____    words _____

        screams _____    babbling _____    phrases _____

        phonemes (speech sounds) _____    jargon _____    echolalic _____

    G.    Can the child name objects, pictures presented either verbally or manually?

    H.    Describe the sounds, words, signs, etc. the child used.

    I.    Does the child use his/her voice communication, i.e., as opposed to self-stimulation?

    J.    Does the child communicate nonverbally?

        Touch the evaluator _____

        Place the evaluator's hand on an object? _____

        Return the object to the evaluator _____

        Points _____    Pulls the evaluator to the desired effect _____

        Gestures _____    Signs _____

    K.    Does the child know what objects are for and how to use them?

    L.    Does the child possess the prerequisites for language?

    M.    If the child communicates in phrases or sentences, try to list 10 examples.

    N.    What other formal instruments or subtests would you use to gather further information about this child's language?

    _____

    O.    What is the child's approximate developmental language level?

V. Socialization Self-Care Skills
    A. Did the child separate easily from the parent(s)?
    B. Was rapport established easily?
    C. Was eye contact established with the evaluator(s)?
    D. Did the child cooperate with the evaluators? Enthusiastically or passively?
    E. Did the child resist performing tasks?
    F. Did the child exhibit any unusual behaviors, i.e., self-stimulation?
    G. Was the child abusive or aggressive?
    H. Did the child interact with people and toys appropriately?
    I. To what extent could the child toilet self?
    J. To what extent could the child wash hands?
    K. To what extent could the child undress and dress?
    L. What further instruments would you use to gather more information?
    M. What was the approximate developmental level?

VI. Other Observations/Impressions

# Medication Effects in Handicapped Preschool Children

*Rune J. Simeonsson, Ph.D.*
*Frank Porter Graham Child Development*
  *Center*
*University of North Carolina*
*Chapel Hill, North Carolina*

*Nancy E. Simeonsson, R.N., B.S.N.*
*Duke University Medical Center*
*Durham, North Carolina*

THE PERVASIVENESS of drug therapy in the medical management of children is reflected by the finding that at least one of every three children seen by a physician is on some form of medication (Haggerty & Roghmann, 1972). Furthermore, the proportion of inpatient children (60%) medicated in hospitals is approximately the same as among adult inpatients, with a mean of 2.5 drugs given per child (Moreland, Rylance, Christopher, & Stevenson, 1978). Drug therapy for handicapped children is undoubtedly even more extensive, given the greater frequency of physical and neurological complications among such children.

## THE NEED TO DOCUMENT DRUG THERAPY

While Greer, Davis, and Yearwood (1977) and May (1976) have commented on medica-

*The preparation of this report was supported in part by the Bureau of Education for the Handicapped, U.S. Office of Education, DHEW, Contract number 300-77-0309. However, the opinions expressed do not necessarily reflect the position or policy of the U.S. Office of Education, and no official endorsement by the U.S. Office of Education should be inferred.*

213

tion problems of handicapped populations in institutions and schools, no summary figures are available regarding the extent of drug therapy in handicapped preschoolers. The lack of such data for preschool children with handicaps is unfortunate, since the success of early intervention often requires the effective meshing of medical and programmatic dimensions. Neisworth, Kurtz, Ross, and Madle (1976) have called for naturalistic assessment of drug effects through a four-step procedure to be carried out by teachers and aides of handicapped children. Inadequate documentation of drug therapy is, however, not unique to handicapped populations, but reflects broader problems in pediatric pharmacology. In a recent article, Rylance (1979) reviewed a number of problems involved with prescribing drugs for infants and children.

Rylance points out that despite the fact that age is a major factor in the outcome of drug therapy, there are few studies of how drugs affect a child's development. Severe, even catastrophic, reactions are too often the result of drug exposure among children. According to Rylance, "paradoxically, the misuse of drugs arising from a lack of relevant data is perpetuated by false ethical issues which prevent the planned and controlled clinical studies that are necessary if further catastrophes are to be avoided" (p. 346). Recognition of the seriousness of these and related problems is evidenced by the convening of an international workshop on the medical, ethical, and legal aspects of pediatric pharmacology (Gross, Boreus, Deutsch, Gladtke, Helge, Mirkin, Morselli, Sereni, & Yaffe, 1980).

Yaffe (1980) has stressed the need for data on the short-term as well as long-term effects of drug therapy. Dimensions of analysis such as drug absorption, distribution, and elimination are as important with handicapped as nonhandicapped children. Of particular relevance for handicapped children are adverse reactions which may "affect the develop-

mental process itself and . . . this type of drug action may be delayed and not apparent for many years after the drug has been administered" (p. 3).

This article summarizes findings pertaining to the use of medication with handicapped preschool children, identifies considerations of special concern in drug therapy with such populations, and proposes implications for practice and research in early intervention. A restriction of the review is that it focuses on issues and findings pertaining to handicapped children under the age of 6. Research summaries covering medication of school-aged and older handicapped children are available elsewhere (Sroufe, 1975; Cohen, 1979), as are materials directed at educators of such children (Gadow, 1979; Lindsey, Leibold, Ladd, & Ownby, 1980). A further restriction is that "nonstandard" therapies of a biochemical nature, such as megavitamin therapy, will not be considered since scientific evaluation of their effectiveness has not been adequate (Golden, 1980).

## CLASSIFICATION OF DRUGS

Drugs administered to children vary widely in purpose and pharmacological action; they range from antibiotics to stimulants. Surveys have shown that more than 50% of hospital prescriptions for children are classified as antibiotic agents (Harte & Timoney, 1980; Moreland et al., 1978). Since antibiotics and other similar drugs are not administered exclusively to the handicapped but to all children, their effects will not be reviewed in detail here.

It should be emphasized, however, that antibiotics can produce adverse reactions (Harte & Timoney, 1980), a fact that should be taken into account in giving them to young handicapped children. Rylance (1979) and Lindsey et al. (1980) have summarized in table form frequently observed adverse effects of drugs commonly given to children. These tables can serve as a useful reference for staff working with handicapped children, and the chart prepared by Lindsey et al. (1980) describes side effects that might be noticed by teachers.

Medication effects of interest here are those associated with drugs administered specifically to alleviate symptoms and problems specifically found in handicapped children. In general such drugs are intended to manage problems of behavior, activity, emotion, or epilepsy. Since some of these drugs are used differently with adults, labels such as *antipsychotics* may be inappropriate. Silver (1979) and Combrinck-Graham, Gursky, and Saccar (1980) have reviewed drugs for children in terms of their primary function (e.g., stimu-

lants, tranquilizers). Table 1 draws these classifications and provides a summary of representative drugs, indications for use, and common side effects. While a variety of these drugs are used with some frequency with older handicapped children (Gittelman-Klein, 1978; Donaldson & Menolascino, 1980) their use with preschool handicapped children appears to be more restricted. In reviewing literature for this article, it was evident that clinical and research studies involving children under the age of 6 were not only limited in number but in focus, dealing primarily with control of seizures or behavior. This is probably due partly to the Food and Drug Administration's not having approved certain drug applications in children. For example, a

**Table 1.** Drugs frequently used in pharmacological management of children and youth

| Classification | Representative drugs (trade name) | Indication for use | Possible side effects[*] |
|---|---|---|---|
| Tranquilizers (Major) | Thorazine | Severe agitation/ psychosis | Drowsiness |
| | Mellaril | psychosis | Incontinence Weight gain |
| (Minor) | Librium | Anxiety | Possible memory loss |
| | Atarax | Anxiety | Drowsiness |
| Antidepressants (not recommended for younger children) | Tofranil | Mood elevation | Drowsiness Constipation |
| | Lithonate | Depression | Gastrointestinal involvement |
| Stimulants | Dexedrine | Hyperactivity | Reduced appetite |
| | Ritalin | Hyperactivity | Reduced growth Increased anxiety |
| Anticonvulsants | Mysoline | Convulsion | Aggressive behavior |
| | Dilantin | Convulsion | Gingival hypertrophy |
| | Zarontin | Convulsion | Allergic reactions |
| Drugs for specific problems | Tofranil | Enuresis | Confusion/dry mouth |
| | Mellaril | Nightmares Tics | Headache/tardive dyskinesis |
| | Haldol | TRS/Gilles de la Tourette Syndrome | Muscle spasm/weakness |
| | Benedryl | Sedative | Drowsiness |

[*]For each drug there are usually a number of side effects; only one or two have been listed as examples.

216 number of the common antidepressants and several tranquilizers are not recommended for children under 12 years of age, and other tranquilizers and at least one stimulant (Ritalin) are not recommended for children under 6 (Campbell & Small, 1978).

## MEDICATION EFFECTS

### Seizure control

Clinical and research reports pertaining to medication for controlling seizures in handicapped infants and children are summarized in Table 2. While some studies involved only infants or preschool children, others included older children and adults. Furthermore, some studies provided specific documentation for the type and severity of handicapping conditions, whereas others defined the population only by the presenting problem of seizures. However, the latter studies are relevant here since seizures are indicative of central nervous system dysfunction, which is a frequent characteristic of handicapped children. The table reveals that the control of seizures in young children involves a variety of drugs of differing effectiveness and range of side effects.

Studies by Knudsen (1979), Leary and Morris (1980), and Coulter, Wu, and Allen (1980) indicate that diazepam and valproic acid are generally effective in managing seizures, particularly petit mal, with only minor side effects.

Phenobarbital administered on a daily or maintenance basis effectively reduced seizures in young children with abnormal developmental histories (Wolf, 1977). It was also found effective in a follow-up study of infants with neonatal status epilepticus although lethargy was a complication (Buda, Joyce, & Zettett, 1979). Clonazepam was found to improve seizure control in epileptic children whose seizures were resistant to other drugs; however, it had a substantial number of severe side effects such as sleep disorder, vertigo, and restlessness (Bensch, Blennow, Ferngren, Gamstorp, Herrlin, Kubista, Arvidsson, & Dahlstrom, 1977).

The other three studies of drug control of seizures documented chronic side effects of phenytoin (dilantin) treatment of mentally retarded epileptic children. Based on the results of retrospective analyses, Iivanainen, Viukari, and Helle (1977) concluded that epileptics with brain damage were particularly susceptible to cerebellar side effects such as balance and coordination disturbances and potential locomotor losses. Phenytoin and/or other anticonvulsant therapy has also been found to result in rickets (i.e., vitamin D deficiency) in retarded epileptic children (Winnacker, Yeager, Saunders, Russell, & Anast, 1977). Another study has shown that where phenytoin was discontinued because of phenytoin intoxication, the result was varied seizure control and improvement in the psychomotor deterioration attributed to the drug intoxication (Meistrup-Larsen, Hermann, & Permin, 1979).

In summary, seizures in young handicapped children can be effectively controlled by drugs with variable side effects from minor to serious. Acute intermittent athetosis, for example, was found to coincide with phenytoin administration to a 3-year-old child with seizures (Zinsmeister & Marks, 1976). As Stores (1975) has cautioned, however, there are some particularly serious effects associated with anti-epileptic medication of certain populations such as the brain damaged and/or

---

*There are some particularly serious side effects associated with anti-epileptic medication of certain populations such as the brain damaged and/or severely handicapped.*

**Table 2.** Studies on use of medication to control seizures in preschool handicapped children

| Author | Purpose of drug study | Subjects' ages | Subject characteristics | Results | Side effects |
|--------|----------------------|----------------|------------------------|---------|-------------|
| Buda et al., 1979 | 12 to 24 mo. follow-up study of high dose phenobarbital in treatment of neonatal status epilepticus | 5 mo.–12 mo. N = 12 | Neonatal status epilepticus | Respiratory depression did not occur All patients survived No further seizures while on maintenance doses Frequency & severity of motor & intellectual deficits on follow-up were lower than previous studies | Lethargy Some psychomotor impairment |
| Bensch et al., 1977 | Double-blind study of clonazepam in treatment of therapy-resistant epilepsy in children | 5 yr. N = 50 | Epilepsy—akinetic seizures, walk but not speak, epilepsy resistant to other drugs | Seizures better controlled when clonazepam added to existing drug treatment | High incidence of unpleasant side effects: hypersalivation, swelling of parotid glands, ataxia, speech disturb., behavior disturb., listlessness, loss of appetite, enuresis nocturna |
| Leary & Morris, 1980 | Effectiveness of sodium valproate in seizure control | 13 mo.–4 yr. 9 mo. (M = 9 yr. 1 mo.) | 24 of 62 S's of subnormal intelligence (N = 62), recurrent epileptic seizures | Most effective in petit mal Good results in myoclonic seizures Full control of psychomotor seizures Overall reduction in no. of anticonvulsants per individual | Few & minor side effects: headaches, drowsiness, nausea, behavior disorders, insomnia |

**Table 2** (continued)

| Author | Purpose of drug study | Subjects' ages | Subject characteristics | Results | Side effects |
|---|---|---|---|---|---|
| Knudsen, 1979 | Rectal valium to treat convulsions in infants & children | 6 mo.–5 yr. N = 44 | Febrile convulsions & epilepsy | Effective in acute treatment; therapeutic effect correlated with duration of convulsion before treatment started. Demonstrated as effective alternative to mode of drug administration | Few side effects |
| Wolf, 1977 | Effectiveness of phenobarbital in prevention of recurrence of febrile convulsions in children | Age not specified N = 300 | "Abnormal" group with significant histories of pre-, peri-, & postnatal abnormalities compared with "normal" group without histories | Significant reduction of febrile seizure recurrence in both normal and "abnormal" group found with daily phenobarbital administration, compared to phenobarbital administration with onset and duration of fever in controls (no phenobarbital) | |
| Meistrup-Larsen et al., 1979 | Discontinuation of di-phenylhydantoin (DPH) intoxication | (5–24 yr.) (M = 16.2 yr.) N = 21 | Mental retardation with severe epilepsy | 3 mo. and 1 yr. after withdrawal of DPH considerable clinical improvement in psychomotor areas and convulsive status | |

| | | | | | |
|---|---|---|---|---|---|
| Winnacker et al., 1977 | Investigation of complications of anticonvulsant therapies involving combinations of phenobarbital, phenytoin, & primidone | 2–16 yr. N = 41 | Mental retardation with epilepsy | Slight but significant decrease in concentrations of serum calcium, phosphorus, and vitamin D, and increase in serum alkaline phosphatase values compared to retarded persons who receive anticonvulsant therapy | Vitamin D deficiency (Rickets most marked in children with (a) primidone included in therapy (b) largest number of drugs for longest duration and blood levels of phenobarbital significantly higher than other patients |
| Iivanainen et al., 1977 | Effect of phenytoin intoxication | 3–37 yr. (M = 16.3 yr.) N = 131 | Mental retardation with epilepsy | Phenytoin intoxication diagnosed retrospectively in 56% of sample | Brain-damaged persons particularly susceptible to drowsiness, nystagmus, balance and coordination disturbances, dizziness, limb ataxia, loss of locomotion |
| Coulter et al., 1980 | Valproic acid with other anticonvulsants | 0–21 yr. N = 100 | Epilepsy; borderline through severe mental retardation; motor deficits (ataxia, hemiparesis, quadriparesis, no deficit) | Seizure control improved across age groups—best results in petit mal and less in handicapped | Overall incidence side effects high including: 3 deaths, edema, coma, mild hepatic dysfunction, and leukopenia |

220

severely handicapped. Further brain damage, for example, has been found in older retarded children and adults following chronic hydantoin intoxication (Vallarta, Bell, & Reichert, 1974). Systematic monitoring of individual cases in particularly important in drug therapy of children when multiple medications are used (Berman, 1976).

### Behavior change

While substantial research exists on the use of medication to influence behavior of school-age populations, particularly hyperactive children (Barkley, 1977), there are very few such studies involving preschool handicapped children. The ones reviewed are summarized in Table 3.

Most of the studies have been of children classified as autistic, with varying levels of mental retardation. The two studies examining the effectiveness of haloperidol obtained positive findings of reduced symptoms and increased appropriate behavior resulting from drug treatment (Cohen et al., 1980; Campbell, Anderson, Meier, Cohen, Small, Samit, & Sacher, 1978). Side effects reported in the study by Campbell et al. (1978) included changes in motor activity and disposition. Cohen et al. (1980) found a rebound effect of worse behavior when the medication was discontinued.

In an earlier study, Campbell, Fish, Shapiro, and Floyd (1971) investigated the role of imipramine on behavior of autistic and schizophrenic preschoolers. Only 2 of 10 children treated were rated as improved by an independent "blind" observer, and a number of negative side effects were found.

In the only behavior study found involving nonautistic children, the effects of methylphenidate (Ritalin) were investigated with hyperactive preschool children of normal intelligence (Schleifer, Weiss, Cohen, Elman, Cvejic, & Kruger, 1975). While parents reported positive drug-related changes in hyperactivity, changes were not observed on measures of school behavior and psychological functioning. Additionally, negative side effects on mood and behavior reduced the frequency of overall improvement. Findings of the study were also complicated by the fact that improvement was observed in hyperactive children over time regardless of drug treatment.

Studies have also compared the differential effectiveness of haloperidol and fluphenazine in the treatment of young autistic and schizophrenic children. While both drugs were found to result in improvement, fluphenazine was associated with greater frequency of side effects (Faretra, Dooher, & Dowling, 1970; Engelhardt, Polizos, Waizer, & Hoffman, 1973). In a somewhat different context, Campbell, Small, Hollander, Korein, Cohen, Kalmijn, and Ferris (1978) administered triiodothyronine to preschool autistic children in a controlled study. Differential effects were not attributable to drug treatment. (While lower IQ children responded more favorably, no consistent pattern of subject characteristics was associated with drug responsiveness.)

In three studies involving 3- to 6-year-old psychotic and other severely handicapped children, Campbell and her associates (1972a, b; 1973) examined the effectiveness of four pharmacologic agents on symptoms and behavior. A comparison of lithium and chlorpromazine revealed no differences attributable to drugs on symptom scores (1972a), but triiodothyronine (1972b) and liothyronine (1973) resulted in symptom improvement. Each of the four drugs, however, was associated with side effects such as tachycardia, diarrhea, and motor retardation.

The variability in the above findings may reflect in part the likelihood that drug therapies interact with environmental variables to influence outcome. In this regard, Campbell and Small (1978) found that drug therapy was enhanced when it was combined with behavior therapy. This suggests that the benefits of drug therapies are more likely to be realized if they are seen as part of an overall treatment program.

## VARIABILITY OF EFFECTS

Positive results have been found for drug therapy in both seizure management and behavior control. Negative side effects ranging from mild behavioral disturbances to structural damage have also been reported. General conclusions are difficult to draw given the variety of drugs administered, the frequency of polypharmacy (simultaneous administration of two or more drugs), and the variations in experimental control of reported studies. Differences in subject characteristics within and across studies also restrict comparisons of findings.

Several factors may further contribute to variability of findings and need to be considered in the evaluation of drug treatment for handicapped children. One potential source of variable findings (Stores, 1975) is individual differences in the form of idiosyncratic reactions unrelated to dosage or drug concentrations. Such individual differences may account for the finding that imipramine, for example, has a toxic dose range so broad that a low dose (8 mg/kg) was lethal for one child and a massive dose (112 mg/kg) was survived by another (Gualtieri, 1977). This is a problem of some concern since recent data have shown that not only is imipramine more commonly prescribed (probably for enuresis) than other tricyclic antidepressants in the 0 to 9 age group, but more poisonings are also attributable to this drug in this age group (*FDA Drug Bulletin*, 1980).

A second factor of significant proportion that influences drug response of children is drug interaction. Handicapped preschool chil-

dren are quite often administered two or more drugs at the same time. While drug interactions account only for a part of adverse reactions, their consequences are likely to be of greater importance than other negative effects (Rylance, 1979). Administration of an antibiotic such as chloramphenicol (for bacterial meningitis) in conjunction with dilantin can result in a twofold increase in the serum concentration of the dilantin (Meissner & Smith, 1979). The extent of drug-drug interaction is further illustrated in a study in which two or more of seven anticonvulsants were administered concomitantly. Recognition of drug interactions provides a basis from which to examine apparent overdoses as well as nonresponse to specific drugs (Windorfer & Sauer, 1977). A table listing drug interactions that may be seen with some regularity in children has been summarized by Rylance (1979), and can serve as a valuable reference for those concerned with the practical management of children who are receiving multiple drugs.

## RESEARCH DIRECTIONS

Research regarding medication effects in preschool handicapped children is relatively limited compared to the extensive literature on older children and adults with a variety of developmental and learning problems. This may actually reflect the early state of the art of drug therapy with young children in general and young handicapped children in particular.

The ethical, legal, and medical dimensions of pediatric pharmacology are receiving increasing attention among professionals in the field (Gross et al., 1980). A particular concern is that developmental variables may influence as well as be influenced by drug therapy. Yaffe (1980) states that there should "be a constant awareness of the changes in drug dosages that are determined by altera-

Table 3. Studies on the use of medication to control behavior of preschool handicapped children

| Author | Purpose of drug study | Subjects' ages | Subject characteristics | Results | Side effects |
|---|---|---|---|---|---|
| Campbell et al., 1978 | Comparison of haloperidol & behavior Rx | 2.6–7.2 yr. | Autistic | Significantly superior to placebo, decreasing certain symptoms. Combination Rx most effective in acquisition of imitative speech | Excessive sedation. Decreased motor activity, depressed affect, excitement, insomnia, increased motor activity, increased irritability, acute dystonic reaction |
| Campbell et al., 1971 | Effect of imipramine on behavior | 10 subjects 2–6 yr. (M = 3.5 yr.) | Autistic and schizophrenic; intellectual level: low average to severe mental retardation | Mixed effects: 5 children improved, decreased irritability, decreased apathy, decreased withdrawal, decreased hypoactivity | Increased psychotic speech, increased behavioral disorganizat., increased excitation |
| Cohen et al., 1980 | Behavioral effects of haloperidol | 2.1–7.0 yr. (M = 4.7 yr.) | Profoundly to mildly retarded; autistic | Reduced stereotypy. Increased imitative speech. Increased attending, increased learning. Decreased withdrawal | Strong effect of age on response to medication, related to metabolism. When medication discontinued, rebound effect, worse behavior |
| Schleifer et al., 1975 | Hyperactivity in preschoolers & effect of methylphenidate | 3 yr. 4 mo.–4 yr. 10 mo. (M = 4.08 yr.) | (IQ 86–124) hyperactive children with minimal brain dysfunction | Parents reported decreased hyperactivity in home, no differences in nursery school setting or on psychological tasks as a function of treatment | Negative effect on mood. Negative effect on relationship with peers. Sadness, irritability, hugging, clinging, solitary play, poor appetite, difficulty going to sleep |

| Campbell et al., 1978 | Effects of triiodothyronine | 2 yr. 3 mo.–7 yr. 2 mo. (M = 4 yr. 5 mo.) N = 30 | Autistic, intellectual level range from bright normal to profound retardation | No specific drug-associated changes, time accounted for changes. Lower IQ level associated with drug responsiveness | Fluctuating blood pressure & mild & transient tachycardia |
|---|---|---|---|---|---|
| Faretra et al., 1970 | Comparison of haloperidol & fluphenazine | 5–12 yr. N = 60 | Inpatient psychotic, severely impaired schizophrenic | Both drugs similarly effective in producing overall improvement. Haloperidol more effective in reduction of provocativeness and autism, also acted more quickly | Some extrapyramidal symptoms—controllable by contramedic |
| Englehardt et al., 1973 | Comparison of fluphenazine & haloperidol | 6–12 yr. N = 30 | Outpatient schizophrenic functioning at mod. to severe retard. levels | Both drugs similar on overall efficacy | Extrapyramidal side effects associated with fluphenazine controllable by reduction or contramedication |
| Campbell et al., 1972b | Comparison of triiodothyronine & dextroamphetamine | 3–6 yr. N = 16 | Psychotic, chronic brain syndrome, avg. to severe mental retardation | Triiodothyronine resulted in significant improvement in overall symptomatology and had antipsychotic and stimulating effects | Tachycardia |
| Campbell et al., 1972a | Compare lithium & chlorpromazine | 3–6 yr. N = 10 | Severely disturbed, schizophrenic, autistic, average to severe retardation | No significant differences between drugs on symptom scores | Lithium toxicity—motor retardation. Chlorpromazine—motor retardation, irritability |
| Campbell et al., 1973 | Effects of liothyronine | 3–6 yr. (M = 3.7 yr.) N = 20 | Psychosis, chronic brain syndrome, avg. to severe retard. | Significant improvement in symptom (e.g., attention span, speech modulation, communication) | Transient tachycardia, mild diarrhea |

224

> *Developmental variables may influence as well as be influenced by drug therapy.*

tions and processes of dispositions at different ages" (p. 3). Sprague and Sleator (1976), studying drug management of older learning disabled children, found that optimal social behavior was achieved with dosages 2 to 3 times those required for optimal cognitive behavior. The implication of these findings is that there is a need not only for differential drug dosages as a function of outcome desired (e.g., social versus attending behavior), but that the desired outcome may change with the age of the child.

Then there is the question of the extent to which drug therapy may influence development itself. As Yaffe (1980) indicates, particular caution needs to be exercised when children receive medication over an extended period of time and some drug effects may not be evident right away. While the problem of long-term drug effects does not appear to have been studied in children, adolescent and adult epileptics treated with anticonvulsants for one or more years have been studied by Herha and Obe (1976). Chromosomal damage was significantly higher in the treated epileptics as compared to a control group. There was also evidence that the type of damage differed with the type of anticonvulsant administered. These findings support Yaffe's (1980) recommendation for "developmental pharmacology" in which the "safe and effective use of drugs is to base their prescription upon scientific data obtained for the particular age group under consideration" (p. 3). The Neisworth et al. (1976) procedures for in-situ data collection seem promising in providing a means for monitoring drug effects in the natural setting. This seems especially pertinent for handicapped populations who may differ from nonhandicapped peers in age as well as in medical and psychological status.

## PRACTICAL IMPLICATIONS

The questions raised about drug therapy with children warrant caution in the use of medication and show the need for systematic research on drug effectiveness and effects. With the expansion in medicine of drug treatment in general, it is likely that the use of drugs in treating handicapped preschool children will also increase. Thus it is important that teachers and other direct care staff become more aware of and involved in dimensions of drug therapy. Specific ways in which direct care staff can facilitate drug treatment of handicapped children include the following:

1. Secure detailed information about each drug administered to children in the program, with emphasis on purpose of drug, expected effects, adverse reactions, and contraindications, if any.

2. Seek cooperation of the child's physician to develop a drug therapy plan that complements overall treatment program for child. Family medication records may be useful in monitoring such a plan (Bleiyer, 1975).

3. Incorporate systematic documentation of drug therapy into records assessing child's status and progress. Dosage and schedule documentation can (a) yield information on drug therapy patterns over time, and (b) provide insights on possible relationships between drug therapy and behavioral or developmental status. Such documentation seems particularly relevant for children with severe handicaps, who are very likely to be given anti-seizure medication. Recognition of their problem has led to the development of an experimental behavior assessment instrument, Carolina Rec-

ord of Infant Behavior (Simeonsson, 1979), of which documentation of a child's medication status is an essential part. Ongoing research seeks to demonstrate the value of this strategy to expand and qualify behavioral and developmental assessment (Simeonsson, Huntington, & Parse, 1980).

Securing a balance in drug therapy between achieving outcomes and minimizing adverse reactions should be a cooperative venture of physicians, parents, and staff involved with the handicapped youngster. Essential to such a

venture should be the recognition that the value of medication is to "facilitate changes in the child such that certain responses become more or less likely to occur. However, whether or not such responses actually occur must rely on additional efforts at restructuring the crucial environmental variables which greatly influence the child's long-term psychological adjustment" (Barkley, 1977, p. 158). This recognition places drug therapy in proper perspective in an overall treatment program and seems consistent with the best interest of the young handicapped child.

## REFERENCES

Barkley, R.A. A review of stimulant drug research with hyperactive children. *Journal of Child Psychology and Psychiatry*, 1977, *18*, 137–165.

Bensch, J., Blennow, G., Ferngren, H., Gamstorp, I. Herrlin, K.M., Kubista, J., Arvidsson, A., & Dahlstrom, H. A double blind study of clonazepam in the treatment of therapy-resistant epilepsy in children. *Developmental Medicine and Child Neurology*, 1977, *19*, 335–342.

Berman, P.H. Management of seizure disorders with anticonvulsant drugs: Current concepts. *Pediatric Clinics of North America*, 1976, 23(3), 443–459.

Bleiyer, W.A. Surveillance of pediatric adverse drug reactions: A neglected health care program. *Pediatrics*, 1975, *15*, 308–310.

Buda, F.B., Joyce, R.P., & Zettett, P.G. Use of high dosage phenobarbital in the treatment of neonatal status epiliplicus: A preliminary report. *Military Medicine*, 1979, *144*, 456–459.

Campbell, M., Fish, B., Shapiro, T., & Floyd, A. Jr. Imipramine in preschool autistic and schizophrenic children. *Journal of Autism and Childhood Schizophrenia*, 1971, *1*, 267–282.

Campbell, M., Fish, B., Korein, J., Shapiro, T., Collins, P., & Koh, C. Lithium and chlorpromazine: A controlled crossover study of hyperactive severely disturbed young children. *Journal of Autism and Childhood Schizophrenia*, 1972, 2, 234–263. (a)

Campbell, M., Fish, B., David, R., Shapiro, T., Collins, P., & Koh, C. Response to triiodothyronine and dextroamphetamine: a study of preschool schizophrenic children. *Journal of Autism and Childhood Schizophrenia*, 1972, 2, 343–358. (b)

Campbell, M., Fish, B., David, R., Shapiro, T., Collins, P., & Koh, C. Liothyronine treatment in psychotic and

nonpsychotic children under 6 years. *Archives of General Psychiatry*, 1973, *29*, 602–608.

Campbell, M., Anderson, L.T., Meier, M., Cohen, I.L., Small, A.M., Samit, C., & Sacher, E.J. A comparison of haloperidol and behavior therapy and their interaction in autistic children. *Journal of the American Academy of Child Psychiatry*, 1978, *17*, 640–655.

Campbell, M., & Small, A.M. Chemotherapy. In B.B. Wolman, J. Egan, & A.O. Russ (Eds.), *Handbook of treatment of mental disorders in childhood and adolescence*. Englewood Cliffs, N.J.: Prentice-Hall, 1978.

Campbell, M., Small, A.M., Hollander, C.S., Korein, J., Cohen, I.L., Kalmijn, M., & Ferris, S. A controlled crossover study of triiodothyronine in autistic children. *Journal of Autism and Childhood Schizophrenia*, 1978, *8*, 371–381.

Cohen, M.J. (Ed.). *Drugs and the special child*. New York: Gardner Press, 1979.

Cohen, I.L., Campbell, M., Posner, D., Small, A.M., Triebel, D., & Anderson, L.T. Behavioral effects of haloperidol in young autistic children: An objective analysis using a within subjects reversal design. *Journal of the American Academy of Child Psychiatry*, 1980, *19*, 665–677.

Combrinck-Graham, L., Gursky, E.J., & Saccar, C.L. Psychoactive agents. In S.J. Yaffe (Ed.), *Pediatric pharmacology*. New York: Grune & Stratton, 1980.

Coulter, D.L., Wu, H., & Allen, R.J. Valproic acid therapy in childhood epilepsy. *Journal of the American Medical Association*, 1980, 244(8), 785–788.

Donaldson, J.Y., & Menolascino, F.J. Therapeutic and preventive intervention in mental retardation. In G.P. Sholeyar, R.M. Benson, & B.J. Blinder (Eds.),

**226**

*Emotional disorders in children and adolescents.* New York: Spectrum Publications, 1980.

Engelhardt, D.M., Polizos, P., Waizer, J., & Hoffman, S.P. A double-blind comparison of fluphenazine and haloperidol in outpatient schizophrenic children. *Journal of Autism and Childhood Schizophrenia,* 1973, *3,* 128–137.

Faretra, G., Dooher, L., & Dowling, J. Comparison of haloperidol and fluphenazine in disturbed children. *American Journal of Psychiatry,* 1970, *126,* 1670–1673.

*FDA Drug Bulletin,* 1980, *10*(3). Rockville, Md.: Dept. of Health and Human Services.

Gadow, K.D. *Children on medication: A primer for school personnel.* Reston, Va.: Council for Exceptional Children, 1979.

Gittelman-Klein, R. Psychopharmacology in children. *Drug Therapy,* 1978, *8,* 137–147.

Golden, G.S. Nonstandard therapies in the developmental disabilities. *American Journal of Diseases of Children,* 1980, *134,* 487–491.

Greer, J.G., Davis, T.B., & Yearwood, K. Drug treatment: Factors contributing to high risk in institutions. *Exceptional Children,* 1977, *43*(7), 451–453.

Gross, F., Boreus, L.O., Deutsch, E., Gladtke, E., Helge, H., Mirkin, B.L., Morselli, P.L., Sereni, F., & Yaffe, S.J. Medical, ethical and legal aspects of clinical trials in pediatrics. *European Journal of Clinical Pharmacology,* 1980, *18,* 121–127.

Gualtieri, C. T. Imipramine and children. A review and some speculations about the mechanism of drug action. *Disorders of the Nervous System,* 1977, *38,* 368–375.

Haggerty, R.J., & Roghmann, K.J. Non-compliance and self-medication—Two neglected aspects of pediatric pharmacology. *Pediatric Clinics of North America,* 1972, *19,* 101–115.

Harte, V.J., & Timoney, R.F. Drug prescribing in paediatric medicine. *Journal of the Irish Medical Association,* 1980, *73,* 157.

Herha, J., & Obe, G. Chromosomal damage in epileptics on monotherapy with carbamazepine and diphenylhydantoin. *Human Genetics.* 1976, *34,* 255–263.

Iivanainen, M., Viukari, M., & Helle, E.P. Cerebellar atrophy in phenytoin treated mentally retarded epileptics. *Epilepsia,* 1977, *18,* 375–386.

Knudsen, B. Rectal administration of diazepam in solution in the acute treatment of convulsions in infants and children. *Archives of Disease in Childhood,* 1979, *54,* 855–857.

Leary, P.M., & Morris, S. Clinical experience with sodium valproate in children. *South American Medical Journal,* 1980, 866–867.

Lindsey, C.N., Leibold, S.R., Ladd, F.T., & Ownby, R. Jr.

Children on medication: A guide for teachers. *Rehabilitation Literature,* 1980, *41,* 124–126.

May, E. Drugs in use in school for severely subnormal children. *Child: Care, Health and Development,* 1976, *2,* 261–266.

Meissner, H.C., & Smith, A.L. The current status of chloramphenicol. *Pediatrics,* 1979, *64,* 348–356.

Meistrup-Larsen, K.I., Hermann, S., & Permin, H. Chronic diphenylhydantoin encephalopathy in mentally retarded children and adolescents with severe epilepsy. *Acta Neurologica Scandinavica,* 1979, *60,* 50–55.

Moreland, T.A., Rylance, G.W., Christopher, L.J., & Stevenson, I.H. Patterns of drug prescribing for children in hospital. *European Journal of Clinical Pharmacology,* 1978, *14,* 39–46.

Neisworth, J.T., Kurtz, P.D., Ross, A., & Madle, R.A. Naturalistic assessment of neurological diagnoses and pharmacological intervention. *Journal of Learning Disabilities,* 1976, *9*(3), 22–25.

Rylance, G. Prescribing in infancy and childhood. *British Journal of Hospital Medicine,* 1979, *22,* 346–354.

Schleifer, M., Weiss, G., Cohen, N., Elman, M., Cvejic, H., & Kruger, E. Hyperactivity in preschoolers and the effect of methylphenidate. *American Journal of Orthopsychiatry,* 1975, *45,* 38–50.

Silver, L.B. Drug therapy with children and adolescents. In M.J. Cohen (Ed.), *Drugs and the special child.* New York: Gardner Press, 1979.

Simeonsson, R.J. *Carolina Record of Infant Behavior.* Unpublished manuscript, University of North Carolina at Chapel Hill, 1979.

Simeonsson, R.J., Huntington, G.S., & Parse, S.A. Expanding the developmental assessment of young handicapped children. *New Directions for Exceptional Children,* 1980, *3,* 51–74.

Sprague, R., & Sleator, E. Drugs and dosages: Implications for learning disabilities. In R.M. Knights & D. Bakker (Eds.), *The neuropsychology of learning disorders.* Baltimore: University Park Press, 1976.

Stores, G. Behavioural effects of anti-epileptic drugs. *Developmental Medicine and Child Neurology,* 1975, *17,* 647–657.

Sroufe, L.A. Drug treatment of children with behavior problems. In Horwitz et al. (Eds.), *Review of child development research, Vol. 4.* Chicago: University of Chicago Press, 1975.

Vallarta, J.M., Bell, D.B., & Reichert, A. Progressive encephalopathy due to chronic hydantoin intoxication. *American Journal of Diseases of Children,* 1974, *128,* 27–34.

Windorfer, A., & Sauer, W. Drug interactions during anticonvulsant therapy in childhood: Diphenylhydan-

toin, primidone, phenobarbitone, clonazepam, nitraze-
pam, carbamazepin and dipropylacetate. *Neuropadia-
trie*, 1977, *8*, 29–41.

Winnacker, J.L., Yeager, H., Saunders, J.A., Russell, B., &
'Anast, C.S. Rickets in children receiving anticonvulsant
drugs. *American Journal of Diseases of Children*,
1977, *131*, 286.

Wolf, S.M. The effectiveness of phenobarbital in the
prevention of recurrent febrile convulsions in children
with and without a history of pre-, peri- and postnatal
abnormalities. *Acta Paediatrica Scandinavica* 1977, *66*,
585–587.

Yaffe, S.J. Clinical implications of perinatal pharmacology. *European Journal of Clinical Pharmacology*, 1980,
*18*, 3–7.

Zinsmeister, S., & Marks, R.E. Acute athetosis as a result of
phenytoin toxicity in a child. *American Journal of
Diseases of Children*, 1976, *130*, 75–76.

# Index